Promoting Success with At-Risk Students: Emerging Perspectives and Practical Approaches

ALL HAWORTH BOOKS & JOURNALS ARE PRINTED ON CERTIFIED ACID-FREE PAPER

LC
4691
P73
1990

Promoting Success with At-Risk Students: Emerging Perspectives and Practical Approaches

Louis J. Kruger
Editor

The Haworth Press
New York • London

Promoting Success with At-Risk Students: Emerging Perspectives and Practical Approaches has also been published as *Special Services in the Schools*, Volume 5, Numbers 3/4 1989.

© 1990 by The Haworth Press, Inc. All rights reserved. No part of this book may be reproduced or utilized in any form or by any means, electronic or mechanical, including photocopying, microfilm and recording, or by any information storage and retrieval system, without permission in writing from the publisher. Printed in the United States of America.

The Haworth Press, Inc., 10 Alice Street, Binghamton, NY 13904-1580
EUROSPAN/Haworth, 3 Henrietta Street, London WC2E 8LU England

Library of Congress Cataloging-in-Publication Data

Promoting success with at-risk students : emerging perspectives and practical approaches / Louis J. Kruger, editor.
    p. cm.
    Includes bibliographical references.
    ISBN 0-86656-922-7
    1. Underachievers—United States. 2. Motivation in education. 3. Special education—United States. I. Kruger, Louis J. II. Maher, Charles A., 1944-   .
LC4691.P73   1990
371.93—dc20   89-29916
                                                                                      CIP

Promoting Success with At-Risk Students: Emerging Perspectives and Practical Approaches

CONTENTS

Promoting Success with At-Risk Students   1
    Louis J. Kruger

PART I: ISSUES IN IDENTIFICATION AND ASSESSMENT

Social Status as a Predictor of At-Risk Children   7
    Barbara Hanna Wasik

  Behavioral and Cognitive Correlates of Children's
    Sociometric Status   9
  Intervention Efforts   12
  Measurement of Social Status   14
  Use of Sociometric Measurement with At-Risk Students   17

Diagnosis of Youth At-Risk for Suicide, Pregnancy, and Drug and Alcohol Abuse   25
    David A. Sabatino
    Robert R. Smith

  Who Comprises the Group of At-Risk Youth?   27
  Substance Abuse   28
  Suicide   29
  Pregnancy   32

The Diagnostic Dilemma	33
A Policy Issue	38

PART II: CLASSROOM-BASED APPROACHES IN PROMOTING STUDENT SUCCESS

Behavioral Self-Management with At-Risk Children — 43
F. Charles Mace
Michael C. Shea

Theoretical Models of Behavioral Self-Management	45
Self-Monitoring	46
Self-Evaluation	50
Self-Reinforcement	52
Self-Instruction	55
Suggestions for Implementing Self-Management Procedures in the Classroom	57
Conclusion	60

The Individualized Contingency Contract for Students: A Collaborative Approach — 65
Louis J. Kruger

Identification of the Student's Problems	67
Preconditions to Contract Development	70
Involvement of Student and Parent	71
Contract Development	72
Writing the Contract	76
Incorporating Cognitive Interventions into the Contract	79
Implementation Issues	83
Concluding Comments	86

Individualized Education and Applied Behavior Analysis — 89
Wayne C. Piersel
Steven W. Lee

Applied Behavior Analysis	90
Individualized Education	92
Applied Behavior Analysis and Behavior Modification	95
Conclusion	104

Improving the Study Skills of At-Risk Students   **109**
    Judy L. Genshaft
    Patricia M. Kirwin

Review of the Literature	110
Introduction to Study Skills Techniques	113
Issues and Guidelines	126
Conclusion	128

Time Management in the Classroom: Increasing Instructional Time   **131**
    Cathy Collins

Nature and Scope of the Relationship Between Student Failure and Teachers' Misuse of Time	131
Assisting Teachers in Better Managing Their Own Time	140
Suggestions for Future Practices and Applied Research	150

Providing Opportunities for Student Success Through Cooperative Learning and Peer Tutoring   **155**
    David W. Peterson
    Janice A. Miller

Defining Peer-Influenced Academic Interventions	157
Comparison of Peer Tutoring and Cooperative Learning Methods	162
Research on Cooperative Learning	163
Research on Peer Tutoring	165
Developing and Implementing Cooperative Learning Programs	166
Developing and Implementing Peer Tutoring Programs	168
General Issues in Planning and Evaluating Peer-Influenced Academic Interventions	171
Conclusion	173

PART III: SCHOOL-WIDE APPROACHES IN PROMOTING STUDENT SUCCESS

Keeping Students in School: Academic and Affective Strategies — 179
  Gary Natriello
  Aaron M. Pallas
  Edward L. McDill
  James M. McPartland

Academic Success in School — 181
Strengthening the Connection of Students to the Academic Program of the School — 183
Positive Relationships in School — 188
Conclusion — 192

Promoting Parent Involvement in Schools to Serve At-Risk Students — 197
  Diane L. Smallwood
  Mary Katherine Hawryluk
  Ellen Pierson

Educational Roles for Parents — 198
Promoting Parent Involvement: Guidelines for School Professionals — 204
Conclusions — 211

Preventing Classroom Discipline Problems: Promoting Student Success Through Effective Schools and Schooling — 215
  Howard M. Knoff

Definitions — 217
A Prevention Perspective for School Discipline Problems — 218
Effective Schools and Schooling Approaches: A Focus on Prevention — 221
Conclusion — 235

The School-Based Prevention of Childhood Crises — 241
  Jonathan Sandoval

Definition and Theory — 242
Four Types of Crisis Prevention — 245

Competence Enhancement Programs	252
System Focused Prevention	253
Research Needs	254
Conclusion	255

Reducing Academic Related Anxiety — 261
Thomas J. Huberty

Trait and State Anxiety	262
Indicators of Anxiety	262
When Anxiety Becomes Problematic	263
Types of Anxiety Disorders	263
Anxiety and School Performance	264
Interventions with Anxious Students	266
Conclusion	274

ABOUT THE EDITOR

Louis J. Kruger, PsyD, is Assistant Professor of Education and Coordinator of the School Psychology Program at Tufts University, Medford, Massachusetts. He teaches courses and presents workshops about behavior management and consultation. He is a consultant for public schools and community agencies on the planning and evaluation of services for at-risk and special needs students. Before joining Tufts University, Dr. Kruger held a variety of special services positions in public schools and mental health agencies including school psychologist, adjustment counselor, and supervisor. He is a member of several professional organizations, including the Council for Exceptional Children, National Association of School Psychologists, American Educational Research Association, and the American Psychological Association. Dr. Kruger has written numerous articles, book chapters, and technical reports on topics related to at-risk and special needs students.

Promoting Success with At-Risk Students

Louis J. Kruger

Tufts University

SUMMARY. A rationale is presented for special services providers to work with at-risk students. It is assumed that collaboration between services providers in special education and regular education can enrich both delivery systems. Finally, an overview of the papers contained in this publication is presented.

A fundamental assumption of the group of papers in this publication is that promoting student success in regular and special education are complementary and interdependent processes. It follows from this assumption that special services providers can indirectly improve special education by lending their knowledge and skills to help students in regular education. The following example illustrates the importance of collaboration among special and regular education staffs. It involves the area of prereferral intervention, that is, systematic provision of an intervention prior to the referral for special education evaluation (Graden, Casey, & Christenson, 1985). Johnny Jones's parents recently divorced and, concomitantly, Johnny's school performance began to decline. After consulting with Johnny's teacher, and interviewing Johnny and Johnny's parents, the school psychologist concluded that Johnny's recent poor performance was probably related to the parents' divorce. Fortunately, the school which Johnny attended had a support group for children of divorced parents (for a description of such a group, see Epstein, Borduin, & Wexler, 1985). Therefore, instead of recommending a special education evaluation for Johnny, the school psychologist

---

Requests for reprints should be directed to: Louis J. Kruger, Department of Education, Tufts University, Medford, MA 02155.

© 1990 by The Haworth Press, Inc. All rights reserved.

recommended that Johnny first attend the support group for children of divorced parents. The group was organized and led by a school counselor. Following ten meetings of the group, Johnny's teacher informed the school psychologist that Johnny's performance had returned to its previously satisfactory level. Though it cannot be said with certainty that attending the support group improved Johnny's school performance, the intervention might have helped prevent a referral for a special education evaluation and possible subsequent placement in special education. In this example, two special providers were involved with the case prior to referral for a special education evaluation. This type of involvement with regular education can help improve special education by reducing the number of referrals for special education evaluations and thereby possibly increasing the quality of special education evaluations. Other examples of how collaboration among regular and special education staff might improve both special and regular education are possible. Nonetheless, the point being emphasized is this: When regular education fails to meet the needs of students, an increased burden is placed upon special education to meet their needs. Therefore, it is in the best interest of both special education students and students at-risk for special education that special services providers be involved with regular education.

It is both the best and worst of times for special education. Never before have such large financial resources been devoted to the education of special needs students. During the 1985-1986 school year, at least 18 billion dollars were spent on special education in the United States (Department of Education, 1988). However, with increased spending of monies for special education has come increased scrutiny and criticism of special education. Particularly troubling are the lack of data supporting the efficacy of special education (see, e.g., Glass, 1983). The growing criticism of current special educational programs coupled with an increased emphasis on prevention (Zins & Forman, 1988) has led to a call for special services providers to become more involved with regular education (Reschly, 1988).

The papers herein reflect emerging perspectives and practical approaches relative to the need for special services providers to become more involved in regular education. In particular, the papers emphasize the importance of promoting success with at-risk students in regular education. In this context, at-risk students are defined as those regular education students who are in danger of dropping out of school, academically failing, or being referred for a special education evaluation. Success is defined as the consistent application of age-appropriate social skills and the consistent attainment of academic achievement commensurate with the student's abilities. Specifically, the papers address what skills and knowledge are needed by special services providers in order to help at-risk students and what assessment or intervention approaches can be used with these students.

Part I is composed of two papers which deal with issues relative to the identification and assessment of at-risk students. In the first paper, Wasik discusses the rapidly developing area of assessing the social status of students. She points out that students' social status among peers can be used to predict both academic and social success. In this regard, assessment of social status has promise for being an important approach to early identification of at-risk students. Wasik also provides practical suggestions for how social status might be assessed in schools. In the second paper of Part I, Sabatino and Smith argue that many of the students who are at-risk for school problems also are at-risk for suicide, pregnancy, or drug and alcohol abuse. The students' school related problems often are difficult to disentangle from their problems outside of the school. Proceeding from this premise, the authors critique the traditional approach for assessing at-risk students and propose a viable alternative.

Part II is composed of six papers which present important classroom-based approaches to helping at-risk students succeed in school. In the first paper, Mace and Shea discuss behavioral self-management and point out the notable advantages of delegating to students the responsibility for managing their own behavior. The authors review the latest research and theory about behavioral self-management and its components (self-monitoring, self-evaluation, self-reinforcement, and self-instruction). Furthermore, Mace and Shea provide clear examples of how behavioral self-management can be implemented in regular education classrooms with at-risk students. Next, Kruger discusses how contingency contracts can be individualized to meet the needs of at-risk students. He views contingency contracts as a possible means to facilitate collaboration among regular education teachers, special services providers, the at-risk student, and the at-risk students' parents. Kruger also suggests how cognitive interventions might be incorporated into contingency contracts. In the third paper of Part II, Piersel and Lee address how the principles of applied behavior analysis can be used to individualize regular education for at-risk students. Particularly important, the authors stress approaches to individualization that are practical to employ in the regular education classroom. Peirsel and Lee discuss the personalized system of instruction, curriculum-based assessment, instructional monitoring and feedback, as well as other approaches. Next, Genshaft and Kirwin address the fundamental but often neglected topic of improving students' study skills. They discuss the relevance of several study skills to academic success. In addition, Genshaft and Kirwin suggest that multiple methods should be used to improve students' study skills. In the fifth paper of Part II, Collins suggests how special providers can help regular education teachers learn how to improve both the teachers' and at-risk students' use of time in the classroom. The purpose of improving time management is to increase time devoted to instruction. Collins presents several checklists and forms which can be used to facilitate the teaching of time management to teachers. In the final paper of Part II, Peterson and Miller review two classroom-based interventions, cooperative learning and peer tutoring, both of which use students as change agents. Sarason (1982) has eloquently argued for the need to find non-professional personnel to assist in public education. Cooperative learning and peer tutoring are two practical examples of how students can be creatively used to help their at-risk peers.

The five papers of Part III deal with approaches to promoting success with at-risk students that can occur outside the classroom. In the first paper, Natriello, Pallas, McDill, and McPartland discuss programs that are designed to prevent students from dropping out of school before they graduate. This paper is particularly timely given the growing concern about the dropout rate in many large city

PART I:
ISSUES IN IDENTIFICATION AND ASSESSMENT

Social Status as a Predictor of At-Risk Children

Barbara Hanna Wasik
University of North Carolina

SUMMARY. The purpose of this paper is to review the importance of children's social status as a predictor of social and academic success in school. Behavioral and cognitive correlates of social status are described, and the research on intervention strategies is discussed. Procedures for assessing children's social status are reviewed with a discussion of advantages and disadvantages of each procedure. Suggestions are made for the use of assessment and intervention procedures by classroom teachers. The author calls for a priority in the schools for promoting conditions that facilitate social acceptance of children.

"Joey plays by himself all day and I'm concerned." "Judy was not picked by anyone when I asked the children to write down who

---

Requests for reprints should be directed to: Barbara Hanna Wasik, School of Education, The University of North Carolina at Chapel Hill, CB #3500, Peabody Hall, Chapel Hill, NC 27599-3500.

© 1990 by The Haworth Press, Inc. All rights reserved.

they wanted to do their project with." "Thomas is always hitting someone and no one will sit by him at lunch." "Renee seems to be either really liked or really disliked by the children." These statements, typical of ones made daily by teachers across the country, reflect concerns with children's social behaviors and peer interactions and the need to consider the relation between social and academic behavior.

Children's peer relations have been an area of intrigue for educators and psychologists for most of this century. Peer relations have been studied to obtain information on children's friendship patterns (Hartup, 1979, 1983) and to obtain knowledge of individual children's social status among their peers. More recently, social status has been seen as an important part of understanding children's social adjustment and in identifying children at-risk for social and academic failure.

The increased importance attached to social status can be attributed, in part, to the classic study by Cowen, Pederson, Babigian, Izzo, and Trost (1973), in which the social status of elementary-age children was found to be a strong predictor of children's later social adjustment, and to the work reported by Roff, Sills, and Golden (1972) and Coie, Dodge, and Cappotelli (1982) showing relationships between peer status and social adjustment, or by Bonney (1971) and Yellott, Lien, and Cowen (1969) on the relationship between social status and academic performance.

Of particular concern to education professionals has been the social acceptance of children with special needs. Research findings have shown that educable mentally handicapped and learning disabled children have lower social status than their nonhandicapped peers (Bruininks, 1978a, 1978b; Clark, 1964; Goodman, Gottlieb, & Harrison, 1972; Gottlieb, 1978). Low achieving children as well as learning disabled and educable mentally handicapped have also been found to differ from normally achieving children on peer status (Bender, Wyne, Stuck, & Bailey, 1984).

Quay and Jarrett (1984) found that for Head Start children mental age was more positively correlated with social acceptance than chronological age. Their data are consistent with the earlier findings by Jennings (1975) and Rardin and Moan (1971) that support a positive relationship between cognitive ability or mental maturity and social acceptance. Quay and Jarrett suggest that the high correlation between mental age and social acceptance may contribute to Gottlieb's (1978) findings of low popularity for mainstreamed children.

Social status has also been equated with self-esteem, self-confidence, and locus of control, though it may best be considered an indicator of a child's overall social competence. Social competence is a concept used to integrate various child social characteristics. Social competence has been equated by Argyle (1969) with social skill and defined by others as the ability to relate effectively with people. Putallaz and Gottman (1982) have presented a definition of social competence that is particularly useful for those concerned with the identification of at-risk children. They propose that social competence be considered "as aspects of social behavior that are important with respect to preventing physical illness or psychopathology in children and adults" (p. 7). In their recent detailed review of the literature on the predictive value of children's social status, Parker and Asher (1987) concluded that there was strong support for social status to predict later behavior, especially school performance.

White (1979), in addressing the relationship of low social competence to psychopathology, noted that "Children thus handicapped need to acquire enough sense of competence to make true interaction possible and in this way allow social needs to be satisfied" (p. 11). Thus, not only is social competence given an important place in children's development, it is viewed as an area of intervention in which deficiencies can be corrected. Before considering the research on intervention procedures for these children, the behavioral and cognitive correlates of children's sociometric status will be reviewed.

BEHAVIORAL AND COGNITIVE CORRELATES OF CHILDREN'S SOCIOMETRIC STATUS

Several hypotheses have been made over time to account for children's low peer acceptance. Attention has been devoted to physical characteristics such as attractiveness (e.g., Vaugh & Langlois, 1983), maturity, and athleticism status. Research on such characteristics is important because it facilitates understanding on children's peer relationships. Other characteristics, however, provide information with more utility for addressing problems in peer relations.

Two characteristics previously considered to be important components of social status were assertiveness and the frequency of peer interactions. Training in assertiveness has been based upon an assumption that it was a prerequisite for social competence. Bornstein, Bellack, and Hersen (1977) provided training in social skills to nonassertive children with a social skills training package that included instructions, feedback, behavioral rehearsal, and modeling. Though gains in social skills were obtained in the experimental setting, there was no assessment of effects in the classroom. In a follow-up study, Beck, Forehand, Wells, and Quante (1978) also found changes in the experimental setting, but did not find generalization in the natural setting or on sociometric scores. Not only do these studies fail to show generalization to the natural setting, but there is an absence of evidence closely linking assertiveness with social competence.

The frequency of a child's interactions has also been assumed to be an important component of social acceptance. Empirical investigations of efforts to increase children's frequency of interactions have resulted in inconsistent findings, with O'Connor (1972) demonstrating a successful effort to increase children's frequency of interaction through modeling, whereas Gottman (1977) was unable to replicate the findings. No evidence exists, however, relating the simple frequency of interaction with social status (Putallaz & Gottman, 1982).

Research on other behavioral characteristics of children shows stronger relationships with social status. These characteristics include children's attentiveness, aggression, fighting, and withdrawal. The data support a general picture of popular children being more on-task and demonstrating more prosocial or positive behaviors (Hartup, 1983; Vosk, Forehand, Parker, & Rickard, 1982) than unpopular children. Unpopular children include both rejected and neglected children and it is important to distinguish these children because problematic behaviors are typically characteristic of the rejected child, not the neglected child. Rejected children are observed to be less attentive than other children (Coie & Kupersmidt, 1983;

Lahey, Green, & Forehand, 1980; Vosk, Forehand, Parker, & Rickard, 1982) and to demonstrate higher rates of aggression (Dodge, 1983). They are described by their peers as children who fight, disrupt things, and prefer to be alone (Wasik, 1987). Dodge (1983) also found that rejected boys engaged in more antisocial behavior, in contrast to popular children, who were more cooperative. Neglected boys generally did not engage in antisocial actions.

In studying children with emotional and behavioral problems resulting in hospitalization, Asarnow (1988) found that children with externalizing disorders (conduct or attention deficit disorders) and children with concurrent depressive and externalizing disorders were the most rejected, least liked, and least socially competent children. Symptomatology was the best predictor of peer rejection, whereas social and intellectual competence predicted peer acceptance.

Recent attention has focused on the behavior of children in group settings, both newly created groups and ways children enter groups. Coie and Kupersmidt (1983) studied how social status developed in young boys' groups and found clear distinctions for popular and unpopular boys, with popular boys engaging in more active social interactions, less solitary behavior, and more norm setting behaviors. Rejected boys were aversive, active, talkative, and less attentive than other children, whereas neglected boys were not interactive or talkative and tended to withdraw or ignore the aggression of others.

Researchers have also investigated a very specific characteristic of group behavior, namely, how children enter ongoing groups. Putallaz and Gottman (1981) found that when entering groups, unpopular children tend to call attention to themselves by being disagreeable, asking informational questions, and referring to themselves. Further, an investigation by Putallaz (1983) showed that children who contributed relevant conversation when they entered a new group were more likely to have higher social status than children whose conversation was less relevant to the group's activity.

In studying the cognitive correlates of social status and children's social cognition, the ability to characterize others and make inferences about their covert psychological experiences has received considerable attention (Shantz, 1983). Social cognition is often described in terms of perspective-taking and one can examine a child's ability to perceive another's emotions, perceptions, or thoughts. Vosk and her colleagues obtained data showing that children who had high peer acceptance correctly identified more emotions than socially rejected children (Vosk et al., 1982). Another characteristic that has been studied is the attributions children give to the behavior of others. Dodge and Frame (1982) found that rejected children attribute more hostile behaviors to peers than do accepted children.

Children's problem solving has also been studied in relation to their social status, with a correlation found between children's social status and the use of prosocial problem solving strategies (Richard & Dodge, 1982; Rubin & Daniels-Beirness, 1983). Further research is needed, however, to determine if training in such skills influences children's social status.

INTERVENTION EFFORTS

Once it is known that a child's peer relations are problematic, it is important to consider appropriate interventions. In addressing peer status we are not speaking simply of high or low popularity, but rather those children whose behavior with their peers is characterized by social rejection, few opportunities for good social development, and possible feelings of anger, frustration, depression, and isolation.

As noted earlier in this paper, some variables associated with poor peer relations are not modifiable (e.g., ethnic status, physical appearance). But we can address behaviors of the child that are problematic (e.g., fighting, disruption, poor social skills) and we can model, prompt, and reinforce prosocial behaviors on the part of the child and his or her peers. A number of strategies for improving a child's social acceptance have been investigated. These include coaching children directly, modeling, using peers as change agents, reinforcing prosocial behaviors, teaching problem solving skills, and academic skill training. More detailed information on intervention strategies is available in writings by Gresham (1981), Hops (1982), Ladd and Asher (1985), and Wanlass and Prinz (1982).

Of particular interest is a recent intervention effort reported by

Coie and Krebbiel (1984) in which they evaluated the effects of alternative intervention programs with fourth graders who were both socially rejected and having academic problems. Children were assigned to one of four groups: academic skills training, social skills training, both academic and social skills training, and control. They found that children who received academic skill training not only improved in math and reading, but also improved in the social preference scores they received from peers. These findings are important and merit serious consideration by school personnel. In the same study, Coie and Krebbiel (1984) found that children who received only social skills training did not improve in their sociometric status. The authors caution that the social training procedures may not have been intensive enough and may not have addressed the children's particular needs. Oden and Asher (1977) did find that teaching children social interaction concepts led to gains in social acceptance and the gains were evident at a one-year follow-up. They did not find concomitant gains in positive social behavior.

Weincott, Corson, and Wilchesky (1979) implemented an intervention program with twenty teachers, each of whom had referred a child whose social behavior was clearly below that of classroom peers. Teachers were taught to implement a combination of symbolic-modeling, role playing, and individual and group-reinforcement contingencies. The program, implemented in the classrooms for ten weeks, resulted in significant gains in the child's observed social behavior and in teacher ratings.

Extensive work has been done by Hops, Walker, and Greenwood (1979) in developing a classroom intervention program for socially withdrawn children. Their set of procedures includes four major components: direct instruction in specific social skills, a peer-pairing arrangement, a token-reinforcement system with a group back-up, and a verbal-correspondence procedure. Hops (1982) has reported that withdrawn children who have been in studies in which all four components of their program have been used showed gains in social interaction. Information is still needed, however, on the effectiveness of each component and on the long-term effectiveness of the intervention program.

In summary, intervention efforts seem to work best if the intervention extends over a long time period and if it takes place in the natural setting. Classroom teachers may well be in the best position to bring about changes in children's social behavior. The time they spend with children far exceeds any time a psychologist or counselor could work with the child, thus providing for a longer intervention. Also, teachers can prompt and reinforce certain behaviors across the day in a way that makes such interactions part of the daily routine. Further research, however, is essential on all intervention strategies, with a focus on which intervention procedure is appropriate for which child.

In considering intervention efforts, it is important to recognize that identifying a problem does not lead to automatic solutions. Each child must be viewed individually and that child's patterns of social interactions analyzed. One child may actually lack specific social skills that can benefit by coaching and practice. A second child may have an attention deficit with other problems, and possibly need medication as well as other classroom intervention procedures. A third child might benefit from both academic skills training and social skills training.

MEASUREMENT OF SOCIAL STATUS

Sociometric measures can be divided into three types: nominations, ratings, and paired comparisons (Hymel, 1983; Wasik, 1987). The traditional and most-often used method is the nomination method. This method, developed by Moreno (1934), has each child nominate a restricted number of his or her peers for a set of positive and negative questions, for example, "Name the three children you like the best," or "Name the children you do not like to play with." The resulting information can be used to identify children's rankings as most or least liked, obtained by summing the positive and negative nominations separately. Children with the highest number of positive nominations are typically referred to as popular children, those with the highest number of negative nominations are considered unpopular or rejected. Children who receive neither kinds of nominations are referred to as neglected.

The use of negative nominations, however, is, at times, controversial because of the belief that it may be harmful to have children nominate peers for negative statements, and has led some educators to suggest that one only obtain positive nominations. Hayvren and Hymel (1984) have addressed these concerns in an article focused on the ethical issues of sociometric testing. From an analysis of behavioral observations made before and after sociometric testing, as well as 10 minutes after the testing, they concluded that peer interactions were not altered as a result of peer positive or negative nominations and they did not believe the concerns with negative nominations were warranted.

Obtaining both positive and negative nominations makes possible the identification of other categories of social status. One system for deriving categories has been used by Coie et al. (1982). A "controversial" category is obtained by adding positive and negative nominations. Negative nominations can also be subtracted from positive nominations, with children scoring high being described as "preferred." The use of both positive and negative nominations provides information from which one cannot only describe children as popular or unpopular, but also as neglected, rejected, controversial, or preferred. This system of derived scores is based on early work by Perry (1979) who saw derived scores extending the information available from nomination data.

The second most frequently used sociometric measure is the class rating method. This method was described by Thompson and Powell (1951) and has been popularized by Asher, Singleton, Tinsley, and Hymel (1979). To obtain the class ratings, each child is asked to rate each peer in the class according to a specific question, e.g., "How much do you like this child?" Older children are asked to respond on a scale from 1 to 3 or from 1 to 5. Younger children are typically presented with three "faces," one smiling, one neutral, one frowning, and are asked to point to the one that best fits how they feel about the child. Children's responses are then summed across each category. This method allows one to identify the most liked and least liked children in the class. It has an advantage over the nomination method in that it provides for the rating of every child by all the other children. It is limited, however, in that it does not make possible the distinction of rejected and neglected children, a distinction that is important for making decisions on intervention procedures.

The third method is the paired-comparison method, first described in 1933 by Koch, and later used by Cohen and Van Tassel (1978). Each child is presented with every possible combination of two classroom peers and is asked to state a preference for one of the peers in response to a question such as "Which one do you like to play with the best?" This method has the advantage of asking children to make comparisons between two children, an easier task than making judgments comparing one child to all other children in the class. This method is also superior in that fewer assumptions are required concerning the psychometric properties of the data. It is, however, very time consuming and may not provide information more useful than the other procedures.

With children who can read and write, one can ask them to write down nominations for questions on the restricted nomination procedure, or ask them to circle a rating on the class rating form. With preschoolers and children in kindergarten and first grade, sociometric measures need to be obtained in a one-to-one situation, with the assessor asking the child questions and writing the responses. To facilitate children's memory of all their classmates, Marshall and McCandless (1957) used a picture-sociometric procedure, in which pictures of all the children in the room are placed randomly on a board for each child to see when making nominations.

An alternative peer nomination procedure is sometimes used to provide additional information on children. This procedure calls for children to nominate peers who best fit particular descriptors, such as "Who is the child in your class who helps others and shares?" "Who is the child in your class who likes to be alone?" and "Who is the child in your class who fights?" This procedure is based on the Bower Class Play procedure (Bower, 1960), in which children are nominated for particular roles in a play. Hops and Lewin (1984) have suggested that this procedure can be used to help validate information from sociometric measures. It can also provide information helpful in planning for children. For example, one might find that a rejected child is also the child identified by most of the children as a child who fights a lot, whereas another rejected child is inattentive and disruptive.

USE OF SOCIOMETRIC MEASUREMENT WITH AT-RISK STUDENTS

Do sociometric measures have a place in public schools? The current research provides sufficient support to warrant their use for both intervention and research purposes. For intervention purposes, certain guidelines should hold. First, professional judgment is as necessary in viewing sociometric data as it is with any other assessment data. Results that indicate a child may have social problems need to be corroborated by other data such as direct observation of the child's behavior, information from parents, teacher impressions, and child interviews. Other psychological assessment may be indicated. It is not recommended that one set up an intervention program based solely on sociometric data. Rather, it is important to identify the specific child characteristics that appear to be contributing to the low social acceptance and to identify environmental variables that may be influencing the child's behavior. One can then focus interventions on those behavioral, cognitive, and environmental variables that would likely make a difference. Furthermore, teachers may well be advised to look for specific areas of competence on the part of a child with a high likelihood of being rejected, and help identify and develop those areas of competence, thereby giving the child an area in which both the child and others can recognize the child's competence.

For formal assessment of social status, it is recommended that one use the nomination procedure with both positive and negative nominations because this procedure provides the most help in identifying children who may need special attention to their social status (Wasik, 1987). Teachers who do use sociometric measures need to become familiar with the differences in procedures recommended for children of different ages. For preschoolers and kindergarten children, investigators recommend interviewing children individually and providing them with pictures of their classmates to help them remember all their peers (see, e.g., Marshall & McCandless, 1957). For children in the third grade or older, investigators typically use a group administration procedure. At the first and second grade levels, empirical work is needed to determine if group assessment will yield comparable data to individual assessment.

Teachers can typically call on psychologists or counselors in their school to assist in the assessment of social status. In classrooms where teachers have assistants, the assistants could help carry out the individual assessment. It is particularly desirable to involve other school support personnel when one is concerned about an individual child's social adjustment for the child's problems may call for further assessment, intervention, and parental involvement.

In addition to the formal procedures for assessment of social status, it is possible to provide guidelines for teachers to informally identify children who would likely have a low peer acceptance. Teachers can note those child characteristics that are highly predictive of low social status, including such handicapping conditions as cognitive delays, hyperactivity, and learning disabilities. Second, the teacher can make note of children who exhibit behaviors correlated with social rejection, such as fighting and bossiness. They can observe children who fail at attempts to engage their peers in social interactions and they can identify children who are verbally or physically rejected by other children. Such information is frequently used by teachers to facilitate each child's classroom adjustment and to refer children as needed for further assessment.

Because sociometric measurement is time consuming to collect and summarize, one might ask if teacher judgment of peer status is a sufficient measurement procedure. Gronlund (1959) considered teachers' judgments of children's popularity to be in close agreement to children's judgments of popularity. More recently, Kennedy (1988) has also considered teacher ratings to be valid substitutes for peer judgments. Landau, Milich, and Whitten (1984), however, in studying teacher and peer ratings of kindergarten children, found that high agreement existed on a popularity dimension, but that teachers were not as accurate as peers in identifying rejected behavior.

Before a teacher decides to rely exclusively upon his or her own judgment, two points should be considered. First, it seems wise for a teacher to make a self-comparison of how closely one's own judgments parallel those of one's students. Areas of discrepancies may vary from teacher to teacher, with some teachers being more sensitive to particular social behaviors. Learning one's areas of discrepancy could help a teacher better identify children's peer status in the future. Second, the reason for the teacher's assessment has to be considered. If the objective is to pair children for working together, such assessment may more than adequately meet the objective. If, on the other hand, the purpose is to identify rejected children for a specific intervention program, peer assessment may be warranted. Furthermore, it is important to recognize that teachers and peers may respond to child characteristics in a different way, with one more concerned than the other about particular child behaviors. These areas of discrepancy need to be pursued to determine the value of different judgments over time.

One of the most important ways to use sociometric measurement is to facilitate the early identification of children whose peer relations are predictive of poor school achievement, continued social rejection, and a high likelihood of school dropout. In a collaborative effort with a North Carolina school system, we have been studying the possibility of using sociometric data in the early identification of children at-risk for school failure. As part of this effort, the preschool screening program at one school was extended into the kindergarten year and during that time sociometric information was obtained individually from all the children.

Because little documentation existed in the literature on the reliability of sociometric data with young children, we first determined the consistency of kindergarten children's sociometric responses over time. Children were assessed four months after the beginning of the school year, allowing time for the children to become familiar with their classmates, and again five months later, providing as much time as possible between the two assessment occasions. The results showed that sociometric measurement is a relatively reliable and valid measure for kindergarten children and can justifiably be used for the early identification of at-risk children (Wasik, 1987).

To investigate children's sociometric status and school success, teachers were asked to indicate for each child in her class whether that child was at-risk for school failure, in particular, grade retention. Children were identified as no risk, moderate risk, or high risk. The social status of the children in each group was then analyzed, showing strong and significant differences for the high risk group compared to the other two groups. The high risk group was characterized as being less liked, more disliked. They also were nominated significantly more often as children who upset things, start fights, ask for help, and cry (Wasik, Wasik, & Frank, 1988). From these data it seems clear that a close relationship between social and academic achievement not only exists, but can be documented as early as the first few months in school.

Such data, combined with other current evidence in using sociometric status as a predictor of at-risk children, is compelling and provides support for including such assessments in the early identification of children. It is equally important, however, to work towards identifying important subgroups of children within the at-risk categories. Furthermore, we must recognize that the identification of a subgroup does not readily lead to appropriate interventions. Within such groups, the particular problems of individual children must be identified before decisions can be made on appropriate interventions.

Children's social competence must not be taken lightly. The correlation of social competence with behavioral and cognitive difficulties, and the long-term poor prognosis of children with particular social problems should assure a high priority in our schools for promoting conditions that facilitate social acceptance of each child. Such a priority should be on par with academic success, for the interwoven nature of children's social and academic behavior suggests that success in one area frequently depends upon success in the other.

REFERENCES

Argyle, M. (1969). *The psychology of interpersonal behavior*. London: Penguin.

Asarnow, J. R. (1988). Peer status and social competence in child psychiatric inpatients: A comparison of children with depressive, externalizing, and concurrent depressive and externalizing disorders. *Journal of Abnormal Child Psychology, 16*, 151-162.

Asher, S. R., Singleton, L. C., Tinsley, B. R., & Hymel, S. (1979). A reliable sociometric measure for preschool children. *Developmental Psychology, 15*, 443-444.

Beck, S., Forehand, R., Wells, K. C., & Quante, A. (1978, November). *Social skills training with children: An examination of generalization from analogue to natural settings*. Paper presented at the annual meeting of the Association for Advancement of Behavior Therapy, Chicago.

Bender, W. N., Wyne, M. D., Stuck, G. B, & Bailey, D. B. (1984). Relative peer status of learning disabled, educable mentally handicapped, low achieving, and normally achieving children. *Child Study Journal, 13,* 209-216.

Bonney, M. E. (1971). Assessment of efforts to aid socially isolated elementary school pupils. *Journal of Educational Research, 64,* 359-364.

Bornstein, M. R., Bellack, A. S., & Hersen, M. (1977). Social skills training for unassertive children: A multiple-baseline analysis. *Journal of Applied Behavior Analysis, 10,* 183-195.

Bower, E. M. (1960). *Early identification of emotionally handicapped children.* Springfield, IL: Charles C. Thomas.

Bruininks, V. L. (1978a). Actual and perceived peer status of learning disabled students in mainstream programs. *Journal of Special Education, 12,* 51-58.

Bruininks, V. L. (1978b). Peer status and personality characteristics of learning disabled and nonlearning disabled students. *Journal of Learning Disabilities, 11,* 484-489.

Clark, E. (1964). Children's perceptions of educable mentally retarded children. *American Journal of Mental Deficiency, 68,* 602-611.

Cohen, A. S., & Van Tassel, E. (1978). A comparison of partial and complete paired comparisons in sociometric measurement of preschool groups. *Applied Psychological Measurement, 2,* 31-40.

Coie, J. D., Dodge, K. A., & Coppotelli, H. (1982). Dimensions and types of social status: A cross-age perspective. *Developmental Psychology, 18,* 4, 557-570.

Coie, J. D., & Krebbiel, G. (1984). Effects of academic tutoring on the social status of low-achieving, socially rejected children. *Child Development, 55,* 1465-1478.

Coie, J. D., & Kupersmidt, J. B. (1983). A behavioral analysis of emerging social status in boys' groups. *Child Development, 54,* 1400-1416.

Cowen, E. L., Pederson, A., Babigian, H., Izzo, L. D., & Trost, M. A. (1973). Long-term follow-up of early detected vulnerable children. *Journal of Consulting and Clinical Psychology, 41,* 438-446.

Dodge, K. A. (1983). Behavioral antecedents of peer social status. *Child Development, 54,* 1386-1399.

Dodge, K. A, & Frame, C. L. (1982). Social cognitive biases and deficits in aggressive boys. *Child Development, 53,* 620-635.

Goodman, H., Gottlieb, J., & Harrison, R. (1972). Social acceptance of EMRs integrated into a nongraded elementary school. *American Journal of Mental Deficiency, 76,* 412-417.

Gottlieb, J. (1978). Observing social adaptations in schools. In G. P. Sacket (Ed.), *Theory and applications in mental retardation (Vol. 1).* Baltimore: University Park Press.

Gottman, J. M. (1977). Toward a definition of social isolation in children. *Child Development, 48,* 513-517.

Gresham, F. M. (1981). Social skills training with handicapped children: A review. *Review of Educational Research, 51,* 139-176.

Gronlund, N. E. (1959). *Sociometry in the classroom*. New York: Harper.
Hartup, W. W. (1979). Peer relations and the growth of social competence. In M. W. Kent & J. E. Rolf (Eds.), *Primary prevention of psychopathology: Vol. 3. Social competence in children* (pp. 150-170). Hanover, NH: University Press of New England.
Hartup, W. W. (1983). Peer relations. In P. Mussen (Ed.), *Handbook of child psychology (Vol. 4)*. New York: Wiley & Sons.
Hayvren, M., & Hymel, S. (1984). Ethical issues in sociometric testing: The impact of sociometric measures on interaction behavior. *Developmental Psychology, 20*, 844-849.
Hops, H. (1982). Social skills training for socially withdrawn/isolated children. In P. Karoly & J. Steffen (Eds.), *Enhancing children's competencies* (pp. 39-97). Lexington, MA: Lexington Publishing Co.
Hops, H., & Lewin, L. (1984). Peer sociometric forms. In T. H. Ollendick & M. Hersen (Eds.), *Child behavioral assessment: Principles and procedures* (pp. 124-147). New York: Pergamon Press.
Hops, H., Walker, H. M., & Greenwood, C. R. (1979). PEERS: A program for remediating social withdrawal in the school setting: Aspects of a research and development process. In L. A. Hamerlynck (Ed.), *The history and future of the developmentally disabled: Programmatic and methodological issues*. New York: Bruner/Mazel.
Hymel, S. (1983). Preschool children's peer relations: Issues in sociometric assessment. *Merrill-Palmer Quarterly, 29*, 237-260.
Jennings, K. D. (1975). People versus object orientation, social behavior and intellectual abilities in children. *Developmental Psychology, 11*, 511-519.
Kennedy, J. (1988). Issues in the identification of socially incompetent children. *School Psychology Review, 17*(2), 276-288.
Koch, H. L. (1933). Popularity in preschool children: Some related factors and a technique for its measurement. *Child Development, 4*, 164-175.
Ladd, G. W., & Asher, S. R. (1985). Social skills training and children's peer relations. In L. L. Abate & M. Milan (Eds.), *Handbook of social skills training and research* (pp. 219-244). New York: Wiley.
Lahey, B. B., Green, K. D., & Forehand, R. (1980). On the independence of ratings of hyperactivity, conduct problems, and attention deficits in children: A multiple regression analysis. *Journal of Consulting and Clinical Psychology, 48*, 566-574.
Landau, S., Milich, R., & Whitten, P. (1984). A comparison of teacher and peer assessment of social status. *Journal of Clinical Child Psychology, 13*, 44-49.
Marshall, H. R., & McCandless, B. R. (1957). Relationships between dependence on adults and social acceptance by peers. *Child Development, 28*, 413-419.
Moreno, J. L. (1934). *Who shall survive? A new approach to the problem of human intervention*. Washington, DC: Nervous and Mental Disease Publishing.
O'Connor, R. D. (1972). Relative efficacy of modeling, shaping, and the com-

bined procedures for modification of social withdrawal. *Journal of Abnormal Psychology, 79,* 327-334.

Oden, S., & Asher, S. R. (1977). Coaching children in social skills for friendship making. *Child Development, 48,* 495-506.

Parker, J. G., & Asher, S. R. (1987). Peer relations and later personal adjustment: Are low-accepted children at risk? *Psychological Bulletin, 102,* 357-389.

Perry, J. C. (1979). Popular, amiable, isolated, rejected: A reconceptualization of sociometric status in preschool children. *Child Development, 50,* 1231-1234.

Putallaz, M. (1983). Predicting children's sociometric status from their behavior. *Child Development, 54,* 1417-1426.

Putallaz, M., & Gottman, J. (1981). An interactional model of children's entry into peer groups. *Child Development, 52,* 986-994.

Putallaz, M., & Gottman, J. (1982). Conceptualizing social competence in children. In P. Karoly & J. J. Steffen (Eds.), *Improving children's competence: Advances in child behavioral analysis and therapy* (Vol. 1) (pp. 1-33). Lexington, MA: Lexington Books.

Quay, L. C., & Jarrett, O. S. (1984). Predictors of social acceptance in preschool children. *Developmental Psychology, 20,* 793-796.

Rardin, D. R., & Moan, C. D. (1971). Peer interaction and cognitive development. *Child Development, 42,* 1685-1689.

Richard, B. A., & Dodge, K. A. (1982). Social maladjustment and problem-solving among school-age children. *Journal of Consulting and Clinical Psychology, 50,* 226-233.

Roff, M., Sills, S. B., & Golden, M. M. (1972). *Social adjustment and personality development in children.* Minneapolis: University of Minnesota Press.

Rubin, K. H., & Daniels-Beirness, T. (1983). Concurrent and predictive correlates of sociometric status in kindergarten and grade 1 children. *Merrill-Palmer Quarterly, 29,* 337-351.

Shantz, C. U. (Ed.) (1983). Popular, rejected, and neglected children: Their social behavior and social reasoning. *Merrill-Palmer Quarterly, 25.*

Thompson, G. G., & Powell, M. (1951). An investigation of the rating-scale approach to the measurement of social status. *Educational and Psychological Measurement, 11,* 440-445.

Vaugh, B. E., & Langlois, J. H. (1983). Physical attractiveness as a correlate of peer status and social competence in preschool children. *Developmental Psychology, 19,* 561-567.

Vosk, B., Forehand, R., Parker, J., & Rickard, K. (1982). A multi-method comparison of popular and unpopular children. *Developmental Psychology, 18,* 571-575.

Wanlass, R. L., & Prinz, R. J. (1982). Methodological issues in conceptualizing and treating childhood social isolation. *Psychological Bulletin, 92,* 39-55.

Wasik, B. H. (1987). Sociometric measure and peer descriptors of kindergarten children: A study of reliability and validity. *Journal of Clinical Child Psychology, 16,* 218-224.

Wasik, B. H., Wasik, J. L., & Frank, R. (1988, August). *Sociometric characteristics of children at risk for school failure*. Presented at the American Psychological Association meeting, Atlanta, Georgia.

Weincott, M. G., Corson, J. A., & Wilchesky, M. (1979). Teacher mediated treatment of social withdrawal. *Behavior Therapy, 10*, 281-294.

White, B. L. (1979). Social competence. In M. Kent & J. Rolf (Eds.), *The primary prevention of psychopathology: Promoting social competence and coping in children (Vol. 3)*. Hanover, NH: University Press of New England.

Yellott, A. W., Lien, G. R., & Cowen, E. L. (1969). Relationships among measures of adjustment, sociometric status, and achievement in third graders. *Psychology in the Schools, 6*, 315-321.

Diagnosis of Youth At-Risk for Suicide, Pregnancy, and Drug and Alcohol Abuse

David A. Sabatino
Robert R. Smith

West Virginia College of Graduate Studies

SUMMARY. The intent of this paper is to overview three selected subgroups of at-risk youth. These subgroups are: suicidal adolescents, pregnant teenagers, and drug and alcohol abusers.

Alternatives to traditional diagnostic procedures will be examined from the perspective of determining whether they can effectively and efficiently provide information necessary to develop a client management plan. A continuing diagnostic process providing the data base for a client information system is proposed. Such diagnostic practices can promote the early recognition of at-risk behaviors, thus increasing the general awareness, or early recognition, that may be crucial to preventive efforts.

Discussion is provided for the use of the term at-risk. In this paper, the term is used to mean more than an adolescent who is simply at academic risk and prone to dropping out (being stopped or pushed out) of school. As used here, the at-risk group includes a number of students who are not only failing academically, but display unwanted social-personal behaviors, leading to possible adjudication or requiring community based support services, while some may even be in life-threatening circumstances.

Problem behavior theory (Jessor & Jessor, 1977) states that two requirements must exist to generate deviant behavior. First, adolescents' nonconforming attitudes and values must converge with their attempts to claim adult status. Rather than attempting to achieve

---

Requests for reprints should be directed to: David A. Sabatino, Division of Behavioral Studies and Humanities, West Virginia College of Graduate Studies, Institute, WV 25112.

© 1990 by The Haworth Press, Inc. All rights reserved.

maturity through acceptable passage into the adult social order (the completion of school, entry into the labor force, marriage, and childbearing), they enter into what they perceive to be adult behaviors (smoking, drinking, drugs, precocious sexual activity, norm-violating and disruptive behavior). Secondly, a number of these behaviors may serve to produce a single at-risk factor. Each at-risk factor reduces the opportunity for successful entry into adult life. There may be some unknown serial effect or order of occurrence among at-risk behaviors in adolescents. Clearly, academic and social failure remain the most frequently reported relational factors, probably because they are more easily observed and do not have the same grave legal or social-personal implication as do many of the other indicators (McDill, Natriello, & Pallas, 1987).

Recent research (Lowery, 1986) has delineated a profile of at-risk students that most teachers can describe from experience: (a) a developing pattern of poor achievement; (b) discipline problems; (c) lack of motivation; (d) poor attendance; and (e) gradual academic, emotional, and physical withdrawal from school and a competitive peer social group (Miller & Norman, 1979). These students are confronted with depreciating achievement motivation, having internalized learned helplessness, demonstrated as a loss of self-reliance and self-determination (Weiner, 1974). Management plans dealing with the specific aspects of regard for self are rarely stated in instructional objectives. If learned helplessness is the impeding factor in the successful involvement in school, it must be countered with a learning approach that facilitates the learning of self-helpfulness (Klein & Seligman, 1974).

The use of a self-control curriculum has been an excellent intervention approach for learned helplessness (Glasser, 1987). Learned helplessness is not corrected by continuing remediation. It is a learned behavior and, as such, can be extinguished and replaced with new positive behaviors. Intervention requires continued task orientation with an ongoing supportive relationship. It includes teaching that each human response requires decision making and that the decision making process must be based on realistic, and substantive feeling and thought (information). Students learn that decision making enables them to gain control of their lives. Information is power which provides freedom and self direction, that in turn provides on-task direction for task completion.

WHO COMPRISES THE GROUP OF AT-RISK YOUTH?

There are over four million handicapped children, approximately 12%, who attend the public school each year (National Center for Educational Statistics, 1987). Yet, only 60 to 80% of all entering students emerge from the public schools academically and socially successful (National Commission on Excellence in Education, 1983). Mann (1987) confirms that between 17% and 26% of the school age youth either drop-out or are stopped-out of school before graduation. Well over 10 million children will not be promoted this academic year. Grade retention has increased 25% since 1977. Even with the 12% handicapped group removed, there remains approximately 10 to 20% of the total school age population who do not qualify for special education. This poorly defined at-risk population appears to struggle with a variety of threatening obstacles. A partial listing of selected threatening obstacles include (Weitz, 1987):

1. Twenty-two percent of the homeless in this country are under the age of 18.
2. One in five children is born to a single parent.
3. One million teen-age women annually contact chlamydia, the fastest growing sexually transmitted disease and a leading cause of infertility and infant pneumonia.
4. Forty percent of the school age youth are from single parent families, foster homes, or nonrelative living arrangements.
5. Approximately 1.7 million children were reported as abused or neglected in 1984, a 40% increase since 1981.
6. Thirteen hundred babies are born daily to teen-age mothers, half of whom are unwed. America leads all European countries in teen-age pregnancies by at least a two to one ratio.
7. Hard drug use among teen-agers is at an all-time high with 6.2% reporting regular use and .04% reporting daily use.
8. Teen-age suicide is at a record high, with an increase of over

400% in the last 20 years. An estimated 5,000 deaths are attributed yearly to adolescent suicides.
9. Fifty three percent of the female drug users are sexually active, with a range of inappropriate reported behaviors which includes incorrigibility, truancy, running away, theft, and prostitution.
10. The number of children with AIDS is increasing. The first report in 1986 indicates 240 children with AIDS are under 13 years old.

SUBSTANCE ABUSE

Drug and alcohol use by teenagers has reached epidemic proportions and is considered by the United States Congress to be a major threat to the welfare of this nation. At least 23% of today's school age youth have used drugs at least once in the last month (Bennett, 1987). Shockingly, 75% of all drugs used by youth are purchased on school grounds. Today one in every six 13-year olds has used marijuana. And, marijuana is now 5 to 20 times stronger than it was 10 years ago.

Alcohol use is extremely common among adolescents. Jalali, Jalali, Crocetti, and Turner (1981) report that 80 to 91% of juveniles sampled reported regular use of alcohol. Drinking is considered by adolescents to be a socially normative, adult modeled behavior. The belief prevails among young people that drinking enhances social recognition, augments cognitive or motor function, and generally increases the degree of control in confronting life's problems (Sher & Levenson, 1982). One recent study (Mann, Chassin, & Sher, 1987) reports that adolescent problem drinkers believe their use of alcohol provides personal control and social enhancement. Alcohol is the ultimate tonic for youth who are academically and socially uncomfortable.

Marijuana use has been associated with "amotivational syndrome." Research on marijuana indicates it produces memory loss, distorts perceptions and, in some cases, causes paranoia and psychosis (Bennett, 1987).

Cocaine is the fastest growing drug, particularly in the cheap but potent form called crack. When smoked, crack produces instant feelings of extreme euphoria. Repeated use can cause addiction within days.

A variety of other chemical agents produce equally serious consequences. Phencyclidine (PCP) interrupts intellectual controls resulting in unpredictable and violent behaviors. Lysergic acid (LSD) produces illusions and hallucinations. Users of inhalants, (glue, gas, and solvents) suffer nausea, nosebleeds, fatigue, lack of coordination, and loss of appetite. Long term use can result in renal disease, hepatitis, even brain damage and death.

Drugs interfere with memory, sensation, and perception. They distort experiences and reduce self-control leading users to harm themselves or others. They impair academic learning through interference with the ability of the nervous system to receive, code, classify, and synthesize information. The user has a false sense of well being. Drug use erodes self discipline and the desire to achieve in school. Continued drug use causes a serious decline in grades. But, once drug use is discontinued, grades often improve (Bennett, 1987).

Heavy drug users report twice the number of unexcused absences from school versus those reported by nonusers. Drop-outs are twice as likely to be drug users, with four out of every five drop-outs using drugs regularly (Rhodes & Jason, 1988). Heavy drug users are three times more likely to vandalize school property. Students on drugs create a climate of apathy, disruption, and disrespect for others. Thirty-two percent of the teenagers calling the National Hotline sold drugs, whereas 64% said they stole from family, friends, or employers to buy drugs (Bennett, 1987). Another emphatic conclusion to this brief discussion of drugs is that more than half of all adolescent suicides are drug related.

SUICIDE

Suicide is the second leading cause of adolescent deaths in the United States (Spirito, Halverson, & Hart, 1985). In the United States, trauma remains the primary cause of death for those under age 30 (Trunkey, 1985). There is a plausible link between suicide and trauma. A depressed adolescent may die of trauma from an automobile accident that was a purposeful act. Adolescent suicide has increased 400% over the last 20 years. Females far out number male attempters. Male attempters have a much higher completion rate (Allen, 1987). The most common method of suicide is drug overdose. Drugs and alcohol are frequently used in combination with other suicidal behaviors. The most common recurring theme verbalized as a reason for committing suicide is depression. Depression is expressed through sexual promiscuity, school failures, and atypical sleeping and eating habits. Notable among depression related behaviors are increased complaints of physical illness. Fifty percent of the adolescents attempting suicide saw a doctor in the preceding month and 25% within the preceding week (Donovan & Jessor, 1985).

There is little empirical data available on the possible relationship between various social and psychological factors and attempted suicides. The most prevalent belief is that suicide is multi-determined. The relationship between hopelessness, depression, and suicidal intent has been studied in children (Kazdin, French, Unis, Esveldt-Dawson, & Sherick, 1983). Hopelessness alone was not a significant variable. But, hopelessness in combination with other variables became a principal factor in differentiating those who contemplate suicide but do not attempt it from those who do attempt it. One major factor that differentiates suicide attempters from ideators is social skills deficits. This powerful predictor of adolescent suicide attempters was reported by Strauss, Forehand, Frame, and Smith (1984). Their work indicates that social skill deficiencies are the inability of students to effectively obtain desirable social and academic outcomes. The result, a loss of social esteem and positive peer recognition, in combination with hopelessness (a loss of peer recognition may generate hopelessness), remains the most robust of predictors.

There is mounting evidence that unmanageable academic and social stress, coupled with depression, is the best predictor of suicide. Spirito, Halverson, and Hart (1985) examined the relationship between social skills and depression in adolescent suicide attempters. Their findings (drawn from self-report data) indicated low positive correlations between student depression and social skills; social skills which are needed to cope with problems of everyday living. Teacher observations failed to report the depression. They did recognize the absence of social skills that prevented the students from solving academic and social issues related to everyday school life. The variance between student and teacher reports suggests that teachers are not aware of the severity of the student's depression. Students and teachers do agree that the absence of appropriate social skills is associated with reduced coping capacity and prevailing feelings of hopelessness.

In 1974, Schaffer found that a large proportion of 12- to 14-year-old students who committed suicide were physically large and intellectually superior. Schnuer (1976) reviewed the current literature and found that the gifted are subject to pressures and tend to be less emotionally stable. More recently, Leroux (1986) noted that teachers and counselors are frequently unaware of the conflicts and stresses being experienced by gifted students. This group of exceptional students is not considered to have overwhelming social-personal adjustment difficulties. Nonetheless, gifted or talented students may feel increased pressures to achieve academically. Beck (1967) notes gifted children demonstrate heightened sensitivities to historic cycles of human suffering and the absence of social amelioration. These sensitivities might result in a sense of hopelessness for these particularly sensitive students that is frequently unrecognized by the professional educational community.

Sadly, 57 suicide attempts are confirmed each day, 13 of which are successfully completed (Pfeffer, Conte, Plutchik, & Jerrett, 1980). As many as 50% of the unsuccessful attempters try again; 10% within the same year (Pfeffer, 1981). One of the major issues with teenage suicide is recognizing when it should be taken seriously, and when it is a message with another meaning. The safest response to the issue of recognition is to obtain mental health referrals on all those that verbalize or show any indicators, such as either a lack of perceived social skill success, or hopelessness in any of its many forms. A suicidal threat, by even a non-suicidal student, may be an awkward attempt to obtain a listener. That fact alone suggests that any person in a working relationship with an adolescent, or even preadolescent, must have enough knowledge to observe behaviors, respond realistically but calmly, and make referrals through a preplanned and policy guided structure to the appropriate internal or external (to the school) mental health professional.

The prevailing attitude of the adult community is critical to effectively preventing suicide. Any verbalization or observed behavior that reflects withdrawal or despair is worthy of school, community, and family concern. Suicide must be recognized as a very real issue. By understanding its symptoms, a prevention effort can be initiated by adding the social skills and eliminating the conditions for perceived hopelessness. The question is the extent to which the prevailing attitudes will encourage the educational community to focus on the students' concerns and not simply reflect academic achievement concerns of school officials (Walker, 1980).

PREGNANCY

Anastasiow (1983) raises a question: Why should special educators be concerned with 1.2 million adolescents who bear over 550,000 offsprings each year? His contention is that a disproportionate number of their offspring will become future consumers of special education. Society has traditionally associated pregnancy with marriage, subsequent to the transition from adolescence into adulthood. This transition is marked by behaviors which define evolving maturity including graduation, employment, marriage, and parenthood (Hogan, 1981). Deviations from the time table and from sequential achievement of these events may result in negative consequences (Marini, 1984). The number of illegitimate births increased from 15% of the total teen births in 1960 to 48% in 1984 (National Center for Health Statistics, 1984).

It is significant to note that many of the same factors associated with adolescent drug use are also predictors for teenage pregnancy. These youth tend to be less religious, participate more frequently in delinquent activities, have poorer relationships with their parents, are heavily involved in peer culture, may be depressed, have low self esteem, and are high in other risk taking behaviors (Donovan & Jessor, 1985). Minority racial status, parents who fail to achieve a high school education, families with low educational aspirations are among the most consistent identifying factors (Hofferth & Hayes, 1987) associated with teenage pregnancy.

Yamaguchi and Kandel (1987) recently examined the risk factors in a group of adolescent women and found that premarital pregnancy is directly related to a loss or disruption in family roles. Mitchell (1984) identifies the leading predictive variables for teen pregnancies as: cohabitation, race, poor grades, high peer activity level, use of illicit drugs other than marijuana, and having dropped out of high school. Premarital sex and pregnancy may be used as a punitive measure against one's own parents. This behavior may reflect a need for security (and the fulfillment of that need) or it may reflect the need for peer status as an adult.

THE DIAGNOSTIC DILEMMA

Since the time of Binèt (1903), educators have complained that diagnosis, as used in medicine, is not applicable to the instructional process. Those faced with the management of at-risk youth agree that entry-level diagnosis does not take into consideration the constantly changing interpersonal relations and environmental circumstances faced by these adolescents. In this context, we will examine the concept of employing continuing diagnosis for the development of appropriate programming directed at the prevention, reduction, or elimination of at-risk behaviors prior to returning the student to a traditional educational environment. Such a radical departure in diagnostic practice requires a significant change in the traditional roles of the classical diagnostician and other support service personnel.

Another major concern, in opposition to traditional assessment practices with at-risk adolescents, is a dependence on diagnostic classification as an answer to the conflicts faced by these youth. Forness (1983) notes that traditional practices of assessing adolescents' behavioral problems is adequate for identification. Beyond the purpose of identification, traditional assessment data provides little usable information to guide the educational management of these troubled youth. One example is the ambiguity in the language of U.S. Public Law 94-142 concerning the role of the diagnostician. The individualized educational plan was designed to be written by the principals or their designee, or other appropriate educators, such as special services providers. The role of diagnosticians is not clear, except that they are to interpret diagnostic data. This practice removes the value and impact of describing behaviors and places greater emphasis, if not reliance, on the more easily used and reported test data. Test interpretation requires that scores be obtained from intellectual, developmental, and academic achievement tests, which reflect a limited sample of the social-personal development of at-risk students. The interpretation of scores is clearly not the same as observing or ascertaining behavior for the purpose of preventing or managing it. Management of at-risk adolescent behavior requires the development of hypotheoretical constructs (Kelly, 1955) capable of generating interventions.

There is literature (Heinlein, Nelson, & Hohenshil, 1984; Sabatino, Paulson, Allen, & Sedlak, 1984) to suggest that assessment practices with adolescents should ascertain the degree to which students can demonstrate academic, social/personal, and vocational skills necessary for independent living. Alternatives to traditional instructional support in curriculum areas such as consumerism, recreational and leisure activities, getting and keeping a job, lifestyle management, partnering and parenting skills, career information, general job knowledge, and specific job skills should also be identified and planned for at-risk students (Smith, Jenkins, Petko, & Warner, 1979). Clearly, adolescent behavioral and learning problems cannot be separated (Siperstein, Bopp, & Bak, 1978). To reduce the threat of failure, educators should begin to utilize diagnostic procedures that also provide information about the quality of adolescents' decision-making capability. Social/personal and vocational interests, aptitudes, and career knowledge levels should be ascertained among at-risk adolescents, forming a client information system that can be used to validate a management plan.

Dependence on the special education diagnostic model to establish a management plan for at-risk students may not be effective (Sabatino & Miller, 1979). A comparison of the behaviors for the two groups, handicapped vs. at-risk, exhibits some overlap as both student groups generally do not succeed academically and socially in school. But, the reasons for the absence of success are based on dissimilar behaviors. Some mild mentally retarded, learning disabled, and/or behaviorally disordered students could also be at risk. However the majority are not. A 16-year-old mild mentally retarded student, who is developmentally achieving academically at his predicted level and demonstrating commensurate social skills, is not necessarily at-risk. He is not demonstrating developmentally regressive behaviors nor is there threat to his personal well being. A 16-year-old intravenous drug user who is homeless, sexually active, and rapidly developing hopelessness that is contributing to depression, may be in a life-threatening situation.

One point of confusion is that the term at-risk historically referred solely to academic risk (Coker, Medley, & Soar, 1980). It was used in reference to preschool and early school age children who were predictably going to underachieve academically. Currently, educators use "at-risk" as a behavioral term suggesting the student is at-risk academically (a potential drop-out), at-risk behaviorally (demonstrating regressive behaviors), at-risk socially, used by correctional educators to describe students who will be adjudicated or recidivate (Combs, 1981).

In the absence of a universal use or understanding of the term, this paper defines "at-risk" as behavior that is developmentally regressive (does not demonstrate progressive growth), inhibits social skill achievement, and may be threatening to the student's well being. The importance of diagnostically isolating at-risk behaviors is that the causative conditions and social-environmental interactive forces may vary greatly in posing threatening or regressive conditions. One of the most critical, if not the most critical, diagnostic procedures is to differentiate surface relationship factors, such as blame bearing, or imaginary horrors, or manipulative or attention seeking behaviors, which camouflage the real causative factors.

It is not safe to assume that only academic and social failing students are at-risk (Edgar, Horton, & Maddox, 1984). In contrast to the previously described 16-year-old mentally retarded boy achieving at an expected grade level with commensurate social skill development, let us consider a 16-year-old child, with one abortion, who manifests a borderline personality with histrionic associated characteristics. Although of high average intelligence, she is barely passing some academic subjects. She is shy, relates well to other students, is attractive, and active in church, band, chorus, and a number of other community and school activities. She displays responsive, responsible behaviors in school and at home for a week or so. Then she becomes passively angry, runs away, and is absent for several days. During those periods she is seen with older men, drinking, and using drugs. Now she will no longer live with her parents, roams the community and is also believed to be pregnant. She is oppositional in response to her mother, and feels her father supports only her mother and never her. She has contemplated suicide and has been involved in one serious car accident, suggestive of a suicide attempt.

The brief case synopsis describes an adolescent who feels she has no family support. She feels rejected by her father. The borderline personality characteristics suggest limited self-control and a strong desire to be passively directed by others. She no longer trusts her own decision-making capacity but tends to generate behaviors orchestrated by others, primarily the peer group. She inflicts pain on her parents in an effort to force them to acknowledge her discomfort, which she blames on them. When she is able to cope, she assumes the "princess role" (associated with a histrionic personality characteristics) and seeks acceptable recognition by assuming parent pleasing behaviors such as the tasks of cooking, cleaning, and being socially responsive. During periods of despondency she desires to be a victim of others. She was hospitalized last week as a result of life-threatening circumstances.

Upon release in two to six weeks, a support structure must be built that can manage her at school or in a home related environment, and in the community. Her career goal is to become a cosmetologist. That is a realistic desire. Her current vocational program in practical nursing is the one area she finds enjoyable. This should become the center of her school experience. The prevailing attitude of the school must be changed and an advocacy/support structure developed. This case illustrates the need for a dynamic diagnosis, one that supplies continuing feedback and related data obtained in response to the specific activities and objectives present in the case management plan. Critical to the educational aspect of that management plan is a clear focus on her social development, so that it becomes the central curriculum theme and takes precedence over any academic considerations. That aspect will require a significant change in the prevailing attitude of the school.

The point to be made by this vignette is that the test, written report, special educational diagnostic placement model, all commonly utilized in the public schools, will not be effective with at-risk students. It simply does not provide an appropriately detailed description of the contributing behaviors. What, then, is essential in a comprehensive assessment?

A comprehensive assessment begins with a study of the immediate and extended family systems and focuses on school, community, and family resources that can be developed to provide emotional support structures for the student. Assessment should include consideration of such psychological constructs as achievement motivation, and impulse control. Personality functioning should be described with the clarity required in using the five axes from the *Diagnostic and Statistical Manual of Mental Disorders* (American Psychiatric Association, 1987), with a particular note to severity (axes four and five). Additionally, the range of skills needed for interpersonal success, independent living, and street survival should be considered. An analysis of social-personal behaviors that relate to adaptation and adjustment, willingness to learn (teachability), and the types and strengths of social pressures should also be included. Diagnosis can involve the use of several psychological constructs such as those developed by social learning theorists, such as locus of control and perceived social need status, for the purpose of assessing the decision-making capability or the need to be directed by others, including the peer group.

Career development providing specific social, academic, and vocational skills to obtain realistic goals are extremely important. It is not merely an issue of having these goals well developed, but identifying the social-personal developmental status, and knowing what academic, vocational, or social-personal data is needed and where it can be obtained in order to develop achievable career goals.

The following five points (Simon, 1986) may have some utility in the continuing diagnostic process with at-risk adolescents:

1. Ascertain the awareness, range and intensity of feelings directed to self and others.
2. Ascertain the personal (self) and environmental (social and family) limitations that inhibit interpersonal relationships.
3. Ascertain the boundaries of self-identity.
4. Ascertain any despondency, loneliness, hopelessness, and depression. Determine the emotional support base in family, ex-

tended family, or advocacy relationship, with peers, teachers, or significant others.
5. Ascertain the personality integration and capacity of the student to respond appropriately with self-initiated and self-regulated behaviors to the social/personal cues and needs of others.

A POLICY ISSUE

The number of at-risk youth in trouble in the school has stretched the larger society until there is no longer room for the homeless or the incarcerated. There is not enough treatment available for the drug and alcohol abusers who, at six million strong, are epidemic in proportion. The heart-break and loss of human resource in the death of an adolescent is beyond measure, especially when we have little means of understanding the despair that generates the hopelessness and depression resulting in suicide. The legacy (Maslow, 1960) that any generation leaves to the next generation is the best of times, and for far too many illegitimate babies only the worst of times. H. G. Wells, the noted historian said it best when he wrote, "the race is on between education and catastrophe." Who then will speak for the at-risk students? It is our contention that a different educational environment is needed; one based on prevention, and therefore, early recognition of a wide range of social and personal behaviors.

BIBLIOGRAPHY

Allen, B. P. (1987). Youth suicide. *Adolescence*, 22, 271-290.
American Psychiatric Association. (1987). *Diagnostic and statistical manual of mental disorders* (3rd ed.) (rev. ed.). Washington, DC: Author.
Anastasiow, N. J. (1983). Adolescent pregnancy and special education. *Exceptional Children*, 49, 396-401.
Beck, A. T. (1967). *Depression: Clinical, experimental and theoretical aspects*. New York: Hoeber.
Bennett, W. J. (1987). *What works: Schools without drugs*. Washington DC: U.S. Department of Education.
Binèt, A. (1903). *L'etude experimentale de intelligence* [An experimental study of intelligence]. Paris: Schleicher.
Coker, H., Medley, D. M., & Soar, R. S. (1980). How valid are expert opinions about effective teaching? *Phi Delta Kappan*, 62, 131-134.

Combs, A. (1981). Humanistic education: Too tender for a tough world? *Phi Delta Kappan, 62,* 446-449.

Donovan, J. E., & Jessor, R. (1985). Structure of behavior in adolescence and young adulthood. *Journal of Consulting and Clinical Psychology, 53,* 890-904.

Edgar, E., Horton, B., & Maddox, M. (1984). Planning for public school students with developmental disabilities. *Journal for Vocational Special Needs Education, 6*(2), 15-18.

Forness, S. R. (1983). Diagnostic schooling for children or adolescents with behavioral disorders. *Behavior Disorders, 8,* 176-190.

Glasser, W. (1987). The key to improving schools: An interview with William Glasser. *Phi Delta Kappan, 68,* 656-662.

Hofferth, S., & Hayes, C. (1987). *Risking the future: Adolescent sexuality, pregnancy, and childbearing* (Vol. 2). Washington, DC: National Academy Press.

Hogan, D. P. (1981). *Transitions and social change: The early lives of American men.* New York: Academic Press.

Hohenshil, T. H. (1984). Vocational aspects of school psychology: 1974-1984. *School Psychology Review, 13,* 503-509.

Jalali, B., Jalali, M., Crocetti, G., & Turner, F. (1981). Adolescents and drug use: Toward a more comprehensive approach. *American Journal of Orthopsychiatry, 51,* 120-130.

Jessor, R., & Jessor, S. L. (1977). *Problem behavior and psychological development: A longitudinal study of youth.* New York: Academic Press.

Kazdin, A. E., French, N. H., Unis, A. S., Esveldt-Dawson, K., & Sherick, R. B. (1983). Hopelessness, depression, and suicidal intent among psychiatrically disturbed inpatient children. *Journal of Consulting and Clinical Psychology, 51,* 504-510.

Kelly, G. A. (1955). *The psychology of personal constructs.* Vols. 1 and 2. New York: Norton.

Klein, D. C., & Seligman, M. E. (1974). Reversals of performance deficits and perceptual deficits in learned helplessness and depression. *Journal of Abnormal Psychology, 85,* 11-26.

Leroux, J. A. (1986). Suicidal behavior and gifted adolescents. *Roeper Review, 9,* 77-79.

Lowery, D. (1986). An advocacy service for the difficult-to-serve adolescents. *Guidance & Counseling, 1*(5), 30-34.

Mann, D. (1987). Can we help dropouts? Thinking about the undoable. In G. Natriello (Ed.), *School dropouts: Patterns and policies* (pp. 3-19). New York: Teachers College.

Mann, L. M., Chassin, L., & Sher, K. J. (1987). Alcohol expectancies and the risk for alcoholism. *Journal of Consulting and Clinical Psychology, 55,* 411-417.

Marini, M. M. (1984). The order of events in the transition to adulthood. *Sociology of Education, 57,* 63-84.

Maslow, A. (1960). Some basic propositions of a growth and self-actualization psychology: Perceiving, behaving, becoming. *ASCD Yearbook*.

McDill, E. L., Natriello, G., & Pallas, A. M. (1987). A population at risk: Potential consequences of tougher school standards for student dropouts. In G. Natriello (Ed.), *School dropouts: Patterns and policies* (pp. 106-147). New York: Teachers College.

Miller, I. W., & Norman, W. H. (1979). Learned helplessness in humans: A review and attribution-theory model. *Psychological Bulletin, 86*, 93-118.

Mitchell, M. F. (1984). Reducing the risks of teenage pregnancy. *Mobius, 4*(3), 20-25.

National Center for Educational Statistics. (1987). Washington, DC: U.S. Government Printing Office.

National Center for Health Statistics. (1984). *Vital statistics of the United States*. Washington, DC: Government Printing Office.

National Commission on Excellence in Education. (1983). *Nation at risk*. Washington, DC: Secretary of Education, U.S. Department of Education.

Pfeffer, C. R. (1981). Suicide behavior of children: A review with implications for research and practice. *American Journal of Psychiatry, 138*, 154-159.

Pfeffer, C. R., Conte, H. R., Plutchik, R., & Jerrett, J. (1980). Suicidal behavior in latency age children: An out-patient population. *Journal of American Academy of Child Psychiatry, 19*, 707-710.

Rhodes, J. E., & Jason, L. A. (1988). *Preventing substance abuse among children and adolescents*. New York: Pergamon Press.

Sabatino, D. A., & Miller, T. L. (1979). *Describing learner characteristics of handicapped children and youth*. New York: Grune & Stratton.

Sabatino, D. A., Paulson, D., Allen, D., & Sedlak, R. A. (1984). Integrating vocational education: Techniques. *Techniques: A Journal for Remedial Education and Counseling, 1*, 53-66.

Schaffer, D. (1974). Suicide in childhood and early adolescence. *Journal of Child Psychology and Psychiatry, 15*, 275-291.

Schnuer, G. (1976). Emotional disturbance and giftedness. *Gifted Child Quarterly, 20*, 470-477.

Sher, K. J., & Levenson, R. W. (1982). Risk for alcoholism and individual differences in the stress-response-dampening effect of alcohol. *Journal of Abnormal Psychology, 91*, 350-367.

Simon, J. I. (1986). Day hospital treatment for borderline adolescents. *Adolescence, 21*, 561-571.

Siperstein, G. H., Bopp, M.J., & Bak, J.J. (1978). Social status of learning disabled children. *Journal of Learning Disabilities, 11*, 98-102.

Smith, R. R., Jenkins, W. O., Petko, C. M., & Warner, R. W., Jr. (1979). An experimental application and evaluation of rational behavior therapy in a work release setting. *Journal of Counseling Psychology, 36*, 519-525.

Spirito, A., Halverson, J., & Hart, K. (1985, November). *The relationship between social skills and depression in adolescent suicide attempters*. Paper presented at the Annual Meeting of the Association for Advancement of Behavior Therapy, Houston, TX.

Strauss, C. C., Forehand, R., Frame, C., & Smith, K. (1984). Characteristics of children with extreme scores on the Children's Depression Inventory. *Journal of Clinical Child Psychology, 13*, 227-231.

Trunkey, D. D. (1985). Trauma care systems. *Medicine Clinics of North America, 2*, 913-922.

Walker, W. L. (1980). Intentional self-injury in school-age children. *Journal of Adolescence, 3*, 217-228.

Weiner, B. (1974). *Achievement motivation and attribution theory*. Morristown, NJ: General Learning Press.

Weitz, J. H. (1987). America's children: Growing up at risk. *State Government News*, 8-9, 26.

Yamaguchi, K., & Kandel, D. (1987). Drug use and other determinants of premarital pregnancy and its outcome: A dynamic analysis of competing life events. *Journal of Marriage and the Family, 49*, 257-270.

PART II: CLASSROOM-BASED APPROACHES IN PROMOTING STUDENT SUCCESS

Behavioral Self-Management with At-Risk Children

F. Charles Mace
Michael C. Shea

Rutgers University

SUMMARY. This paper presents an overview of the use of behavioral self-management techniques with students at-risk for academic or behavioral problems. The major components of self-management are reviewed (self-monitoring, self-evaluation, self-reinforcement, and self-instruction) with illustrations from the educational literature. The two major theoretical models of self-management (cognitive-behavioral and operant) are discussed, followed by suggestions for practitioners on how they may design and implement self-management programs for students identified as at-risk for special education placements. Self-management techniques may help to prevent at-risk students from being placed in restrictive special education placements.

Requests for reprints should be directed to: F. Charles Mace, Graduate School of Applied and Professional Psychology, Rutgers University, Piscataway, NJ 08854.

© 1990 by The Haworth Press, Inc. All rights reserved.

The use of self-management techniques has grown steadily since their introduction in the late 1960s. They have been utilized to remediate a variety of problems in many groups and individuals, encompassing a variety of ages and populations. Because self-management techniques are generally self-administered and often use positive reinforcement techniques to affect behavior change, they have become increasingly popular among both educators and parents (Witt & Elliott, 1985). Other advantages of self-management techniques which may contribute to their increasing acceptability in the classroom include: (a) the flexibility of self-management techniques allows them to be utilized with a variety of different academic and social behaviors, (b) self-management techniques reduce the amount of time teachers devote to implementing and managing interventions (by involving students in the implementation of self-management methods), and (c) self-management techniques are compatible with the consultation model of service delivery (see Bergan, 1977, and Lentz & Shapiro, 1985 for further discussion of this model), thus allowing more students to be served with current student/staff ratios.

These qualities of self-management make it a potentially valuable tool for use with students at-risk for educational and/or behavioral problems that may lead to special education placement. For example, self-management procedures have been successful in improving reading, math, and handwriting skills, increasing prosocial classroom behavior, as well as decreasing aggression, off-task, and various disruptive behaviors (Mace & Kratochwill, 1988). Because these target behaviors are observed frequently in children with educational or behavioral handicaps (Gardner, 1977), self-management strategies appear well-suited to this population.

Further, self-management methods may be applied as a prereferral intervention that may avert a time-consuming psychoeducational assessment process that is oriented toward diagnosis and special educational placement (Curtis, Zins, & Graden, 1987). Successful application of self-management techniques at this stage may avoid restrictive educational placements that have not been shown to be more beneficial than mainstreaming approaches (Algozzine, Christenson, & Ysseldyke, 1982).

Our objectives in this paper are to introduce the reader to the major components of self-management: self-monitoring (SM), self-evaluation (SE), self-reinforcement (SR), and self-instruction (SI) along with examples from the literature illustrating the application of these self-management components in educational settings with various student populations, but particularly with those at-risk for special education placement. We begin with a brief overview of the two major theoretical models of self-management because the models emphasize different self-management components and mechanisms responsible for behavior change. Following an overview of self-management components, suggestions for practitioners designing and implementing self-management techniques for at-risk students will be offered.

THEORETICAL MODELS OF BEHAVIORAL SELF-MANAGEMENT

Much of the conceptual and procedural developments in behavioral self-management have been influenced by two theoretical models. Proponents of the cognitive-behavioral view have proposed a multistage process of self-management which consists of various components. This model has the student monitor his/her own behavior, evaluate it against a standard, and deliver rewards to himself/herself based on whether or not the standard is met. Much of this process can occur covertly; thus, the cognitive-behavioral model is one which emphasizes covert thought processes rather than environmental contingencies in the self-management process.

The operant model, on the other hand, views self-managed behavior as a product of environmental contingencies. Nelson and Hayes (1981) have proposed an operant model of self-management in which the individual arranges the environment to improve one's discrimination of and response to environmental contingencies, which operant theorists believe ultimately control an individual's behavior. The operant model proposes an interactive relationship between a student's behavior and the environment. This relationship is one where the individual acts to alter his/her environment which, in turn, may alter his/her behavior through reinforcement contingencies.

The cognitive-behavioral and operant models have been very influential in the development of self-management procedures. Therefore, as part of the discussion of the components of self-management, we will briefly present each theory's position regarding the mechanisms believed to be responsible for the effects produced by each component.

SELF-MONITORING

Self-monitoring (SM) is the simplest of the self-management components to utilize in the classroom. It only requires that the student observe his/her behavior in the classroom. Hence, this makes SM a procedure which could be used with at-risk students in many classroom situations.

Self-monitoring is a two-step process (Nelson, 1977). The first step, self-observation, requires that the student be able to discriminate the presence or absence of his/her own target behavior(s). Second, the student self-records the occurrence of one or more dimensions of the target behavior (e.g., frequency or duration). Self-monitoring from the operant tradition involves the production of permanent physical recordings (e.g., data sheets, mechanized data collectors, etc.), whereas the cognitive-behavioral model would permit the individual to keep a mental record of the occurrence or nonoccurrence of the target behavior. The accuracy of these recordings can be maximized if the target behaviors selected are operationally defined.

Reactive effects often produced by SM make it a potentially valuable self-management intervention. The reactivity of SM may be defined as the change in the target response(s) that results from the observation and recording of one's own behavior. The change in the target response is usually in the same direction as the target response's valence; hence, behaviors with a negative balance (e.g., out-of-seat) would decrease, whereas those considered positive would increase (e.g., on-task) (Nelson, 1977). The reactive benefits of SM have been utilized in a large number of psychoeducationally-based studies with favorable results reported across subjects, settings, and problem behaviors (Gardner & Cole, 1988; Shapiro, 1984).

A study by Workman, Helton, and Watson (1982) demonstrated

both the potential effectiveness of SM as an intervention for at-risk students and the ease with which the investigator worked with the classroom teacher in a manner compatible with the consultative model of service delivery. The investigators taught a 4-year-old male pre-school student to self-monitor his on- and off-task behavior and compliance with teacher instructions. The student was instructed to make a mark on a piece of paper each time a timer sounded if he was working on a teacher-assigned task and had been following teacher directions. Reinforcement for these behaviors was not offered. Using this SM procedure, on-task and compliance behaviors increased substantially compared to baseline levels, and were replicated in a ABAB reversal design. Although the teacher was not directly involved in the training phase, teacher participation has been frequently reported in other SM studies. Thus, this procedure might require little adaptation to be used within the consultative framework.

An early study by Gottman and McFall (1972) demonstrated the successful implementation of SM in a group setting. The subjects were 17 high school sophomore students (11 males and 6 females). The subjects were enrolled in a special education program for students identified as at-risk for dropping out of school, and had been labeled by staff at one point as "emotionally disturbed," "culturally disadvantaged," "socially disadvantaged," or "alienated." The subjects were divided into two experimental groups. In one experimental condition, students received a pink card on which they were to place a check mark each time they verbally participated in class (e.g., answering a question or commenting on class material). The other condition consisted of students placing a check mark on a green card each time they *wanted to* verbally participate in the class but did not. The results of this study indicated that when students were in the pink card condition, verbal participation in class increased substantially over baseline levels. Conversely, when the students were in the green card condition, verbal participation decreased substantially as compared to the pink card condition and either stayed the same or decreased as compared to baseline verbal participation. Gottman and McFall also reported some gains in academic achievement that appeared to be a positive side-effect of the SM procedure. Thus, these two studies provide support for the reactivity of SM, as well as demonstrating its utility for classroom use both with individuals and groups identified as at-risk for academic difficulties.

Although the reactivity of SM has received much empirical support in the literature, there exists a substantial number of studies that have demonstrated that SM does not always produce reactive effects. These findings have prompted considerable research aimed at discovering the variables responsible for the reactivity of self-monitoring. Several reviews of this research have identified the following eight variables as being potential contributors to the reactive process (Gardner & Cole, 1988; Mace & Kratochwill, 1988; Nelson, 1977; Shapiro, 1984):

1. *Motivation*—The degree of motivation a student has to change his/her self-monitored behavior affects the probability that reactivity will occur (e.g., if a student verbalizes the desire to finish homework assignments, the probability that reactive effects will occur is greater).

2. *Valence*—In general, positive behaviors (e.g., correct answers) will increase, whereas negative behaviors (e.g., teasing peers) will decrease as a result of SM.

3. *Target behaviors*—Reactivity may increase as a function of the conspicuousness of the target behavior and for undesirable behavior with reliable antecedents (e.g., the probability of reactive effects occurring is greater for self-monitoring out-of-seat behavior which occurs consistently whenever the student is given seatwork to complete, versus self-monitoring off-task behavior which occurs inconsistently during the school day in a variety of classroom situations).

4. *Goals, reinforcement, and feedback*—Setting performance goals and providing feedback on these goals, as well as providing reinforcement for SM can increase the probability of reactivity occurring (e.g., a teacher may set a goal of correctly completing a math worksheet during the class period, provide feedback to the student indicating if he/she met this goal or not, and state beforehand that meeting or exceeding this goal will result in the student earning some predetermined reward).

5. *Timing*—Some studies have demonstrated that reactivity increases if SM occurs before the target response is emitted (e.g.,

students may self-monitor urges to speak out inappropriately in class rather than self-monitoring the actual occurrences of inappropriate classroom verbalizations).

6. *Concurrent monitoring of multiple behaviors* — As the number of concurrently monitored behaviors increases, the probability of reactive effects decreases (e.g., having a student self-monitor on-task, speaking out in class, and disruptive classroom behavior at the same time decreases the probability that reactive effects will occur).

7. *Schedule of SM* — Reactivity can be maximized if continuous versus intermittent monitoring is practiced (e.g., reactivity is more likely when a student self-monitors his/her off-task behavior in all his/her classes rather than in only a portion of them).

8. *Nature of the SM device* — Obtrusive recording devices increase the probability and magnitude of reactive effects (e.g., having a student place a check on a piece of paper located at the top of his/her desk will increase the probability of reactive effects, versus having the student mentally self-monitor the target behavior).

Those interested in a more in-depth review of SM procedures are encouraged to consult Mace and Kratochwill (1988), Shapiro (1984), and Gardner and Cole (1988).

Both the cognitive-behavioral and operant models of self-management offer theoretical explanations for the reactive effects of SM. The cognitive-behavioral model, as proposed by Kanfer and Gaelick (1986), conceptualizes reactivity of SM as a three-stage process (involving SM, SE, and SR) in a multistage model of self-management. First, the individual self-monitors the target behavior. Second, the products of SM lead the individual to evaluate his/her behavior against a personal- or externally-determined criterion (SE). Third, this evaluation automatically cues the delivery of covert consequences (i.e., thoughts and feelings) by the individual that are consistent with their performance (SR). In other words, reactivity of SM is a process which is caused by the student evaluating his/her behavior and providing rewards covertly for meeting or exceeding his/her personal standards for that behavior.

In contrast, operant theorists believe the change in the self-monitored response to be a result of discriminative stimuli or contextual cues in the environment associated with the overt SM procedure (Brigham, 1982; Mace & Kratochwill, 1985; Nelson & Hayes,

1981). The operant model posits that reactivity of SM is occasioned by these "cues" or stimuli surrounding the entire SM process (e.g., the actual self-recording, instructions, SM device, etc.). These cues function to strengthen the relationship between the self-monitored behavior and the controlling environmental consequences. Thus, the operant model emphasizes overt consequences and the cognitive-behavioral model emphasizes covert consequences as being responsible for the reactivity of SM.

These discrepant theoretical accounts of SM reactivity have implications for practitioners. Those favoring the cognitive-behavioral view will combine SM with cognitive strategies for self-evaluation and self-reinforcement. For example, a student self-managing math performance may say to himself/herself "I have finished 5 math problems correctly. My goal is to finish 5 math problems correctly per math class, thus I have met my goal (SE). I am doing a really good job (SR)!" By contrast, the operantly-oriented practitioner will increase the number and salience of cues for the self-monitored response and ensure that there are adequate reinforcement contingencies for desirable behavior. For example, the teacher would provide specific task instructions, specific instructions regarding the behavior to be self-monitored, inform the student that points may be earned for meeting or exceeding the goal set for the self-monitored behavior, and have the student record the self-monitored behavior on a piece of paper located on his/her desk.

SELF-EVALUATION

Self-evaluation is another component of self-management that has received particular attention from cognitive-behavioral theorists (Bandura, 1977; Kanfer & Gaelick, 1986). Proponents of this view consider SE as the second stage of a three-stage self-management process. Self-evaluation consists of the student comparing his/her self-monitored behavior(s) to a self- or externally-determined performance criterion for that behavior(s). The degree to which the student's behavior matches the criterion for this behavior is a cue for the third stage of the process, self-reinforcement. Therefore, the self-monitored behavior(s) acts as a cue which triggers self-evaluation, which in turn acts as a cue for the delivery of self-reinforcement.

Self-evaluation appears to be an effective component of many self-management programs (Rhode, Morgan, & Young, 1983; Spates & Kanfer, 1977). Because it is fairly easy to implement and maintain by a classroom teacher, SE can be easily incorporated into classroom use with a variety of student populations, both individually and in groups. This makes SE a potentially useful procedure for those practitioners intervening at the prereferral level with at-risk students in the regular classroom.

Research conducted by Spates and Kanfer (1977) demonstrates how SE may contribute to a multi-component self-management intervention. Regular education first grade students were trained in the use of the different components of Kanfer's three-stage self-regulation model while engaging in a simple arithmetic task. The students were randomly assigned to three experimental groups and one control group. Experimental groups received various combinations of the self-management components which constitute Kanfer's self-regulation theory (i.e., SM, SE, and SR). The self-evaluation procedure consisted of training the students to say aloud the steps involved in solving triple digit numbers in columns (e.g., "First I should add the two numbers on the right, then I should add the two numbers in the middle, then I should add the two numbers on the left"), and then checking to see if they had done the problems correctly or not. If completed correctly, the children were instructed to say "I am correct," if completed incorrectly, they said "I'm wrong." The children who were in the self-evaluation only experimental group and experimental groups which included the SE component performed better on the arithmetic task than did those students in groups which did not have a SE component. These results supported Spates and Kanfer's (1977) view that SE was a vital component of self-management.

Rhode, Morgan, and Young (1983) employed SE methods in a resource room setting with six behaviorally disordered students. The SE procedure consisted of having the students rate their behavior in the classroom over 15-minute intervals (e.g., attending to task, working on teacher-assigned tasks, among others). At the end of each interval the children rated their behavior on a 6-point scale and compared their rating with that of the teachers. If the students' ratings differed by no more than 1 point from the teacher's, students were permitted to award themselves points which could be exchanged later for toys and snacks. The ratings matching procedure was conducted initially for all intervals, but was faded to 16% of the intervals over a 15-week period. More importantly, this intervention was expanded to the students' regular classroom with continued improvement in the target behaviors. Although this intervention was not implemented before special education placement, it greatly improved the behavior of children whose continued inappropriate behavior would leave them at-risk for a more restrictive placement (e.g., a full-time special education placement). It is possible that similar procedures could be implemented in the regular classroom in a preventative manner with at-risk students.

SELF-REINFORCEMENT

Much controversy surrounds the self-reinforcement component of behavioral self-management. This is in large part due to the differences between the cognitive-behavioral and operant models' conceptualization of self-reinforcement (SR) and the underlying mechanisms thought responsible for this process. In particular, important differences exist between the two models around three key points: (a) designation of stimuli as reinforcers versus designation of stimuli as discriminative stimuli for responding to some external contingency; (b) the contingent relationship between response and subsequent stimulus versus the temporal relationship between response and subsequent stimulus; and (c) internal versus external location of reinforcing stimuli. In response to this controversy, Mace and West (1986) have provided the following definition of SR which is less dependent on a particular theoretical view:

> SR is the process by which an individual, usually under conditions of satisfying a performance standard, comes into contact with a stimulus that is freely available following emission of a response, which in turn increases the probability of the occurrence of the response subject to the performance standard. (p. 151)

In classroom applications of SR a student typically administers rewards to himself/herself under the supervision of school personnel. The student accesses a predetermined reinforcer contingent on meeting or exceeding a performance standard. Reinforcers may be tangible, (e.g., material goods, privileges, or points exchangeable for back-up reinforcers) or intangible (i.e., positive cognitions or feelings), depending on the theoretical perspective adopted. For example, tangible reinforcers are typically associated with operant procedures, and intangible reinforcers are common to cognitive-behavioral approaches. For classroom behavior, it is advisable to select reinforcers which are school related and do not require excessive amounts of teacher time to supervise (e.g., additional free time, extra computer time, and award certificates).

Kapadia and Fantuzzo (1988) demonstrated the use of SR with four learning disabled students placed in a special eduction program. Students were exposed to two different reinforcement conditions in a modified reversal design. One condition consisted of the teacher awarding the students points whereas in the other conditions students awarded themselves points, which in either condition were contingent on a satisfactory number of spelling problems solved correctly. These points could then be exchanged for back-up reinforcers. The authors reported that the number of spelling problems correctly solved increased for both experimental conditions, however, the SR condition resulted in the greatest gains. Research by Edgar and Clement (1981) reported similar results with a SR procedure aimed at improving underachieving black children's academic and social behavior. Students kept track of the number of points they earned which they could exchange later for back-up reinforcers. Points were awarded if the student was engaged in the academic activity each time a tape-recorded beep sounded. Wall (1982) demonstrated the effectiveness of SR in improving the performance of 85 regular education fourth grade students on history, Spanish language, and reading-comprehension tests. The SR procedure consisted of students awarding themselves points based on how many points each child thought they had earned. The points could be exchanged for free time and raffle chances for inexpensive prizes. Although little research has been conducted with at-risk populations at the prereferral level, the range of social and academic difficulties that have been remediated with SR procedures suggests that SR might be an effective prereferral intervention.

The two theoretical models provide contrasting accounts of the mechanisms thought responsible for SR effects. According to the cognitive-behavioral model, SR is a true reinforcement process whereby the individual self-administers a reinforcer contingent on behavior meeting or exceeding a performance criterion (Bandura, 1977; Kanfer & Gaelick, 1986). In Kanfer's three-stage self-regulatory approach, SR represents the third and final stage. Thoughts and feelings of satisfaction or dissatisfaction are believed to occur as a result of prior self-evaluation of the target behavior. These private events are considered reinforcers or punishers which increase or decrease the probability of future occurrences of the target behavior. Thus, for Kanfer and Bandura, SR is a process which allows individuals to control their own behavior by supplying the reinforcers or punishers necessary to reach personal goals.

Operant theory on SR differs from the cognitive-behavioral model on several points. First, self-administered consequences are not believed to be reinforcers which control the target behavior, but are thought to be discriminative stimuli which signal the person to either respond to some environmental contingency or serve as cues which link the target behavior with delayed consequences (Catania, 1975; Malott, 1984; Nelson, Hayes, Spong, Jarrett, & McKnight, 1983). Second, operant theorists see the response/stimulus relationship as temporal rather than contingent. That is, positive cognitions may occur independent of behavior that meets a performance criterion. Because these private events are not *dependent* on behavior, the process is not true reinforcement. Third, whereas private as well as public events are thought to influence behavior (Skinner, 1953), it is not possible to determine the influence of private events empirically due to the lack of acceptable research methodology. Furthermore, public events are thought to have more influence over behavior than private events (Baer, 1984; Malott, 1984). Readers are encouraged to consult Gross and Woljnilower (1984), Jones, Nelson, and Kazdin (1977), and Mace, Belfiore, and Shea (in press) for in-depth reviews of the SR procedures and for support of the contrasting theoretical positions concerning the underlying processes responsible for SR.

SELF-INSTRUCTION

Self-instruction (SI) is a multi-stage process in which students manage their own behavior by applying specific instructions, rules or strategies in order to perform a task or solve a problem. Self-instructions provide the student with a structured sequence of problem-solving steps to perform that increase the likelihood of successful performance.

Meichenbaum and Goodman (1971) introduced SI as an innovative behavioral technique to improve impulsivity of second-grade children placed in a special education class. Researchers and practitioners have since utilized this approach and other SI variations to increase academic performance and alter both positive and negative classroom behavior. Specifically, SI procedures have been employed alone or as part of a multi-component self-management program to improve academic performance in mathematics (Swanson & Scarpati, 1984), reading (Malamuth, 1979), handwriting (Kosiewicz, Hallahan, Lloyd, & Graves, 1982), and written language (Schumaker, Deshler, Alley, & Warner, 1983). SI has also been used to reduce disruptive classroom behaviors such as aggression and off-task behavior (Roberts & Dick, 1982), as well as to increase adaptive classroom behaviors such as on-task, assertiveness, and cooperation (e.g., Kazdin & Mascitelli, 1982).

Most SI research has been conducted with students already placed in special education classrooms. However, in nearly all of these cases, SI may have been an appropriate prereferral intervention as illustrated by the following study.

Malamuth (1979) employed SI methods with fifth grade regular education students identified as poor readers and at-risk for special education placement. Procedures used were a modified version of Meichenbaum and Goodman's (1971) SI approach. The children first observed an adult performing each step of a reading task taken from the curriculum. Students then performed the task while the adult orally instructed the students through each step of the reading task. Next, the students instructed themselves in the task by stating aloud each step to be performed. Following successful performance, students were taught to whisper the instructions to themselves. In the final SI stage, students were told to covertly state each task step. The results indicated that the self-instruction group's performance on the reading task was superior to that of a control group's, and that SI students exhibited concomitant gains over the control group in reducing the amount of reading errors and in increasing attention to the reading task.

Research has yielded inconsistent findings regarding the efficacy of SI procedures. Whereas many studies have reported positive results (e.g., Bornstein & Quevillon, 1976; Fish & Mendola, 1986; Malamuth, 1979), others have reported clinically insignificant or negative effects (Billings & Wasik, 1985; Friedling & O'Leary, 1979; and Robin, Armel, & O'Leary, 1975). Billings and Wasik (1985) attempted without success to replicate Bornstein and Quevillon's (1976) successful study which increased the on-task behavior of three overactive pre-school males. These researchers argued that the inability to replicate Bornstein and Quevillon's (1976) results can be attributed to changes in teacher attention in the Bornstein and Quevillon (1976) study after those students received the SI training. Billings and Wasik contended that the teacher may have attended to the boys' disruptive behavior before the SI training and to their appropriate behavior following SI training, thereby reinforcing the appropriate behavior of the students. Bornstein (1985), in response, argued that there are many variables (i.e., reinforcement, history, population, among others) which can increase or decrease the effectiveness of SI. Although he acknowledged the inconsistent results of the SI literature, he argued that the above variables are the key to these results and research should be aimed at identifying which variables contribute to the success of SI procedures. Bornstein stated that inconsistent results will continue until the methodology is further developed and refined. Regardless, SI remains a very popular and potentially useful component in a self-management intervention.

Both the cognitive-behavioral and operant models offer explanations for SI effects, although the majority of the research is cognitive-behavioral in nature. The Meichenbaum and Goodman (1971) approach has been the most widely used since its inception. The foundation for this model lies in the cognitive-behavioral view that cognitions produce behavior change. Therefore, this model focuses on altering an individual's current inefficient problem-solving cognitions to more efficient problem-solving cognitions. This is achieved through the use of the slow fading from the instructors' models of more efficient cognitions, to the student stating aloud the new cognitions, and finally, the student stating covertly the new problem-solving sequence. That is, the new statements alter the old inefficient cognitions, which in turn are responsible for overt behavior change.

From the operant standpoint, SI is viewed as the adherence to rules an individual constructs or is supplied with to manage their own behavior (Zettle & Hayes, 1982). Roles may be defined as the formulation of a set of discriminative stimuli which describe a contingency (Skinner, 1969). Accordingly, SI statements are one of two sets of controlling discriminative stimuli for a target behavior. One set relates directly to the target behavior and is governed by the standard A-B-C (discriminative stimulus, response, reinforcer) operant paradigm. The other set consists of the SI statements which act as discriminative stimuli describing the contingencies for emitting the target behavior. In other words, the first set are discriminative stimuli, such as the presence of the task, the classroom, time of day, and teacher instructions. The response is completion of the task, following of teacher instructions, etc. The reinforcer or punisher might be teacher praise or loss of privileges. The second set might be the SI statements (e.g., "First I must open my book to the correct page, then I must begin the assignment . . .") which serve to strengthen the contingent relationship described by the first set of rules. This establishes a condition in which SI statements (either covert or overt) may enhance learning, and quite possibly make for more efficient learning than direct consequences alone.

SUGGESTIONS FOR IMPLEMENTING SELF-MANAGEMENT PROCEDURES IN THE CLASSROOM

The following suggestions are intended to guide practitioners in the implementation and maintenance of behavioral self-management programs. They are derived both from the literature and our own practical experience.

1. Practitioners should be aware of and design self-management

programs based on both the skill level and level of functioning of the student and/or group. Young students and students with skill deficits may have difficulty following a self-management program. These students might benefit from pre-intervention training, as well as from procedures designed to be compatible with their existing skills (e.g., specific instruction, demonstrations, and practice).

2. The success of a self-management program can be enhanced through the use of self-recording forms, behavioral checklists, rating scales, and structured behavioral interviews. These make it easier to identify, define, and record discrete target behaviors for which a self-management program is to be designed, as well as help to facilitate a consultative relationship between the practitioner and school personnel. For example, Bergan's model of behavioral consultation, specifically the problem identification interview component, may facilitate identification and clarification of the student's behavior(s) the consultee finds troublesome in class. This can also help in designing and implementing a self-management procedure.

3. To maximize the effects of self-monitoring, the SM intervention should be designed such that the variables surrounding both the occurrence of and consequences for the self-monitored behavior be as clear as possible. This may include obtrusive recording devices, training in SM, explicit information about contingencies, and performance feedback. For example, a teacher could have the student self-record his/her behavior in a book located on the student's desk, provide instruction on the use of the chosen SM technique, provide clear contingencies to the student concerning what he/she needs to do to earn a particular reinforcer, and provide clear feedback to the student on whether or not he/she met the goal that will produce reinforcement.

4. Self-monitoring procedures should be designed as simply and clearly as possible. This will maximize response discrimination as well as avoid interfering with adaptive academic and social behavior. For instance, having a student place a simple check mark on a piece of paper each time he/she engages in a target behavior is much easier than performing an elaborate SM procedure that would require the student to record what he/she was doing, for how long, the time of day, what assignment he/she was working on, etc.

5. Having students set their own performance criteria, self-evalu-

ate, and deliver private consequences may increase the effectiveness of a self-management program, especially when linked to external reinforcement contingencies. This may be achieved by having the student say covertly that he/she has met the goal, as well as having the student receive points that he/she can later exchange for back-up reinforcers.

6. The effectiveness of self-reinforcement techniques may be increased if an externally managed contingency program is implemented along with covert strategies (e.g., in addition to having the student praise his/her behavior, he/she would also receive points exchangeable for back-up reinforcers).

7. The effectiveness of a self-reinforcement program can be enhanced if potential reinforcers are identified and chosen by the student and/or special services providers in conjunction with the classroom teacher before implementation of the SR program. Also, having the student set stringent performance criteria and discouraging the consumption of unearned reinforcers may increase the effectiveness of SR as well. For instance, the student may sit down with the teacher to identify different reinforcers the student would like to work for. The teacher could have the student set goals that are reachable, but are not so easy that he/she would not have to work very hard. Also, for student-controlled delivery of reinforcers, it is important for the teacher to instruct the student not to administer reinforcers unless the performance criterion is reached.

8. To maximize the effectiveness of self-instruction, practitioners should utilize SI to help students put together component skills that they already possess to perform more complex tasks. Self-instruction is not as effective for learning new skill components. (E.g., SI could assist a student who already has the basic skills of addition become more proficient in math addition skills, but would not be as successful in helping to teach a new math skill such as multiplication.)

9. Self-instruction requires planned follow-up along with booster sessions if the effectiveness of SI is to be maintained. It also should be pointed out that SI initially may lower the rate of task completion, thus teachers should plan to utilize other interventions to strengthen and increase student work rate. For instance, it may take time for the student to learn to proficiently perform the SI procedure

for addition problems, thus, until this occurs, the teacher may want to work one-to-one with the student and/or have the student check his/her work with the teacher more frequently.

10. It is highly recommended that all self-management programs be empirically evaluated to determine their effectiveness. This can be achieved by collecting data on the target behaviors at regular intervals (e.g., time-series data). Time-series or other program evaluation designs may be utilized to make confident conclusions concerning the effectiveness of self-management programs (i.e., baseline data prior to implementation of the self-management program may be compared to subsequent experimental conditions when the self-management program is implemented) (e.g., see Bryant & Budd, 1982; Fish & Mendola, 1986; and Rhode, Morgan, & Young, 1983 for examples of self-management time-series research).

11. Finally, as with any type of psychoeducational intervention, all ethical standards governing intervention with students should be strictly adhered to in the implementation and maintenance of self-management programs. Involving both the school personnel and students in designing self-management programs, keeping the intrusiveness of the self-management procedures to a minimum, and designing self-management programs which emphasize positive consequences for desirable behavior while minimizing negative consequences for undesirable behavior, are a few of many activities which may be adopted to ensure that self-management programs meet the highest ethical standards.

CONCLUSION

This paper provided an overview of the use of behavioral self-management with at-risk students. It discussed the major components of self-management: self-monitoring, self-evaluation, self-reinforcement, and self-instruction, as well as presented two major theoretical models' explanations of the underlying mechanisms thought to be responsible for the effects of each component. Finally, suggestions to practitioners regarding the design and implementation of self-management programs were offered. Behavioral self-management is a valuable tool for practitioners because it: (a) is time-efficient and thus can increase the number of students served by existing personnel; (b) emphasizes positive nonintrusive reinforcement procedures; and (c) is designed, administered, and evaluated on an individual basis with input from the student, teacher, and special services provider. These features make self-management particularly suitable for remediating the academic and social problems of students identified as at-risk before they require more intrusive and restrictive interventions.

REFERENCES

Algozzine, B., Christenson, S., & Ysseldyke, J. E. (1982). Probabilities associated with the referral to placement process. *Teacher Education and Special Education, 5,* 19-23.

Baer, D. M. (1984). Does research on self-control need more control? *Analysis and Intervention in Developmental Disabilities, 4,* 211-218.

Bandura, A. (1977). *Social Learning Theory.* Englewood Cliffs, NJ: Prentice-Hall.

Bergan, J. R. (1977). *Behavioral Consultation.* Columbus, OH: Merrill Publishing Company.

Billings, P. H., & Wasik, B. H. (1985). Self-instructional training with preschoolers: An attempt to replicate. *Journal of Applied Behavior Analysis, 18,* 61-68.

Bornstein, P. H. (1985). Self-instructional training: A commentary and state-of-the-art. *Journal of Applied Behavior Analysis, 18,* 69-72.

Bornstein, P. H., & Quevillon, R. P. (1976). The effects of a self-instructional package on overactive preschool boys. *Journal of Applied Behavior Analysis, 9,* 177-188.

Brigham, T. (1982). Self-management: A radical behavioral perspective. In D. Karoly and F. H. Kanfer (Eds.), *Self-management and behavior change: From theory to practice* (pp. 32-59). New York: Pergamon Press.

Bryant, L. E., & Budd, K. S. (1982). Self-instructional training to increase independent work performance in preschoolers. *Journal of Applied Behavior Analysis, 15,* 259-271.

Catania, A. C. (1975). The myth of self-reinforcement. *Behaviorism, 3,* 192-199.

Curtis, M. J., Zins, J. E., & Graden, J. L. (1987). Prereferral Intervention Programs: Enhancing student performance in regular education settings. In C. A. Maher & J. E. Zins (Eds.), *Psychoeducational interventions in the schools: Methods and procedures for enhancing student competence* (pp. 7-25). New York: Pergamon Press.

Edgar, R., & Clement, P. (1981). Teacher-controlled and self-controlled reinforcement with underachieving black children. *Child Behavior Therapy, 2,* 33-56.

Fish, M. C., & Mendola, L. R. (1986). The effects of self-instruction training on homework completion in an elementary special education class. *School Psychology Review, 15,* 268-276.

Fox, D. E., & Kendall, P. C. (1983). Thinking through academic problems: Applications of cognitive behavior therapy to learning. In T. R. Kratochwill (Ed.), *Advances in school psychology* (Vol. 3, pp. 269-301). Hillsdale, NJ: Erlbaum Associates.

Friedling, C., & O'Leary, D. K. (1979). Effects of self-instructional training on second and third grade hyperactive children: A failure to replicate. *Journal of Applied Behavior Analysis, 12,* 211-220.

Gardner, W. I. (1977). *Learning and behavior characteristics of exceptional children and youth.* Boston, MA: Allyn & Bacon, Inc.

Gardner, W. I., & Cole, C. L. (1988). Self-monitoring procedures. In E. S. Shapiro & T. R. Kratochwill (Eds.), *Behavioral assessment in schools: Conceptual foundations and practical applications* (pp. 206-246). New York: Guilford Press.

Gottman, J. M., & McFall, R. M. (1972). Self-monitoring effects in a program for potential high school dropouts: A time-series analysis. *Journal of Counseling and Clinical Psychology, 39,* 273-281.

Gross, A. M., & Woljnilower, D. A. (1984). Self-directed behavior change in children: Is it self-directed? *Behavior Therapy, 15,* 501-514.

Jones, R. T., Nelson, R. O., & Kazdin, A. E. (1977). The role of external variables in self-reinforcement. *Behavior Modification, 1,* 147-178.

Kanfer, F. H., & Gaelick, L. (1986). Self-management methods. In F. H. Kanfer & A. P. Goldstein (Eds.), *Helping people change: A textbook of methods* (3rd ed., pp. 283-345). New York: Pergamon Press.

Kapadia, E. S., & Fantuzzo, J. W. (1988). Effects of teacher and self-administered procedures on the spelling performance of learning-handicapped children. *The Journal of School Psychology, 26,* 49-58.

Kazdin, A. E., & Mascitelli, S. (1982). Behavioral rehearsal, self-instructions, and homework practice in developing assertiveness. *Behavior Therapy, 13,* 346-360.

Kosiewicz, M. M., Hallahan, D. P., Lloyd, J., & Graves, A. W. (1982). Effects of self-instruction and self-correction procedures on handwriting performance. *Learning Disability Quarterly, 5,* 71-78.

Lentz, F. E., & Shapiro, E. S. (1985). Behavioral school psychology: A conceptual model for the delivery of psychological services. In T. R. Kratochwill (Ed.), *Advances in school psychology* (Vol. 4, pp. 191-232). Hillsdale, NJ: Erlbaum Associates.

Mace, F. C., Belfiore, P. J., & Shea, M. C. (in press). Operant theory and research on self-regulation. In B. J. Zimmerman and D. H. Schunk (Eds.), *Self-regulated learning and academic achievement: Theory, research, and practice.* New York: Springer-Verlag.

Mace, F. C., & Kratochwill, T. R. (1988). Self-monitoring: Applications and issues. In J. Witt, S. Elliott, & F. Gresham (Eds.), *Handbook of behavior therapy in education* (pp. 489-522). New York: Pergamon Press.

Mace, F. C., & Kratochwill, T. R. (1985). Theories of reactivity in self-monitoring: A comparison of cognitive-behavioral and operant models. *Behavior Modification, 9*, 323-343.

Mace, F. C., & West, B. J. (1986). Unresolved theoretical issues in self-management: Implications for research and practice. *Professional School Psychology, 1*, 149-163.

Malamuth, Z. N. (1979). Self-management training for children with reading problems: Effects on reading performance and sustained attention. *Cognitive Therapy and Research, 3*, 279-289.

Malott, R. W. (1984). Rule-governed behavior, self-management, and the developmentally disabled: A theoretical analysis. *Analysis and Intervention in Developmental Disabilities, 4*, 199-209.

Meichenbaum, D., & Goodman, J. (1971). Training children to talk to themselves: A means of developing self-control. *Journal of Abnormal Psychology, 77*, 115-126.

Nelson, R. O. (1977). Methodological issues in assessment via self-monitoring. In M. Hersen, R. M. Eisler, & P. M. Miller (Eds.), *Progress in behavior modification* (Vol. 5, pp. 263-308). New York: Academic Press.

Nelson, R. O., & Hayes, S. C. (1981). Theoretical explanations for reactivity in self-monitoring. *Behavior Modification, 5*, 3-14.

Nelson, R. O., Hayes, S. C., Spong, R. T., Jarrett, R. B., & McKnight, D. L. (1983). Self-reinforcement: Appealing misnomer or effective mechanism? *Behavior Research and Therapy, 21*, 557-566.

Rhode, G., Morgan, D. P., & Young, K. R. (1983). Generalization and maintenance of treatment gains of behaviorally handicapped students from resource rooms to regular classrooms using self-evaluation procedures. *Journal of Applied Behavior Analysis, 16*, 171-188.

Roberts, R., & Dick, L. (1982). Self-control strategies with children. In T. R. Kratochwill (Ed.), *Advances in school psychology* (Vol. 2, pp. 275-314). Hillsdale, NJ: Erlbaum.

Robin, A. L., Armel, S., & O'Leary, K. D. (1975). The effects of self-instruction on writing deficits. *Behavior Therapy, 6*, 178-187.

Schumaker, J. B., Deshler, D. D., Alley, G. R., & Warner, M. M. (1983). Toward the development of an intervention model for learning disabled adolescents: The University of Kansas Institute. *Exceptional Education Quarterly, 4*, 45-74.

Shapiro, E. S. (1984). Self-monitoring procedures. In T. H. Ollendick & M. Hersen (Eds.), *Child behavioral assessment: Principles and procedures* (pp. 148-165). New York: Pergamon Press.

Sheinker, A., Sheinker, J. M., & Stevens, L. J. (1984). Cognitive strategies for teaching the mildly handicapped. *Focus on Exceptional Children, 17*, 1-15.

Skinner, B. F. (1953). *Science and human behavior*. New York: Macmillan.

Skinner, B. F. (1969). *Contingencies of reinforcement: A theoretical analysis.* New York: Appleton-Century-Crofts.

Spates, C. R., & Kanfer, F. H. (1977). Self-monitoring, self-evaluation, and self-reinforcement in children's learning: A test of a multistage self-regulation model. *Behavior Therapy, 8,* 9-16.

Swanson, H. L., & Scarpati, S. (1984). Self-instruction training to increase academic performance of educationally handicapped children. *Child and Family Behavior, 6,* 23-39.

Wall, S. M. (1982). Effects of systematic self-monitoring and self-reinforcement in children's management of text performance. *The Journal of Psychology, 111,* 129-136.

Witt, J. C., & Elliott, S. N. (1985). Acceptability of classroom intervention strategies. In T. R. Kratochwill (Ed.), *Advances in school psychology* (Vol. 4, pp. 251-288). Hillsdale, NJ: Erlbaum Associates.

Workman, E. A., Helton, G. B., & Watson, P. J. (1982). Self-monitoring effects in a four-year-old child: An ecological behavior analysis. *Journal of School Psychology, 20,* 57-64.

Zettle, R. D., & Hayes, S. C. (1982). Rule-governed behavior: A potential theoretical framework for cognitive-behavioral therapy. In K. R. Harris & S. Graham (Eds.), *Advances in cognitive-behavioral research and therapy* (Vol. 1, pp. 73-118). New York: Academic Press.

The Individualized Contingency Contract for Students: A Collaborative Approach

Louis J. Kruger

Tufts University

SUMMARY. Individualized contingency contracts can be a powerful intervention for helping at-risk students succeed in regular education. Several issues should be considered relative to developing and implementing the contingency contract. These issues include developing precise definitions of the problem behaviors and prioritizing problem behaviors for contract intervention. In addition, activities should be undertaken that facilitate collaboration among special services providers, regular education teachers, the student in question, and possibly his/her parents. Next, the appropriate contract contingencies need to be selected and the criterion should to be set at the appropriate level of difficulty. The actual writing of the contract encompasses several issues including the use of language and concepts that are both attractive and developmentally appropriate for the student. Guidelines for incorporating cognitive interventions into contracts are presented. Finally, implementation and generalization issues are discussed.

In the contingency contract's most elemental form, it is an agreement between one student and one or more school personnel that specifies (a) the student's problem that is targeted for change, (b) the criterion for improvement of the problem, and (c) contingencies for attaining and/or not attaining the criterion. Though, a contract can be oral or written, I will focus primarily upon written contracts. Kazdin's (1980) review of the research suggests that

---

Requests for reprints should be directed to: Louis J. Kruger, Department of Education, Tufts University, Medford, MA 02155.

© 1990 by The Haworth Press, Inc. All rights reserved.

written contracts may be more effective than oral ones. In most contracts, a positive reinforcer is included as a contingency. A positive reinforcer is defined as a stimulus which follows the occurrence of a behavior and is intended to strengthen that behavior. For example, 15 minutes of free activity time might be used as a positive reinforcer for an elementary school student attaining 75% correct on his/her in-class arithmetic assignments. In addition to a positive reinforcer, a punishment also might be included in a contingency contract. A punishment is defined as a stimulus which follows the occurrence of a behavior and is intended to weaken that behavior. For example, five minutes of recess time might be taken away from a student every time he/she swears at a classmate. Careful deliberation should precede the decision to include a punishment in a contract because of possible negative side effects to the student (e.g., student's imitation of the use of punishment) and ethical and legal concerns about its use (Schwitzgebel & Schwitzgebel, 1980).

Though the contingency contract has its roots in behavior modification (see, e.g., DeRisi & Butz, 1975), recent advances incorporate aspects of cognitive intervention approaches as well. The contingency contract is used to motivate a student to change his/her problem behavior and affords school personnel the opportunity to individualize an intervention to meet the needs of the student (Walker & Shea, 1984). One type of problem behavior is a behavioral excess, that is, a behavior that occurs in excess of what is expected. One example of a behavioral excess might be an elementary school student's daily, verbally aggressive assaults on other students. A second type of problem behavior is a behavioral deficit, that is, a behavior that occurs less than expected. An example of a behavioral deficit is a high school student who only attends three of his/her six classes each day. The contingency contract is especially wellsuited to helping at-risk students succeed in regular education because of its flexibility in addressing a wide array of school related problems, including social and academic ones. Also, the contract provides a convenient vehicle for fostering cooperation between special and regular education service providers because of the importance of collaboration in developing and implementing the contract.

In general, research has supported effectiveness of contingency contracts (Kazdin, 1980). For example, researchers (Brooks, 1975; Spencer-Dunbar, 1976) have found that written contracts can improve student attendance of school truants. Bristol and Sloane (1974) developed contracts for students who were experiencing academic difficulty. As part of the contract, the students agreed to record their academic progress. After the contract was implemented, students improved their test scores. Contracts that include the student's parents also can be an effective means of improving student academic work. For example, Schumaker, Hovell, and Sherman (1977) found that students' grades improved after the implementation of a daily report card and a parent delivered contingency system.

IDENTIFICATION OF THE STUDENT'S PROBLEMS

The first step in developing a contingency contract for the purpose of helping a student succeed in regular education involves the identification of the student's problems and assets. A primary activity is to develop a problem definition that is sufficiently clear and specific so that the problem behavior can be measured in a quantitative manner. Quantification of the problem behavior is essential to ascertaining the current strength of the problem behavior which, in turn, has implications for determining an appropriate criterion for the first contract. A regular classroom teacher, for instance, might complain about a student's verbal aggression. Because there are many different types of verbal aggression, it is not clear from the teacher's statement what type(s) of verbal aggression the student exhibits. One method of clarifying what the teacher means by verbal aggression is to assist the teacher in developing a narrative record of the verbally aggressive incidents. At minimum, the narrative record should include: (a) the specific problem behavior exhibited by the student, (b) when the problem behavior occurred, (c) what classroom activity was occurring at the time of the incident, and (d) how the teacher responded to the incident (for an example of a narrative recording form, see Sulzer-Azaroff & Mayer, 1986). Collecting data about how the teacher responds to the problem behavior can help determine what contingencies might be successful or unsuccessful in motivating the student. Also, a special services provider can explore with the teacher what contingencies might be successful with a particular student.

After the problem behavior has been specifically defined, examples of its occurrence should be used to further elucidate the definition. In regard to verbal aggression between students, the following definition might be developed: "Derisive laughter, verbal threat, or teasing directed from one student to another student." An example of teasing might be one student calling another student "gorilla breath," and an example of a verbal threat might be, "Your ass is grass after school." *Non-examples* can be used to clarify closely related behaviors that are not included in the problem definition. A non-example of verbal aggression might be assertive comments such as, "Don't call me by last name. It gets me mad."

Though there are many possible methods of quantifying the occurrence of the problem behavior, three methods, in particular, deserve discussion with respect to contingency contracts: review of permanent products, frequency recording, and ratings of behavior. Review of permanent products is most appropriate when the behavior to be measured generates a durable record of the problem behavior. If the problem behavior concerns incorrectly completed in-class written assignments, then a product in the form of the student's completed assignments should be available for inspection. Furthermore, this permanent product can be quantified by calculating the percentage of correct assignments completed by the student. Frequency recording involves directly observing the problem behavior and counting the number of times it occurs. Counting should always occur with respect to a consistent interval of time, for example, the number of times a student leaves his/her seat without permission during successive 15 minute intervals. Frequency recording is most appropriate when the problem behavior (a) has a clear beginning and end, (b) is transitory, and (c) is approximately equivalent in duration each time it occurs (Sulzer-Azaroff & Mayer, 1986). Behavior rating can be used for problem behaviors that cannot be appropriately measured by either frequency recording or review of permanent products. The latter type of problem behaviors include those in which duration is an important dimension, such as off-task student behavior. Though there are more precise observation methods than behavior ratings for measuring these types of problem behaviors (e.g., duration recording, momentary time-sampling), the more precise methods are often impractical to use in the regular education classroom where there is one teacher for twenty or more students. Ratings of the problem behavior should occur with respect to a specific time intervals, 8:30 to 9:00 a.m., 9:00 to 9:30 a.m., etc. Typically, behavior rating scales have between three and seven anchor points. In regard to off-task behavior, for example, a teacher might use a five-point scale, where 1 indicates that the problem behavior occurs almost not all, and 5 indicates it occurs almost all the time. Particular caution should be exercised when using behavior ratings because of their sensitivity to personal biases (see, Good & Brophy, 1984, for descriptions of several biases that might affect the accuracy of classroom observations).

When the problem behavior chiefly occurs in one particular classroom, the teacher in that classroom is the logical choice for recording the data. Another option is to have the student observe and record his/her own behavior. Indeed, self-observation has been shown to be an effective intervention with certain students (see, e.g., Kehle, Clark, Jenson, & Wampold, 1986). However, it is unclear under what conditions and with what students self-observation is effective. Moreover, it seems prudent for the teacher to keep a record separate from the student's record to safeguard against inaccurate self-recordings and to minimize the temptation for the student to purposefully alter the self-recordings in order to obtain the positive reinforcer.

It is imperative that data about problem behavior be collected prior, during, and after the implementation of the contract. When data is collected in this manner it becomes possible to view student progress from a longitudinal perspective. However, it may not be important to collect data about the problem behavior throughout the entire school day. For example, the narrative record may reveal that the problem behavior only occurs during "sharing time," therefore, it may be necessary to collect data about the problem behavior only during this time. After the data are collected, the data should be summarized by means of tables, mean occurrence of the problem behavior, and/or graphs. Next, the teacher in collaboration with the special services provider should decide whether or not the problem is occurring at a level that is indeed problematic. Sometimes quanti-

...reveals that expectations for a student's behavior were de-...tally unrealistic. Other times, the mere act of observing ...problem behavior might be sufficient to change the behavior in a positive direction (Gelfand & Hartmann, 1975).

PRECONDITIONS TO CONTRACT DEVELOPMENT

If it is determined that a problem does exist, then the classroom teacher and special services provider need to decide whether or not the problem is most appropriately addressed by a contract. As aforementioned, the overarching purpose of the contingency contract is to motivate a student to change his/her behavior. However, not all problem behaviors are the result of insufficient motivation. Some behavior problems are more closely related to skill deficiencies. A nine-year-old girl might not cooperatively play with her peers because of skill and/or motivational deficiencies. If a skill deficiency exists (e.g., inability to share an object with another child), then a contract, as the primary intervention, might not only be unsuccessful in changing behavior, but also might provide the student with another failure experience. In the example of the nine-year-old girl, she might need to be taught the requisite play skills before a contract can motivate her to consistently perform them.

Also, prior to contract development, school personnel should determine the student's readiness for a behavior contract. The success of a contract is highly dependent upon the student's cooperation. Therefore, the student should exhibit at least a modicum of motivation to change his/her behavior prior to the development of the contract. The student might verbalize his/her desire to change. For instance, a high school student might say, "I'm sick and tired of failing my social studies class." Another important factor to consider relative to a student's readiness for a contract is his/her trust in adults, particularly the adults involved with the contract. For a student to be successfully engaged in the contract, he/she must believe that the adults will fulfill their obligations as specified in the contract. If a student does not trust that a teacher will provide the student with the positive reinforcer when the student reaches the specified criterion, then that student is likely to be minimally motivated by the contract.

Another precondition to contract development is determining whether or not the regular or special education service providers have access to contingencies that will prove sufficiently motivating to a student. Some school related problems might be closely related to factors outside the school environment, such as family problems or peer pressure. In these instances, a contingency contract might be inappropriate or might be included as only one part of larger intervention plan for the student.

Some students will exhibit multiple school related problems, more than one of which are appropriate for intervention by school personnel. Often, it is impractical or overwhelming to the student (and possibly school personnel) for the initial contract to include all of the student's school related problems. When this occurs, school personnel must be able to prioritize the problems. Though no consensus exists among experts on how to prioritize problems for contracts, it has been my experience that is important to select the problem(s) which will most likely result in a successful first contract. If the first contract is successful, the student may increase his/her motivation to succeed, and thereby increase the probability that later contracts also will be successful.

INVOLVEMENT OF STUDENT AND PARENT

Research seems to indicate that contingency oriented interventions are more effective when students are actively involved in either the contract's development or implementation (Salend & Ehrlich, 1983). In regard to contract development, the rationale for the contract should be privately discussed with the student. The rationale should focus on the nature and scope of the student's problem behavior. In regard to adolescents, it is important that they acknowledge the problem behavior and express a desire to change the behavior. Often, adolescents will want to "save face" and therefore be reluctant to openly acknowledge their problem behavior. In these instances, the school personnel should be vigilant for nonverbal and covert indications that the student is motivated to begin the contract. In discussing the rationale for the contract with younger children, it can be helpful to check the extent to which the child is comprehending the rationale. One means of checking this comprehension is to ask the student to paraphrase what the adult has said. Regardless of the student's age or developmental level, school personnel should strive to communicate that their motivation in initiating the contract relates to a desire to help the student, and not to just control him/her.

Next, school personnel decide whether or not the student's parents should be involved in the contract. Parents can be instrumental in identifying contingencies that might motivate a student to change his/her behavior. Parents must be involved if school personnel are considering a home-school contract for implementation. A home-school contract is a contract in which the parents agree to carry out one or more contingencies at home dependent upon their child's school behavior. A pre-implementation consideration to a home-school contract is the extent to which the parents will be able to consistently carry out the contingencies. Moreover, the success of a home-school contract might be highly dependent upon clear and frequent communication between school personnel and the parents. Possible contraindications for a home-school contract include parents and their child who seem to be "locked into control struggles," adolescents who seem particularly sensitive to parental control, and parents who have long work shifts outside the home.

CONTRACT DEVELOPMENT

Contingencies included in the contract should be tailored to the individual student. One fifth grade student, for example, who is interested in baseball might find baseball cards very reinforcing (i.e., the cards motivate the student to change his/her behavior), however, another fifth grade student who is disinterested in baseball, might find the cards minimally reinforcing. Often, a teacher through his/her informal observations of the student in the classroom can identify appropriate contingencies for that student. If a teacher notices that a student likes to bring baseball cards to school and trade them, then it is possible that baseball cards will be appropriate positive reinforcer. In addition to informal observation, appropriate contingencies can be identified by either interviewing the student or giving the student a questionnaire to complete. A questionnaire should only be given when there is a high probability that a student will be able to comprehend the questions and appropriately respond to them in writing. An example of the types of questions that can be incorporated into interview or a questionnaire for a middle school student are presented in Table 1. It is important that the questions be commensurate with the student's current cognitive, social, and language development. Interview or questionnaire data

REINFORCEMENT SURVEY QUESTIONS

1. Who is your favorite adult in school?
2. What do you like to do with him/her?
3. Who is your favorite friend in school?
4. What do you like to do with him/her in school?
5. What is your favorite thing to do in school?
6. If a teacher gave you free-time to do anything you wanted to do in the classroom, what would you do?
7. What is your favorite school subject?
8. What is something you really want?
9. What do you buy when you have money?
10. What would you do if you had one dollar?
11. What would you do if you had ten dollars?
12. What makes you feel happy?
13. What would you like to do if you had a chance?
14. What is your favorite thing to do with your family?
15. What is your favorite thing to do with your friends?
16. What is your favorite thing to do when you are alone?
17. What is the weekend activity or entertainment you enjoy most?
18. What are your favorite games?
19. What are your favorite television programs?
20. What do you want to do when you grow up?

Table 1. Questions that can be used in a survey intended to ascertain what conditions might be reinforcing for a particular student.

coupled with informal observations can be used to rank order objects and activities as possible positive reinforcers for a contract. The most highly ranked objects or activities should: (a) have a high probability of motivating the student, (b) not overshadow the significance of changing the problem behavior, and (c) be practical to deliver on a regular basis.

McAuley and McAuley (1977) recommend the use of token reinforcement systems for elementary school and older students. A token is something that can be accumulated by the student and later exchanged for a previously identified object or activity (Kazdin, 1977). Tokens have at least two important advantages. First, the use of tokens can encourage students to work toward long-term reinforcement as opposed to immediate reinforcement. Recent research has indicated that children who are capable of delaying gratification are more likely to become more socially competent adolescents (e.g., have the ability to form friendships) (Fisher, 1988). Second, it may not be practical to have available continuously the types of objects or activities that older children find positively reinforcing. Points, coupons, and plastic chips are examples of possible tokens. Each time a student, Sally, achieves 75% or higher on an in-class assignment, for example, she might receive a coupon which has a picture of a computer on it (see Figure 1). Once Sally earns five of these coupons she is eligible for 15 minutes of com-

Figure 1. A coupon type of token that might be used in a contingency contract.

puter time. Coupons are particularly attractive as tokens because they: (a) provide concrete feedback about the student's success, and (b) can have graphic designs that are tailored to the student's specific contract. Tokens also are a convenient means of building a bonus clause into a contract. Continuing with the previous example, the student might earn one additional coupon for each time she receives 85% or higher on an assignment. Bonuses might be particularly motivating when the student is achieving considerably below her skill level. Instituting a token system does not absolve the teacher from keeping track of the student's progress; tokens can be lost or stolen. Therefore, teachers need to keep a record of tokens accumulated by the student.

If the contract is intended to address a behavioral excess, then school personnel should consider two alternative contingencies to punishment: differential reinforcement of low rates of responding and reinforcement of alternative behaviors (Sulzer-Azaroff & Mayer, 1986). Differential reinforcement of low rates of responding occurs when a student is positively reinforced for exhibiting a low rate of the problem behavior. For example, a student might be positively reinforced for five or less verbally aggressive behaviors during five consecutive 50 minute English classes. Reinforcement of alternative behaviors involves the positive reinforcement of behavior that is an appropriate alternative to the problem behavior. A more appropriate alternative to verbal aggression might be assertive "I" statements. "I get angry when you interrupt me" is an example of an assertive "I" statement. School personnel should ascertain whether or not the alternative behavior is within the skill repertoire of the student prior to including it in the contract.

The criterion for receiving the first contract's positive reinforcer should be slightly different from the student's pre-contract functioning with respect to the problem behavior. If a behavioral excess is being addressed in a contract, then the criterion should be slightly *lower* than pre-contract functioning. On the other hand, if a behavior deficit is being targeted for change, then the criterion should be slightly *higher* than pre-contract functioning. For example, if pre-contract frequency recording indicates that a student is, on the average, teasing other students six times a week (a behavioral excess), then the reinforcement criterion for the first contract might be five times or less. Setting an easily attainable criterion for the first contract helps ensure that the student will initially view the contract as a worthwhile endeavor and that adults can be depended upon to fulfill their obligations. In short, the purpose of the first contract is to begin a "self-reinforcing upward cycle," where improved behavior stimulates self-efficacy, which in turn stimulates improved behavior, which then stimulates self-efficacy, and so forth. When the student's behavior improves, the criterion for the positive reinforcer in the later contracts can be made more difficult. I recommend that school personnel determine the criterion for the contracts; many behavior problem students have unrealistically optimistic expectations about how much they can change in a relatively brief period of time.

In contrast to criterion setting, the students should have considerably more control over the type of positive reinforcer they receive. Nonetheless, they should not be free to choose any positive reinforcer they desire. Instead, the aforementioned rank ordering of positive reinforcers can be used as a vehicle of presenting students with a short list of positive reinforcers (i.e., approximately, two to five) that are practical to deliver and potentially attractive to the student. Then, the student can pick the positive reinforcer he/she wants from this brief menu.

WRITING THE CONTRACT

After the criterion for the positive reinforcer and the positive reinforcer have been determined, school personnel can begin the actual writing of the contract. The contract should be succinct and have brief sentences. It is imperative that the written contract be on a developmental level commensurate with the student's abilities. The opening statement or statements of the contract should describe the relevant assets of the student. The description of assets helps the contract begin on a positive note. Next, the problem behavior should be described. Third, a rationale for the contract is provided. This rationale should explain how changing the problem behavior can benefit the student. By addressing potential benefits, it is hoped that the student's intrinsic motivation to change can be stimulated. Fourth, the criterion for the positive reinforcer is stated in simple, quantitative terms. Fifth, the positive reinforcer must be described. Sixth, the dates during which the contract is in effect and the date when the contract will be reviewed should be given. Finally, spaces should be provided for all the relevant parties, student, teacher, special services provider, and possibly parents, to sign the contract. Though the signing of the contract may strike some professionals as superfluous, it might be an important part of motivating the student to improve. In fact, one experienced teacher told me that she would not implement a contract with a student who refused to sign the contract. This teacher went on to say that the student's refusal to sign the contract might be indicative of the student's unwillingness to cooperate with adults and, therefore, the contract may not be an appropriate intervention at that time. The student's signature can be construed as a form of public acknowledgement that the student has a problem and is willing to work on this problem. Additional components, such as a punishment for the student not reaching the criterion, can be added to the contract.

Figure 2 illustrates a contract with two additional components: a bonus for attendance that exceeds the minimum required for the presumed positive reinforcer and a punishment (loss of late-night privileges) for failure to reach the criterion. The inclusion of punishment would be justifiable only if two conditions were apparent. First, the adults involved in the contract decided that a positive reinforcer, by itself, might be insufficient to motivate Roger to attend more classes. Second, the parents were capable of carrying out the presumed punishment in a business-like manner, so that Roger's disappointment about losing late-night privileges were not exacerbated. An attempt is made to stimulate Roger's intrinsic motivation by pointing out to him that attending school is an intermediate step toward acquiring his house on the shore. Also, important to note are the messages that the relevant adults in Roger's life are working cooperatively with each other, and they care about Roger's welfare. These messages are most clearly expressed in the last sentence of the first paragraph, which begins, "We want to help Roger. . . ."

Roger's contract is an example of a contract with a specific time line. In order to receive the positive reinforcer, he had to attend 15 classes within the period of one week. However, it is possible to write a contract that has a *free-floating* time line. With a free-float-

Official Contract: Helping Roger Dodge Failure

Roger Skipit, a 9th grade student at Oceanview High, is a friendly and personable teenager, who enjoys helping teachers with their classroom chores. However, Roger is at risk of repeating the 9th grade because of his poor attendance. On the average, Roger only attends 2.6 classes each day. We want to help Roger to succeed in school so that he can get a good job and earn enough money to get something he really wants - a house on the shore.

We, the undersigned agree to the following contract:

If school attendance sheets indicate Roger attended at least 3 of his assigned classes **each** day during the week of March 10 - 14 (a total of 15 classes), then Ms. Halpren will allow Roger to help her in the school store for 3 hours @ $4/hour on Friday, March 14.

Bonus: For every 2 classes Roger attends beyond the 15 classes required by the contract, Ms. Halpren will give him a coupon good for 1 free hamburger and soft drink.

Penalty: If Roger misses all classes on 2 or more days during the week of March 10 - 14, then he will lose his late-night privileges (11:30 P.M.) for the weekend nights of March 14 and 15 and must be home by 8:00 P.M. each night.

_____
(Roger Skipit, Student)

_____
(Ms. Halpren, Teacher)

_____
(Dr. Elliot, School Counselor)

_____
(Mr. or Mrs. Skipit, Roger's Parents)

This contract will be reviewed and possibly renegotiated on March 14.

Figure 2. An example of a contract with two contingencies: a positive reinforcer (paid work) and a punishment (loss of late-night priveleges).

ing time line, Roger still can be required to attend 15 classes in order to receive the positive reinforcer. However, he would receive the positive reinforcer immediately after attending the 15th class, regardless of when this occurred. Thus, it would be possible for Roger to receive the positive reinforcer before, on, or after Friday, March 14, depending on when he attended his 15th class. The free-floating time line has two potential advantages. First, it allows the student greater control over when he/she will receive the positive reinforcer. This control might facilitate the generalization of the improved behavior after the contract has been discontinued. Second, it decreases the possibility that the student will fail to reach the criterion. With the free-floating time line, the uncertainty concerns *when* the criterion will be attained, not *if* it will be attained. A free-floating time line may be especially appropriate for those students who are more motivated to avoid failure than they are motivated to succeed. Nonetheless, there are two potential disadvantages to the free-floating time line. First, it might provide insufficient motivational pressure for those students who are not very fearful of failing and are very capable of behaving more appropriately. Second, it can be inconvenient and impractical to deliver a positive reinforcer immediately after the criterion is reached, no matter when it is reached. In summary, the decision to implement a free-floating or specific time line should be based on several considerations, including one's knowledge about the student's motivations, as well as the situational constraints and available resources.

INCORPORATING COGNITIVE INTERVENTIONS INTO THE CONTRACT

In addition to using the contract as a means for motivating the student to succeed, the contract also can be used in conjunction with cognitive interventions; that is, interventions that are intended to help the student more clearly understand his/her behavior problems and possible alternative behaviors. Research (e.g., Dodge, Murphy, & Buschbaum, 1984) has indicated that children, who are neglected or rejected by peers, seem to have deficits in their social cognitions that are independent of other skills, such as verbal skills. An example of a type of cognitive intervention that can be used with a contract is the molar label intervention (Parad, 1978). A molar label is a rubric for two or more topographically similar behaviors. Often, the label is a metaphor which has special appeal or meaning to the student. The hypothesized function of the label is to help the student cognitively organize his/her problem behaviors. Figure 3 presents an example of a contract with two molar labels that are similar to ones actually used for a socially withdrawn and isolated eighth grade student who had difficulty appropriately participating in group discussions. In this contract, the metaphor, "falling off the track" denotes four conceptually related behaviors. The "track" metaphor was used because the student was especially fond of trains which, of course, travel on railroad tracks. The negative molar label, "falling off the track," is counterpointed with a positive molar label, "connecting on the right track," which denotes three socially appropriate alternative behaviors. School personnel should clearly explain the significance of the labels being used and provide concrete examples of the behaviors they denote. Furthermore, when both a positive and negative label are used, school personnel should explain to the student the relationship between the two labels. In the aforementioned example, school personnel should ensure that the student understands that "on the right track" refers to socially appropriate alternative behaviors that can replace the undesirable "off the track" behaviors. Instead of punishing the student for exhibiting "falling off the track behaviors," the student is positively reinforced for emitting a low rate of the inappropriate behavior. Moreover, the student also must demonstrate the socially appropriate alternative behaviors to receive the positive reinforcer. The student's strong interest in trains is viewed as an asset and is incorporated into the positive reinforcer. The use of the first person pronoun is intended to communicate to the student that she must begin to take the responsibility for changing her problem behavior. Little research has been published about molar labeling. However, two case studies conducted in a residential facility suggest that molar labeling coupled with a contingency contract hold promise for changing children's behavior (Gilbert & Christensen, 1980).

Another way of incorporating a cognitive intervention into a contract, is to have the student self-observe. Figure 4 is an example of a form that can be used in conjunction with a contract for the purpose

Connecting on the Right Track: An Official Contract

I, Helen Recluse, usually get good grades and I am respected for my academic work. However, I want to be "one of the girls" and have teenage friends. Unfortunately, I often choose not to communicate with others or actively participate in groups. When I'm not participating or communicating, I'm **falling off the track** that leads to friendships. **Falling off the track** during in-class discussions involves one more of the following behaviors:

1. Talk about a topic no one else is talking about
2. Talk about inappropriate topics (e.g., my scary dreams)
3. Interrupt others comments
4. Do not respond to comments directed to me

I want to stop **falling off the track** and want to connect **on the right track** with others. When I'm connecting **on the right track**, I :

1. Talk about the same topics the group members are talking about
2. Wait for others to finish their comments before speaking
3. Respond to comments directed at me

Each time I do one of the **off the track** behaviors during group discussion time I will get an **off the track** point. Each time I do one of the **on the right track** behaviors I will get an **on right the track** point. If I get **4** or fewer **off the track** points and **4** or more **on right the track** points for the next 3 group discussions, then I will be able to lead a group discussion about the future of rail transportation in the early 21st century.

_____
(Helen Recluse, Student)

_____
(Mr. Coleman, Teacher)

_____
(Ms. Filene, School Psychologist)

This contract will be reviewed and possibly renegotiated on October 22.

Figure 3. An example of a contract with a positive (on the right track) and negative molar label (off the track).

BEHAVIOR RATINGS OF STUDENT BY STUDENT AND TEACHER

Dates:

Behavior to be Decreased:
Verbal Aggression - teasing, provoking, & threatening

Behavior to be Increased:
Appropriate Assertiveness - making "I" statements about how you feel in a calm tone of voice

RATINGS*

Day of Week	Verbal Aggression		Appropriate Assertiveness	
	Student	Teacher	Student	Teacher
Monday	-----	-----	-----	-----
Tuesday	-----	-----	-----	-----
Wednesday	-----	-----	-----	-----
Thursday	-----	-----	-----	-----
Friday	-----	-----	-----	-----
SUBTOTAL	-----	-----	-----	-----

ADJUSTED TOTAL FOR STUDENT-TEACHER DIFFERENCES:

       -----   -----

*Ratings for verbal aggression: 1 = occurred a lot, 2 = occurred a moderate amount, 3 = occurred very little.

*Ratings for appropriate assertiveness: 1 = occurred very little, 2 = occurred a moderate amount, 3 = occurred a lot.

Total rating points needed for reward : _____ or more

This Week's Reward: _____

Figure 4. An example of a form that can be used by student and teacher to rate the student's behaviors.

of both the student and teacher rating the student with respect to the problem behavior, verbal aggression, and a socially acceptable alternative behavior, using assertive "I" statements. In using such a form, it is important that potential biases, such as others' opinions of the student's behavior, are minimized. Therefore, teacher and student should have separate forms that they fill out independently at the same time of day. Next, a brief meeting can occur to discuss any discrepancies. Students can be penalized when they inaccurately rate their behavior. For example, a student might lose 1 1/4 points for every one point the student's ratings exceed the teacher's ratings. This type of penalty decreases the likelihood that students will intentionally give themselves more favorable ratings so that they can more easily obtain the positive reinforcer.

IMPLEMENTATION ISSUES

An important issue for regular classroom teachers is the extent to which the contract is compatible with the classroom routine. Though it might be feasible and often desirable to have a contract for every student in a special education classroom, it is often not appropriate or practical to do so in a regular education classroom. Sometimes, regular education teachers are concerned that if they implement a contract with one student they will be confronted with an avalanche of requests for contracts, or that the other students will envy the student who has the contract. Implementation of a dependent reinforcement contingency is one possible solution for these problems. Most often, individual contracts have independent contingencies, that is, only the student who has a contract has access to reinforcement. In contrast, school personnel can choose to implement a dependent contingency, where all students in the class have potential access to a positive reinforcer *dependent* upon whether or not the student with the contract attains the criterion (Litow & Pumroy, 1975). For example, all students in a class might have access to 15 minutes of free activity time once a week if the student with the contract attains the criterion of 10 or fewer disruptive behaviors during five consecutive school days. One potential benefit of the dependent contingency is that it might cause the other students to encourage the student with the contract to improve his/her behavior. Another potential benefit is that the student's popularity among peers might increase if he/she frequently reaches the contract's criterion and the entire class receives the positive reinforcer. Therefore, a dependent contingency might be particularly well-suited for socially isolated students. Potential disadvantages of the dependent contingency include excessive peer pressure being placed on the student and peer scapegoating of the student if the student does not attain criterion. Because of these potential disadvantages, it is imperative that school personnel assess three factors prior to deciding to implement a dependent contingency: (a) group dynamics of the classroom, (b) the teacher's ability to manage interpersonal conflicts among students, and (c) the student's ability to cope with peer pressure.

Contracts should be closely monitored and adapted over time. Any changes in the contract should be preceded by a meeting with the student. At this meeting, the rationale for the changes are discussed and the student's concerns about the changes are solicited. It has been my experience that if school personnel have a well-developed rationale for changing the contract, and present the rationale in a clear and constructive manner to the student, then the student usually will be agreeable to the changes. In the unusual instance when the student voices strong opposition to the changes, school personnel should seek to understand the reasons for the opposition and attempt to reach a compromise.

One factor to consider in implementing a contract over an extended time period is *satiation*. Satiation refers to a reduction in the effectiveness of a reinforcement as a result of the reinforcement being repetitively used (Sulzer-Azaroff & Mayer, 1986). When satiation occurs and a student is no longer motivated to change, a new reinforcement should be sought. If school personnel have developed a menu of possible positive reinforcers and rank ordered them, then the student would be able to select one of the remaining positive reinforcers as the next positive reinforcer to be used in the contract.

School personnel should consider changing the contract when the performance level of the student improves. When the performance level improves, for example, the criterion for attaining the positive reinforcer can be made more difficult. Increasing the difficulty level of the criterion can be a means of motivating the student to continue to improve. In order to maximize student success, the changes in the criterion should occur in small increments. If one problem behavior has reached a satisfactory level and a second problem behavior exists, then the second problem behavior can replace the first problem behavior in the contract. However, before this change occurs, school personnel should carefully evaluate whether or not a contract is an appropriate intervention for the second problem behavior.

The contract also can be adapted by increasing the length of time between initiation of the contract and the reinforcement. The purposes of this strategy can be to: (a) improve the student's ability to delay gratification, and (b) decrease the student's dependence on external positive reinforcers for behaving in an appropriate manner. Moreover, increasing the length of time between contract initiation and reinforcement can be conceptualized as a strategy intended to facilitate maintenance of the student's improved behavior over time.

If concrete positive reinforcers (e.g., food, baseball cards) were initially used in the contract, then school personnel should strive to replace the concrete positive reinforcers with more activity-oriented (e.g., creative arts time) or social types of positive reinforcers (e.g., a group game). This strategy can be used to decrease the student's dependence upon concrete positive reinforcers and increase the probability that the student's improved behavior will be maintained over time. It is important that the use of concrete positive reinforcers be gradually faded over a period of weeks so that the student remains motivated to change his/her behavior. For example, if pizza was initially given as a positive reinforcer, then over time, pizza might be combined with a social activity with peers. Finally, the social activity without pizza might be used as the positive reinforcer. Through repeated pairings with pizza, the social activity may attain nearly the same reinforcing effect as the pizza.

Maintenance of improved behavior across time might be facilitated by having the student take an increasingly larger role in designing and monitoring the contract. This strategy might be particularly well-suited for older students, who have the skills and initiative to take considerable control of changing their own behavior. For example, the responsibility for delivering the positive reinforcer can be transferred from the teacher to the student. However, the teacher should monitor the student's use of the positive reinforcer to ensure that the student only self-reinforces when the criterion has been attained.

CONCLUDING COMMENTS

An overview of the issues involved in developing and implementing individualized contingency contracts for the purpose of helping at-risk students succeed in regular education has been presented. Contingency contracts were viewed as a flexible intervention for addressing a wide variety of motivational deficits that may affect student academic and social behavior. Particular emphasis was placed on the importance of collaboration among the student, the student's parents, the regular education teacher, and the special services provider. Growing concern has been voiced about students being subtly coerced into participating in interventions (Adelman & Taylor, 1986). The contingency contract can address this concern by affording students considerable input and control over the contract's design and implementation. Though research has supported the general effectiveness of contingency contracts, no research was found that examines whether different types of written contingency contracts have different effects on different types of students. For example, the following question might be addressed by future research: Are contracts with molar labels more effective with adolescents than with pre-adolescents? It is possible that molar labels might be more effective with adolescents because of their more advanced cognitive development. It is hoped that future research will begin to address such questions so that practitioners will have clearer guidelines about how to tailor contingency contracts for individual students.

REFERENCES

Adelman, H. W., & Taylor, L. (1986). Children's reluctance regarding treatment: Incompetence, resistance, or an appropriate response? *School Psychology Review, 15*, 91-99.

Bristol, M. M., & Sloane, H. N. (1974). Effects of contingency contracting on study rate and test performance. *Journal of Applied Behavior Analysis, 7*, 271-285.

Brooks, B. D. (1975). Contingency management as a means of reducing school truancy. *Education, 95,* 206-211.
DeRisi, W. J., & Butz, G. (1975). *Writing behavioral contracts: A case simulation practice manual.* Champaign, IL: Research Press.
Dodge, K. A., Murphy, R. R., & Buschbaum, K. (1984). The assessment of intention-cue detection skills in children: Implications for developmental psychology. *Child Development, 55,* 163-173.
Fisher, K. (1988, August). Preschool delay tactics predict teen competence. *APA Monitor,* pp. 12-13.
Gelfand, D. M., & Hartmann, D. P. (1975). *Child behavior analysis and therapy.* New York: Pergamon Press.
Gilbert, R., & Christensen, A. (1980). Molar labeling interventions: Two case studies. *Journal of Behavior Therapy and Experimental Psychiatry, 11,* 327-333.
Good, T. L., & Brophy, J. (1984). *Looking in classrooms* (3rd ed.). New York: Harper and Row.
Kazdin, A. (1977). *The token economy.* New York: Plenum Press.
Kazdin, A. (1980). *Behavior modification in applied settings* (rev. ed.). Homewood, IL: Dorsey.
Kehle, T. J., Clark, E., Jensen, W. R., & Wampold, B. E. (1986). Effectiveness of self-observation with behavior-disordered elementary school students. *School Psychology Review, 15,* 289-295.
Litow, L., & Pumroy, D. K. (1975). A brief review of classroom group-oriented contingencies. *Journal of Applied Behavior Analysis, 8,* 341-347.
McAuley, R., & McAuley, P. (1977). *Child behavior problems.* New York: Free Press.
Parad, H. W. (1978, November). *Molar interventions: A synthetic technique.* Paper presented at the meeting of American Association of Psychiatric Services for Children, Atlanta, GA.
Salend, S. J., & Ehrlich, E. (1983). Involving students in behavior modification programs. *Mental Retardation, 21,* 95-100.
Schumaker, J. B., Hovell, M. F., & Sherman, J. A. (1977). An analysis of daily report cards and parent-managed privileges in the improvement of adolescents' classroom performance. *Journal of Applied Behavior Analysis, 10,* 449-464.
Schwitzgebel, R. L., & Schwitzgebel, R. K. (1980). *Law and psychological practice.* New York: Wiley.
Spencer-Dunbar, L. H. (1976). *The effects of contingency management as a means of reducing truancy.* (Report No. UD 022 542.) San Diego, CA: San Diego State University, School of Education. (ERIC Document Reproduction Service No. ED 221 542).
Sulzer-Azaroff, B., & Mayer, G. R. (1986). *Achieving educational excellence: Using behavioral strategies.* New York: Holt, Rinehart, & Winston.
Walker, J. E., & Shea, T. M. (1984). *Behavior management: A practical approach for educators* (3rd ed.). St. Louis: Times Mirror.

Individualized Education and Applied Behavior Analysis

Wayne C. Piersel
University of Nebraska

Steven W. Lee
University of Kansas

SUMMARY. The process of individualizing education for at-risk students is discussed. Three approaches to individualizing education are presented. Applied behavior analysis literature is examined from the perspective of what is known about managing student behavior and the learning process in the regular classroom settings for at-risk students. Examples of how applied behavior analysis can be utilized to individualize education are presented. The position is taken that the use of the principles and procedures gleaned from the applied behavior analysis research permits the teacher to individualize the education experience without the need for substantial additional resources.

Effective teaching is the "expediting of learning" (Skinner, 1968, p. 5). Naturally, it is possible for learning to occur in the absence of teaching, and in fact, much of what we learn does occur as the result of experiences that are not intentional examples of teaching. However, society has determined that certain skills need to be learned by all of its members and has decided that this learning cannot be left to unplanned experiences. As a result, the institution of the school has been created to teach children the essential skills

---

Requests for reprints should be directed to: Wayne C. Piersel, Department of Educational Psychology, 116 Bancroft Hall, University of Nebraska, Lincoln, NE 68588-0345.

© 1990 by The Haworth Press, Inc. All rights reserved.

identified by society. An effective school, from a societal point of view, is one that facilitates effective teaching of what is valued. Effective teaching is the active, deliberate attempt to enhance learning what society values.

The key question for parents of at-risk students, at-risk students, and educators is, "How does one best expedite learning?" Although debate continues on what constitutes effective teaching, there is emerging agreement on what constitutes effective teaching behaviors. For elementary teachers, Rosenshine (1983), Brophy and Good (1986), and White, Wyne, Stuck, and Coop (1983) have identified effective instructional behaviors listed in Table 1 for elementary and secondary school teachers. The results from applied behavior analysis studies (Bushnell, 1978; Reid, 1986) further substantiate the importance of the behaviors identified in Table 1.

Once educators agree on what constitutes good teaching behavior, we are then confronted with the problems of finding means to bring each at-risk student in contact with effective teaching. In other words, educators need to be able to individualize the educational process for every at-risk student to maximize the effect of good teaching behavior. Indeed, one of the major driving forces behind the development and implementation of special education for students with significant learning or behavior difficulties is to provide a setting and sufficient resources in terms of teacher time and curriculum materials to individualize the educational process for handicapped students. To deliver an effective education in the regular classroom to at-risk students as well as typical students also requires a high degree of individualization of the education process. The principles of behavior modification and applied behavior analysis provide one means of implementing individualized education for all students in regular classroom settings.

APPLIED BEHAVIOR ANALYSIS

Applied behavior analysis is based on the fundamental premise that a given teaching technique may not be appropriate for a particular student. Given that students differ in terms of previous experiences, current level of skill, availability and use of learning strategies, and type and frequency of positive and negative consequences,

TABLE 1

Effective Teaching Behaviors for Elementary and Secondary School Classrooms

Elementary	Secondary
1. Structured learning activities	1. Provision of positive and corrective feedback
2. Proceed in small steps at a brisk pace	2. Use of organizers
3. Provide detailed, redundant instructions and explanations	3. High rates of academic responding
4. Provide many examples, models	4. Arrange active student discussion
5. Ask many questions	5. Plan regular reviews of key instructional points
6. Arrange for frequent, overt practice	6. Frequent comprehension checks
7. Provide frequent feedback and correction	7. Frequent, consistent monitoring of performance
8. Provide seatwork assignments in small units	8. Require mastery learning
9. Continue student practice until 90% plus mastery is attained	9. Clear statement of goals and expectations
	10. Set reasonable, attainable goals
	11. Explain rationale for instructional activities
	12. Teach students to be independent

Adapted from Roseshine (1983, 1987), Brophy & Good (1986), and White et al. (1984)

how then does a teacher individualize for each student in the classroom? The need for individualization and the requirement for implementation in a resource-limited environment (i.e., a classroom containing 20 or more students and one teacher) is the basis and motivation for using the principles of behavior modification and the technology of applied behavior analysis in regular classroom settings. What follows is a brief introductory discussion of how the principles of behavior modification and applied behavior analysis can facilitate a teacher's individualization of the teaching process in the regular classroom for at-risk students. Furthermore, this discussion will be limited to the elementary school setting.

INDIVIDUALIZED EDUCATION

Individualized instruction means that a student enters the curriculum at the appropriate skill level, proceeds at his or her own pace, receives immediate corrective feedback, and works on an assigned unit or skill until mastery is achieved before moving onto the next unit or skill. It is clear that individualized instruction is superior to group methods of instructions (Carnine & Silbert, 1979; Paine, Radicchi, Rosellini, Deutchman, & Darch, 1983). However, it needs to be pointed out that individualized instruction does not imply that an individual teacher must work individually with one student and only one student at a given time. In fact, Brophy and Good (1976) note that extended, isolated periods of work are in fact harmful to the learning process. Further, individualized instruction is not unsupervised or only guided independent study. Rather, individualized instruction is planned and delivered based on precise knowledge of the student's current performance.

Individualized instruction matches the student with the curriculum and with teaching tactics and strategies that have the greatest probability of success as determined by the student's immediate learning history. Research strongly suggests that direct instruction is the most effective means of teaching (Paine, Radicchi, Rossellini, Deutchmen, & Darch, 1983; Peirsel, 1987; White, Wyne, Stuck, & Coop, 1983). The term "explicit teaching" (Rosenshine, 1987) has also been utilized to describe effective teaching. The goal of individual education is to increase the amount of engaged learning time for the student in the appropriate curriculum with the appropriate instruction.

Methods of Individualized Instruction

There are four traditional approaches to individualizing instruction. These four approaches include task assignment grouping, homogeneous grouping, personalized system of instruction, and specialized education. The central principles of all approaches to individualized instruction are: (a) each student enters the curriculum at his or her current mastery level, (b) each student proceeds at his or her own pace, and (c) each student masters each objective before progressing to the next objective in the curriculum.

Task Assignment Groupings

Task assignment grouping arranges students together because they need to learn the same task or skill. For example, a task assignment grouping could be formed to instruct in a division skill, or to work on an aspect of reading comprehension. When any student in the task grouping masters the skill that the group is working on, that student is moved on to another group that is working on the next skill in the sequence. Task assignment grouping has the advantage of permitting a teacher to work intensely with a small group of students, thereby increasing the amount of engaged learning time.

Rubin and Spady (1984) describe a math program that uses task assignment grouping. Their description uses the analogy of a ski school. Task assignment grouping includes: (a) all members of the group share the need to learn the same skill at the same time, (b) all group members have previously mastered prerequisite skills, and (c) when a group member demonstrates mastery of the task or skill, that individual moves on to another task assignment grouping. Task assignment is ideally made independent of age, general ability, previous experience, motivation, and learning rate.

Homogeneous Groupings

Homogeneous grouping is similar to task assignment grouping in that both utilize the small group instructional format. However, in homogeneous grouping the students may not have precisely the same skill deficits. Nevertheless, all students share similar skill deficits. For example, students could be grouped according to their respective reading series, rather than the precise reading skill they are mastering. The students advance as a group and students occasionally are moved to another group if they are consistently faster or slower in learning than the members of their current group. Students are not re-grouped as frequently as they are in task assignment groupings. Homogeneous groupings are frequently utilized in regular classrooms. A classroom having three reading groups might be an example of homogeneous grouping.

The direct instructional approach of Carnine and Silbert (1979) and the Exemplary Center for Reading Instruction (ECRI) approach of Reid (1986) use the small homogeneous instructional approach. Choral responding and small group instructional feedback are central features of direct instruction. Choral responding facilitates active student involvement and group feedback permits more immediate and more frequent instructional feedback. Homogeneous groupings permit teachers to give more instruction in a subject area than would be possible utilizing individual instruction.

Personalized System of Instruction

Personalized System of Instruction (PSI) (Keller, 1968) is structured to allow a student to work individually. PSI divides the curriculum into teaching units in which the students read, learn the materials, and pass mastery tests at their own pace. The teacher, with the help of peer tutors, assists students with materials that they need help in mastering. PSI has five defining elements: (a) self pacing, (b) unit mastery, (c) a stress on written materials, (d) use of student tutors or proctors, and (e) use of lectures and discussions to motivate students rather than to provide information.

At the present time, PSI has been utilized primarily in secondary education in content area instruction and in university courses. It has yet to be adapted and fully implemented in the elementary setting to teach basic skills to at-risk students and to students receiving special education services. PSI has been successfully implemented with typical elementary students in regular classroom settings (Darcy-Frederick, Little, Swanson-Williams, Dietz, & Keller, 1981;

Dineen, Clark, & Risley, 1977), and secondary schools (Reid, Archer, & Friedman, 1977). PSI minimizes the amount of teacher instruction while trying to maximize individualization of the learning process and maximizing the amount of engaged learning time.

Special Education

This is viewed by many professionals as the ultimate in individualized education. Students who have been determined to have a handicapping condition have an individual education plan developed and implemented. Typically a specialized teacher works with the student in an individual or small group setting in a location outside the regular classroom. The specialized instruction focuses on the academic areas identified as being deficient.

APPLIED BEHAVIOR ANALYSIS AND BEHAVIOR MODIFICATION

What follows is an overview of the principles gleaned from research in applied behavior analysis and behavior modification. The principles of behavior modification offer the classroom teacher a means to combine principles of effective teaching with individualization of the learning process. Further, applied behavior analysis principles facilitate individualized education without neglecting a segment of the student population and without requiring massive additional resources (Heward, Heron, Hill, & Trap-Porter, 1984; Jenson, Sloane, & Young, 1988). In this regard, the principles and procedures to be discussed are: (a) curriculum-based assessment (CBA); (b) classroom management systems—token programs; (c) peer tutoring; (d) behavioral contracting; (e) daily performance feedback; (f) school-home communication and cooperation; (g) home work; and (h) self-control techniques (self-goal setting, self-monitoring and self-recording, self-reinforcement, and self-analysis). Peer tutoring, behavioral contracting, school-home communication, and self-control are discussed in other papers of this volume in greater detail.

Curriculum-Based Assessment (CBA)

Teachers need to make a variety of instructional decisions regarding each youth in their classrooms during the academic year. As the students progress through the various assignments and subjects, their performance must be evaluated to make necessary modifications and to inform the student and parents of the progress being made. To accomplish any of these functions teachers need to be able to link the assessment data being gathered to the curriculum and instruction being utilized. The current reliance on conventional achievement tests and periodic unit or quarter tests rarely permit the necessary linkage needed for decision making (Deno, 1985; Marston & Magnusson, 1985).

To accomplish the needed linkage of assessment to curriculum and instruction and to permit meaningful monitoring of student performance, the process of curriculum-based assessment (CBA) has been developed. CBA, which is not an entirely new idea (Tucker, 1985), can be defined as the practice of obtaining direct and frequent measures of a student's performance on a series of sequentially arranged objectives derived from curriculum used in the classroom. In developing and utilizing CBA, the teacher needs to engage in the following steps (Blankenship, 1985, p. 234): (a) List the skills contained in the material to be presented, (b) ensure that the resulting list is in a logical order, (c) write an objective for each skill, (d) prepare testing material for each skill for each student, (e) administer the CBA immediately prior to beginning instruction, (f) evaluate the results to determine what skills the students have mastered, and (g) decide the next sequential curriculum step for each student. The CBA is periodically administered throughout the school year to monitor instructional progress and to plan the next step in each student's instructional program (Fuchs, Deno, & Mirkin, 1984).

The initial implementation of CBA will be time consuming in terms of identifying objectives and developing assessment materials. However, once the curriculum has been identified and task analyzed and CBA assessment packages have been developed, they can be utilized repeatedly for each student who is at that point in the curriculum. Because CBA is derived directly from the curriculum, there is a direct linkage of assessment data to what is being taught. CBA directly facilitates student monitoring and feedback to the teacher as well as the to the student and other interested parties, such as parents or administrators. CBA also directly assists in initially individualizing instruction by identifying precisely where the student is presently performing in the curriculum; this identification will form the basis of instruction. The increasing availability of computers and computer software will further enhance the applicability of CBA.

Classroom Management Systems

One of the major difficulties confronting teachers in their efforts to individualize for each at-risk student in their classroom, is the managing of all aspects of the instructional process including positive and negative feedback, positive reinforcement, and management of students who are not directly being taught (i.e., engaged in learning activities not immediately under teacher supervision). Evertson (1987) stresses the importance of having a detailed framework developed and in place prior to the start of the school year to facilitate organization and management of the classroom. Her framework includes: (a) clearly stated classroom rules and procedures, (b) specification of positive and negative consequences, (c) immediate implementation of the framework, and (d) continuous monitoring of student behavior to improve decision making.

A token economy or point system is a management system that allows students to acquire tokens or points for performing previously identified behaviors. The points or tokens can be subsequently exchanged for backup reinforcers. The tokens or points need to be easily dispensed upon the occurrence of selected target behaviors. The backup reinforcers are previously identified activities, objects, events, and privileges that have reinforcing value to the students in the classroom. A token economy is one vehicle which can be used to implement the organization and management framework described by Evertson (1987).

For classrooms and token systems to operate effectively, the rules and procedures must be specifically defined and communicated to all participants. Typically, the rules, positive and negative consequences, backup reinforcers, and provisions for exchanging points for reinforcers are written in large print and prominently posted in the classroom. Students are frequently encouraged to take part in the actual development of the token economy. A token economy permits the teacher to manage many students and ensure compliance with a range of selected procedural rules such as: (a) talking with permission, (b) completing assignments, (c) not interfering with other students' learning, and (d) other desired classroom behaviors. One advantage of the token system is that the teacher can immediately and conveniently reinforce behaviors that he or she wants to continue and can withhold reinforcement when undesired behaviors occur. By tying tokens to completion of assignments and units of instruction, the teacher is enhancing motivation of each at-risk student without the need to be in immediate contact with the student. Further, a token system serves a reminder to the teacher to positively reinforce each student for the occurrence of previously identified appropriate activities.

Although token systems have been most frequently utilized in special education classrooms, they are being increasingly implemented in regular classrooms because of the facilitating value in individualizing instruction and reinforcing feedback in the large class settings. In fact, one of the largest applications of a token economy in the classroom has occurred with at-risk students in the behavioral analysis follow through project (Bushnell, 1978). The students can participate in the operation of the many aspects of the token system including awarding points, recording and charting points, and assisting in delivering backup reinforcers. A point system also provides a means of monitoring student academic and adjustment behavior, provides immediate feedback, and can have instructional value.

Instructional Monitoring and Feedback

The research is surprisingly clear on the importance of monitoring a student's performance during the initial acquisition or learning process (Van Houten, 1980, 1987). The correction of student errors, the reinforcement of correct responding, and immediacy of feedback are all well documented as necessary ingredients of effective teaching. Further, effective monitoring permits the teacher to adjust the instructional process to meet the student's changing needs. Evaluating student responses and providing appropriate feedback in a timely manner is probably the second biggest hurdle to individualizing instruction next to providing each student with materials and instruction at the student's own instructional level. In particular, providing frequent and immediate performance feedback at the appropriate time can be viewed as extremely difficult.

The applied behavior analysis literature (Van Houton, 1980, 1987) indicates that: (a) Feedback should be immediate in the acquisition phase of learning; (b) feedback should always be precise; (c) practice phases need to be short; (d) feedback needs to be differential (distinguishing correct from incorrect responses); (e) student scoring needs to be employed when possible; (f) public posting of performance has motivating and feedback effects; (g) praise for improvement needs to be present to shape initial learning efforts; (h) task-centered peer interactions are educational; and (i) feedback that is coupled with corrective instruction is most effective. Van Houton (1987) makes a distinction between the acquisition stage and the practice or refinement stage. Performance feedback is very important in both stages with the form of the feedback varying depending on the stage. For example, Van Houton suggests that immediate feedback with corrective instruction is essential during the initial acquisition stage. Delayed feedback is harmful during acquisition period because delayed feedback will permit a student to practice an incorrect response; however, delayed feedback can be more appropriately utilized during the refinement or practice stage (Van Houton, 1987).

The behavior analysis research directly suggests that frequent and immediate feedback is most facilitative of learning during initial acquisition phases and is especially important for motor skills. For example, Kazdin and Klock (1973) demonstrated that teacher attention in the form of approval was a potent form of positive feedback for increasing student attending behavior. Activities such as correcting while the teacher circulated about the classroom and having students show the teacher their work before they hand this work in, are two methods that can be utilized to provide monitoring and more immediate feedback.

Two other approaches to monitoring and providing feedback that are less frequently utilized and less demanding of teacher time are peer-monitoring and self-monitoring (Van Houton, 1980, 1987). The use of peers as tutors and checkers has been extensively researched (Maheady & Harper, 1987; Pigott, Fantuzzo, & Clement, 1986). A student selected by the teacher can be designated as a "Peer Checker" for a particular activity. The students would need to have their work checked by the peer prior to turning in the assignment. In some situations only select students would need to have their work checked by the Peer Checker.

Self-correction is the other form of feedback that is typically not systematically taught and utilized. In self-monitoring and self-correction, the student is required to record objectively the occurrence of a given behavior. In particular, self-monitoring is viewed as a means of bridging the gap between when a behavior occurs (completion of an assignment) and when it is reinforced (teacher's evaluation and feedback). Students need to be taught to self-monitor and record and need to be specifically reinforced for engaging in self-recording behavior. It is thought that the form used for self-monitoring acts as a cue to engage in a selected behavior and that the act of self-observing and self-recording also contain prompting or cuing properties (Piersel & Kratochwill, 1978; Peirsel, 1985; Mace & West, 1987).

Peer Tutoring

Peer tutoring can be an extremely valuable asset to the teacher trying to individualize in the classroom. Peers have been effectively utilized as tutors, classroom graders, and as classroom managers (Jenson, Sloane, & Young, 1988). Research has demonstrated that peers have frequently benefited as much from tutoring as have the students who have been the recipient of peer tutoring (Greenwood, Carta, & Hall, 1988; Kalfus, 1984). The use of peer tutors has the effect of extending the amount of engaged learning time, can provide immediate feedback, monitor and repeat assignment instructions, model effective learning behaviors, and provide a potent source of contingent reinforcement for learning.

Peer managers or tutors have been used to reinforce appropriate behavior of other students, to teach specific academic skills, and to model appropriate social skills. In effect, the use of peer and older student tutors permits the teacher to more completely individualize each student's education and implement the important teaching activities outlined in Table 1.

Behavioral Contracting—Individual and Small Group

In many ways "behavioral contracting" is the heart of the individualization process in the classroom. Behavioral contracting, which is also called contingency contracting, is an arrangement between two individuals that states: (a) what student behavior is to be changed, (b) how that student's behavior is to be changed, (c) what the consequences are for producing that change in behavior, and (d) what the consequences are for failing to produce the desired change in behavior. Behavioral contracts can be written between students and teachers, students and parents, and groups of students and teachers. Contracts are viewed as useful for individuals who are capable of entering into agreements and understanding the consequences associated with the agreement. Behavioral contracts represent a means to further individualize instructional programming for at-risk students within an existing classroom management system. Clearly not all students would need to have behavioral contracts at any given time.

School-Home Communication and Cooperation

The Passport

The utilization of the home and of parents represent yet another way to increase the amount of instructional time available. Furthermore, parents are another set of adults who can monitor and provide reinforcing and punishing consequences for student learning behavior. Runge, Walker, and Shea (1975) describe what they call the "passport." Passport is a promising technique for implementing and maintaining teacher to parent communication and cooperation. The passport consists of a spiral notebook that the student, on a daily basis carries to each class. At the end of the day, the passport is brought home to be returned to school the following day. Teachers, janitors, bus drivers, and parents involved with the child's education are encouraged to make notations in the notebook for other concerned adults to read. The frequency and types of comments can be clearly specified to permit assignment of points to targeted behaviors with the student receiving backup reinforcers at home and/ or in a designated classroom.

Daily Report Card

The daily report card is a more specific version of the passport. Typically the daily report card is a pre-made form which lists the critical behaviors by day so that the teacher merely needs to check whether a behavior occurred or did not occur during a period of time. This report card goes home each day for parents to review, sign, and provide consequences as specified in the overall instructional program. The advantage of the daily report card is that once it is developed and implemented, it takes less time to complete each day than the passport. Frequently, unfinished work is attached to the daily report card to be finished by the student at home. Thus school-parent communication can facilitate individualization by extending the situations where reinforcement is delivered and by extending the amount of time out of each day that is available for learning activities to occur. Daily report cards, when used in conjunction with home-based reinforcement programs, have been demonstrated to be effective, efficient, and practical in changing academic and adjustment behaviors in preschool, elementary, and junior high school students (Gresham & Lemanek, 1987). (See Atkeson & Forehand, 1979, for a review.)

Homework

Homework is among the most obvious methods available to individualize instruction and add to the amount of instructional time available. Not so obvious is the role that homework plays in facilitating generalization of newly acquired skills across time and settings. Further, the research (Hall, Delquadri, Greenwood, & Thurston, 1982) is quite consistent that practice spread over time (spaced practice) is more effective than massed practice (practice occurring in a smaller time frame or all at the same time). Homework that is specifically tied to the lesson being taught during the day and that is reviewed on the next day is known to be more effective. Further, when homework is combined with the daily report card, parents can acquire an active role in providing consequences for completion of homework and for ensuring that the homework is completed correctly.

The use of homework in conjunction with the daily report card might be particularly beneficial for the at-risk student. This combination permits the instructional day to be lengthened, permits more individualization in terms of curriculum and time allotted for practice, permits generalization to be systematically addressed, and facilitates immediate feedback regarding the accuracy of the homework when parents carefully monitor student responses and provide feedback.

Self-Control

We have been discussing the use of parents and peers, and increased efficiency as means of more completely implementing individualization in the classroom. Now we are going to examine what each at-risk student can contribute to facilitate their own individualized instructional program.

Teaching students to manage their own behavior through self-control or self-management represents another set of procedures available to permit greater implementation of individualization of instruction. Indeed, John Dewey (1939) stated that "the ideal aim of education is the creation of self-control" (p. 75). Students who have acquired self-control skills are able to perform appropriately in the presence, as well as the absence, of adult supervision. Both typical and atypical learners have been taught to observe, monitor, and alter their own behavior (O'Leary & Dubey, 1979; Piersel, 1987; Piersel & Kratochwill, 1979).

Self-management is made up of several components including: (a) self-statement of the problem, (b) self-monitoring and recording of the occurrence or non-occurrence of the targeted behavior, (c) examination of the self-recorded data, and (d) administering self-reward or self-punishment depending on the relationship of the data to the self-determined goal. Self-control techniques have been employed to enhance handwriting, spelling, reading comprehension, mathematics performance, creative writing, and class discussion, as well as for decreasing undesirable behaviors (Piersel, 1987).

CONCLUSION

We, in the professional educational community, know a number of things about effective instruction of students. Furthermore, the applied behavior analysis literature is becoming increasingly definitive regarding procedures that can enhance the implementation of effective instruction. The utilization of such procedures as teacher attention, curriculum-based assessment, classroom management systems, performance monitoring and feedback, peer tutoring, self-control procedures, parent-teacher cooperation, homework, and behavioral contracting have all been shown to enable the classroom teacher to more readily individualize instruction for the at-risk student.

This paper has not presented an in-depth review and discussion of the behavior principles and behavior technology that has developed to implement behavior principles in classroom settings. Nor has this paper provided an intensive discussion of teaching behavior. Rather this paper has attempted to expose the reader to some of the ways that the principles of behavior modification and applied behavior analysis can be utilized to enhance effective teaching and the individualization of instruction for students in the regular classroom.

Two things remain to be systematically undertaken. Refinement in (a) applied behavior analysis technology and (b) what we know about effective teaching. Also, we need to explore ways to facilitate classroom teachers' utilization of the knowledge base that is available. Finally, ecologically valid demonstrations of individualized instruction with at-risk students using the results of the applied behavior analysis need to receive increased attention.

REFERENCES

Atkenson, B. M., & Forehand, R. (1979). Home-based reinforcement programs designed to modify classroom behavior: A review and methodological evaluation. *Psychology Bulletin*, *86*, 1298-1308.

Blakenship, C. S. (1985). Using curriculum based assessment data to make instructional decisions. *Exceptional Children*, *52*, 233-238.

Brophy, J. E., & Good, T. L. (1986). Teacher behavior and student achievement.

In M. C. Wittrock (Ed.), *Handbook of research on teaching, 3rd Ed.* (pp. 328-376). New York: Macmillan Publishing Company.

Bushnell, D. (1978). An engineering approach to the elementary classroom: The behavioral analysis follow through program. In A. C. Carnine & T. A. Bingham (Eds.), *Handbook of applied behavior analysis* (pp. 523-567). New York: Irvington Publisher.

Carnine, D., & Silbert, J. (1979). *Direct instruction reading*. New York: Charles E. Merrill.

Darcy-Frederick, L., Little, N. M., Swanson-Williams, J., Dietz, S. M., & Keller, F. S. (1981). PSI in the elementary school. *Journal of Personalized Instruction, 5*.

Deno, S. L. (1985). Curriculum based measurement: The emerging alternative. *Exceptional Children, 52,* 219-231.

Dewey, J. (1939). *Experience and education*. New York: Macmillian.

Dineen, J. P., Clark, H. B., & Risley, T. R. (1977). Peer tutoring among elementary students: Educational benefits to the tutor. *Journal of Applied Behavior Analysis, 10,* 231-238.

Everston, C. M. (1987). Managing classrooms: A framework for teachers. In D. C. Berliner & B. V. Rosenshine (Eds.), *Talks to teachers: A Festschrift for N. L. Gage* (pp. 54-74). New York: Random House.

Fuchs, L., Deno, S., & Mirkin, P. K. (1984). The effects of frequent curriculum based measurement and evaluation on pedagogy, student achievement, and student awareness of learning. *American Educational Research Journal, 21,* 449-460.

Greenwood, C. R., Carta, J. J., & Hall, R. V. (1988). The use of peer tutoring strategies in classroom management and educational instruction. *Psychology in the schools, 17,* 258-275.

Gresham, F. M., & Lemanek, K. L. (1987). Parent education. In C. A. Maher & S. G. Foreman (Eds.), *A behavioral approach to education of children and youth* (pp. 153-182). Hillsdale, NJ: Lawrence Erlbaum.

Hall, R. V., Delquadri, J., Greenwood, C. R., & Thurston, L. (1982). The importance of opportunity to respond in children's academic success. In E. B. Edgar, N. G. Haring, J. R. Jenkins, & C. G. Pious (Eds.), *Mentally handicapped children: Education and training* (pp. 107-149). Baltimore: University Park Press.

Heward, W. L., Heron, T. E., Hill, D. S., & Trap-Porter, J. (1984). *Focus on behavior analysis in education*. Columbus, OH: Charles E. Merrill.

Jenson, W. R., Sloane, H. N., & Young, K. R. (1988). *Applied behavior analysis in education: A structured teaching approach*. Englewood Cliffs, NJ: Prentice Hall.

Kalfus, G. R. (1984). Peer mediated interventions: A critical review. *Child and Family Behavior Therapy, 6,* 17-43.

Kazdin, A. E., & Klock, J. (1973). The effect of nonverbal teacher approval on student attending behavior. *Journal of Applied Behavior Analysis, 6,* 643-654.

Keller, F. S. (1968). "Goodbye, teacher. . . ." *Journal of Applied Behavior Analysis, 1,* 79-89.

ace, F. C., & West, B. J. (1986). Unresolved theoretical issues in self-management: Implications for research and practice. *Professional School Psychology, 1*, 165-176.

Maheady, L., & Harper, G. (1987). A class-wide peer tutoring program to improve the spelling test performance of low income, third and fourth grade students. *Education and Treatment of Children, 10*, 120-128.

Marston, D., & Magnusson, D. (1985). Implementing curriculum-based measurement in special and regular education settings. *Educational Children, 52*, 266-276.

Medland, M., & Vitale, M. (1984). *Management of classrooms*. New York: Holt, Rinehart, Winston.

O'Leary, S. G., & Duby, D. R. (1979). Applications of self-control procedures by children: A review. *Journal of Applied Behavior Analysis, 12*, 449-466.

Paine, S. C., Radicchi, J., Rosellini, L. C., Deutchman, L., & Darch, C. B. (1983). *Structuring your classrooms for academic success*. Champaign, IL: Research Press.

Piersel, W. C. (1985). Self-observation and completion of school assignments: The influence of a physical recording device and expectancy considerations. *Psychology in the Schools, 22*, 331-337.

Piersel, W. C. (1987). Basic skills education. In C. A. Maher & S. G. Foreman (Eds.), *A behavioral approach to education of children and youth* (pp. 39-74). Hillsdale, NJ: Plenum Press.

Piersel, W. C., & Kratochwill, T. R. (1979). Self-observation and behavior change: Applications to academic and behavioral problems through behavioral consultation. *Journal of School Psychology, 12*, 151-161.

Pigott, E. H., Fantuzzo, J. W., & Clement, P. W. (1986). The effects of reciprocal peer tutoring and group contingencies on the academic performance of elementary school children. *Journal of Applied Behavior Analysis, 19*, 93-98.

Reid, E. R. (1986). Practicing effective instruction: The exemplary center for reading instruction approach. *Exceptional Children, 52*, 510-519.

Reid, H. P., Archer, M. B., & Friedman, R. M. (1977). Using the personalized system of instruction with low reading ability middle school students: Problems and results. *Journal of Personalized Instruction, 2*, 4.

Rosenshine, B. V. (1983). Teaching functions in instructional programs. *Elementary School Journal, 83*, 335-352.

Rosenshine, B. V. (1987). Explicit teaching. In D. C. Berliner & B. V. Rosenshine (Eds.), *Talks to teachers: A Festschrift for N. L. Gage* (pp. 74-92). New York: Random House.

Rubin, S. E., & Spady, W. G. (1984). Achieving excellence through outcome based instructional delivery. *Educational Leadership, 41*, 37-44.

Runge, A., Walker, J., & Shea, T. M. (1975). A passport to positive parent-teacher communications. *Teaching Exceptional Children, 7*, 91-101.

Skinner, B. F. (1968). *The technology of teaching*. New York: Appleton Century Crofts.

Skinner, B. F. (1984). The shame of American education. *American Psychologist, 39*, 947-954.

Tucker, J. A. (1985). Curriculum based assessment. *Exceptional Children, 52*, 199-204.

Van Houten, R. (1980). *Learning through feedback: A systematic approach for improving academic performance.* New York: Human Sciences Press.

Van Houton, R. (1987). Setting up performance feedback systems in the classroom. In W. L. Heward, T. E. Heran, D. S. Hill, and J. Trap-Porter (Eds.), *Focus on behavior analysis in education* (pp. 114-125). Columbus, OH: Charles E. Merrill.

White, K. P., Wyne, M. D., Stuck, G. B., & Coop, R. H. (1983). *Teaching effectiveness evaluation project* (Final report). Chapel Hill, NC: School of Education, University of North Carolina at Chapel Hill.

Improving the Study Skills of At-Risk Students

Judy L. Genshaft
Patricia M. Kirwin

The Ohio State University

SUMMARY. This paper reviews various definitions of study skills and examines seven specific study skills: discriminate listening, reading methods, memory aids, notetaking, outlining, underlining/highlighting, and test taking skills. Study skills are defined as the specific techniques used to acquire and utilize knowledge (Wise, Genshaft, & Byrley, 1987). Suggestions for effective study skill instruction are offered. Issues important for the development of a study skills program are examined. The authors recommend that more empirical research is needed to determine the effectiveness of study skills and study skills instruction.

This paper will review various definitions of study skills, provide instructional practices for six specific study skills, and then address issues pertinent in the development of a study skills program for a school or district. A rudimentary definition of study skills is that they are the specific techniques that the learner uses to acquire, remember, and utilize knowledge (Wise, Genshaft, & Byrley, 1987).

Study skills instruction, as with any other type of skill instruction, requires that certain basic skills be introduced early in the curriculum so that a foundation for learning more complex skills is established. When students fail to possess these basic skills, the effectiveness of learning a more complex study skill is seriously impaired. For example, to learn the study skill of summarizing, a

---

Requests for reprints should be directed to: Judy L. Genshaft, 356 Arps Hall, Department of Educational Services and Research, Ohio State University, 1945 North High Street, Columbus, OH 43210-1172.

© 1990 by The Haworth Press, Inc. All rights reserved.

child must be competent in categorizing and sequencing information, locating the main ideas, and outlining information.

Acquisition of effective study skills requires practice by the student (Brown, Campoine, & Day, 1981). The rewards of learning these skills are numerous. An example is the advantage of taking reading notes. It can help students to summarize material, to organize material for recall, and also be used as a resource to review material for tests. If notetaking is seldom required as a part of reading assignments, it is very unlikely that students will recognize the value of using such a skill.

A school wide and interdisciplinary commitment is one way to approach study skills instruction in a focused, cohesive manner. Simply mentioning a study skill and expecting students to utilize that skill without further instruction is not effective. If a study skills method is taught to the students by didactic instruction only, the likelihood is that the method will not be used (Gettinger & Knopik, 1985). One study skills plan could allow for the introduction of a study skills program that is extended and reinforced throughout the school year. An example of the steps involved in developing a study skills program can be found in Table 1.

REVIEW OF THE LITERATURE

Study skills may well be one of the most neglected areas in the academic curriculum (Barron, McCoy, Cuevas, Cuevas, & Rachal, 1983). Towle (1982) has referred to study skills as an "invisible" curriculum. Students are expected to learn these skills but are rarely taught them in a systematic way. The National Commission on Excellence in Education (1983) stated that "in most schools the teaching of study skills is haphazard and unplanned" (Davenport, 1984, p. 43). A clear definition of study skills is difficult to find in the literature. Many authors have relied on listing specific skills such as organizing, processing, and using information gained from reading (Salinger, 1983). Others have defined study skills as those skills that have an impact on the development of independence in learning (Dean, 1977). Researchers have organized study skills into a variety of conceptualizations. One focus has been placed on test taking skills (Markel, 1981), particularly as applied to the adolescent with

Table 1

Developing a Study Skills Program
___

Step 1. Write the goals of the study skills program.

Step 2. Write objectives and timelines based on the goals.

Step 3. Identify students who will be the focus of intervention and determine whether students who are experiencing academic difficulties should be included in the program or in a separate, more remedial program.

Step 4. If students experiencing academic difficulties are the targets of the intervention, generate a definition of these students that is quantifiable. For example: the "student experiencing academic difficulties is one who is failing at least one subject"; "all students who have achievement scores that are one standard deviation below aptitude scores are considered students who are at risk of failing academically."

Step 5. Assess all students to determine who falls into the defined category. (Much of this will depend upon the individual school's definition.) The study skills team can develop study skills checklists or use an existing self-check list such as the Cornell Learning and Study Skills Inventory (Pauk & Cassell, 1971) as well as other standardized test scores, grades, and actual observation.

TABLE 1 (continued)

Step 6. Examine study skills curricula and other pertinent materials of the students who are going to be included in the program to determine the techniques.

Step 7. Select the study skills techniques and metacognitive techniques such as rational self-talk. Incorporate them into an organized program that includes methods of evaluation to determine the programs' effectiveness.

Step 8. Implement the study skills program.

Step 9. Evaluate the students' performances. Assess study skills and their impact.

Step 10. Return to step 1 or 5. Set up alternative interventions.

---

learning disabilities. Markel suggests that specifically designed curricula on test taking skills is best taught through a multidisciplinary team approach among educators (special education consultants, regular classroom teachers, supportive personnel such as school psychologists, school counselors).

In Archer and Neubauer's (1981) conception of study skills, time management, test taking behavior, and study/concentration modules are emphasized. Instead of organizing study skills into taxonomies alone, Gettinger and Knopik (1985) have developed four general stages of study skills: (a) studying or processing information; (b) organizing, synthesizing and recording material; (c) practicing or remembering the organized information; and (d) recall and application of information.

The other emphasis from the literature is placed on self-management skills such as anxiety management (Desiderato & Koskinen, 1969), time management, concentration, and reinforcement schedules. All these approaches make clear that the techniques of study skills must be specifically taught and practiced. Presently, research in study skills has been unable to consistently support the benefits of any one technique. Furthermore, no one study skills technique has emerged as markedly superior to others (Armbruster & Anderson, 1981). More direct research on intervention would be valuable in assessing the effectiveness of study skills and test taking techniques with self-management skills.

INTRODUCTION TO STUDY SKILLS TECHNIQUES

Before initiating any study skills program, school staff must emphasize the utility of these skills to increase the likelihood that the students will use the skills. When students acquire proficiency in applying study skills in their school work, they can save time, access information faster and more efficiently, increase their comprehension, and become more independent. The program could teach several study skills in a hierarchical, step-by-step basis. The students are encouraged to select one skill, practice it for a specific period, and then evaluate it to determine if and how the skill was helpful. These determinations may be done on an individual basis with the teacher acting as the monitor.

Too many different study skills exist to be included in this overview. Both Ellis (1984) and Snider (1983) offer comprehensive accounts of many study skills and suggestions for application. The next section addresses seven basic study skills: (a) discriminate listening skills, (b) methods of reading for comprehension, (c) memory aids, (d) notetaking, (e) outlining, and (f) underlining and test taking skills. These skills are included in this paper as illustrative examples of some of the more basic study skills that may serve as the foundation of a study skills program. Discriminate listening may be one of the most necessary skills as it seems to be required in many learning situations. Methods of reading for comprehension are very important as good reading skills are essential for success in school. Using memory aids increases the probability that the learning is available for recall. The ability to take good notes from oral presentations and written material is important in summarizing, synthesizing, and organizing the information. Competent outlining and underlining skills also serve the function of condensing and organizing. These skills will be presented along with suggestions that can be adapted to the unique needs of a school or district.

Discriminate Listening Skills

The task of listening is considered so automatic that many educators neglect to teach rudimentary listening skills. Listening is a difficult task that requires many decisions. Lack of good listening skills and inability to identify situations, such as lectures, where discriminate listening can be applied may be two problems that a student encounters. One approach in teaching discriminate listening skills is for the teacher to review listening skills, evaluate the students on their listening skills, and refer students who are experiencing difficulties to a speech and hearing professional to rule out the possibility of a hearing handicap.

Various steps are required in teaching discriminate listening. The most basic component of listening is to focus both visually and auditorily on the object that requires the attention. Establishing and maintaining eye contact is essential. Students need to be quiet in order to listen. If taking notes, the visual attention should be divided between the teacher and the paper. Another step is to use attending techniques to increase listening skills. One can draw upon previous knowledge to integrate new knowledge. If listeners are aware of the topic to be presented then they can ask themselves what they already know about the subject. If the topic presented is one that listeners have had no previous experience with, they may form associations from previous knowledge.

Teachers may want to facilitate students' listening comprehension by asking them to summarize a lecture (Towle, 1982). Often this will help professionals to spot areas of weakness (e.g., poor vocabulary). Students should be taught to listen for organizational words in lectures such as "in summary," "three major reasons," "the first" (Gettinger & Knopik, 1985). This might increase listening skills as well as enhance notetaking organization. Students can learn to examine the speaker's nonverbal cues that may emphasize a point; for example, pauses and gestures that identify information (Towle, 1982). Teachers may want to place questions throughout the lecture to encourage student participation and check listening comprehension (Gettinger & Knopik, 1985).

Different situations require varying types of listening skills depending upon the listener's degree of involvement. Gettinger and Knopik (1985) identify four different types of listening situations and suggest that students be taught to discriminate among the situations to select a listening strategy. *Marginal listening* is all that is necessary when listening to music, television, or other situations where listening is for purposes of enjoyment. *Appreciative listening* is appropriate for situations, such as a guest speaker presentation, where the listeners do not have to be fully engaged in the act of listening. Students need to use *analytic listening* when the situation requires objective, critical listening such as being in the audience during an oral report. The most important type of listening for students, *focused listening*, is also the one that requires the most effort. Listeners need to focus all of their attention on the speaker (or other types of presentation) which requires a great deal of discipline. If notetaking is not necessary, listeners can direct all their awareness toward the object of attention.

Of great importance is to teach students to first identify the various types of listening situations and then engage in the activities required by the different listening strategies. Teachers may want to present the listening strategies, disseminating a list of the activities required by each one. A teacher may develop class participation sessions where several situations are presented, the students are asked to first identify the listening strategy required, and then asked to list the specific activities involved in the strategy. This could increase students' ability to practice discriminate listening skills.

Methods of Reading for Comprehension

Perhaps it is more appropriate to label reading for comprehension a basic skill rather than a study skill because it is essential for success both in and outside the school environment. Reading for comprehension is a prerequisite to any other study skill. Reading for comprehension differs greatly from reading for enjoyment as it requires understanding and retention of the information. Berger and Perfetti's (1977) research supports a conceptualization of reading comprehension as the interdependence of decoding skills and language comprehension. For the purpose of this paper, reading comprehension is defined as the ability to understand, synthesize, and retain information.

A review of the history of research in reading comprehension can be found in Harris (1968). Unfortunately, there is a paucity of research on the efficacy of reading methods, such as Survey, Question, Read, Recite, and Review (SQ3R) (Wise, Genshaft, & Byrley, 1987). Stahl (1983) collected and compared over 100 different reading methods. No single method of reading comprehension has emerged as more successful than another (Walker, 1986). Until more research is conducted in this field, the best teaching strategy may be to select a reading method based upon the characteristics of the targeted group. Many reading methods can be adapted for use in classes ranging from elementary to postsecondary. Robinson's (1941) SQ3R is one of the oldest reading methods and many newer methods are variations on this concept. SQ3R, a five-step process, may be the most common reading method taught to students (Gettinger & Knopik, 1985). The steps involved in the SQ3R methods will be explained in detail as most of the reading methods involve similar steps. The first step is *survey* where the material is subjected to a quick overview, scanning for cues of organization, such as headings, subheadings, and summaries. In the second step, *question*, each heading and subheading is turned into a question to be answered. This gives a direction to the search for the information. The answers are sought in the next step which is *reading* the material. In the fourth step, *recite*, the questions and answers are reviewed without looking at the material. This can be either orally, subvocally, or by writing notes. *Review*, the final step, is the immediate re-reading of the material to organize ideas and enhance retention.

The methods described below are similar to the SQ3R and use acronyms to facilitate the retention of the steps. The steps in TSQUARE (Bergman, 1975) are: *take* the text, *survey* the text, formulate *questions* based on the text, *underline* important concepts, *answer* the questions, *review* the material, and *expand* on the material. Similarly, Eanet and Manzo's (1976) REAP asks the reader to: *read* the material, *encode* or transform the material into his/her language, *annotate* by taking notes, and *ponder* or think about the material. The steps of PQ4R (Thomas & Robinson, 1977) are: *preview* the information, develop *questions*, *read* for the answers, *reflect* on the information, *recite* from memory, and *review* the information.

Riley's S2RAT (Lange, 1983) is another method for increasing reading comprehension. The S2RAT is a reading program that is useful as it assists students with reading difficulties and simultaneously challenges more advanced students (Lange, 1983). It emphasizes learning new or difficult vocabulary words, which is a different focus than the methods mentioned previously. Students also are given the opportunity to develop the skills of independence and responsibility. In Lange's program, the goal is to improve reading skills by helping the students master new words outside of the required spelling lists. The steps of S2RAT are:

S	Selected	The students select words for their lists.
R	Reviewed	The teacher reviews each of the student's lists.
R	Return	The lists are returned so the students can begin to learn them.
A	Activities	Students select activities that involve using the words (for example, discover homonyms for the word).
T	Testing	The students work in dyads, testing each other on the words.

The level of sophistication of the materials and the students may influence which reading strategy is selected. Walker (1986) suggests avoiding over reliance on any one reading system, but rather allowing students to be shown how a reading system can increase study skills.

Using Memory Aids

Although it is impossible to assess the capacity of an individual's memory, common beliefs hold that all one experiences is forever encoded in the brain and can be retrieved using the correct pathways (Carlson, 1986). Everyone has experienced the frustration of being aware that one possesses specific knowledge but cannot easily retrieve it when searching for it. Memory aids are techniques that are used to increase retention of information (Ellis, 1984). If students cannot competently retain and recall information they are going to have difficulty in using study skills. Memory aids can be used in conjunction with or separately from other study skills to increase the probability that what is being studied will be committed to long-term memory.

One way to teach the use of memory aids is to separate the presentation into three or four modules taught over a multi-week span. From the presentations, the students select two or three memory aids they wish to practice. A log of studying activities is kept by the students in order to assess the frequency with which the memory aids are being used. The effectiveness of these memory techniques could be evaluated subjectively, by the student's opinion, or more objectively, by the results on pencil and paper tests. The students and the teacher may want to compare their perceptions of the evaluations to determine if the memory aids are being used effectively and efficiently.

Using visualization, creating a mental picture of the concepts to be remembered, is a memory technique (Mangrum, 1983; Snider, 1983). This technique engages both hemispheres of the brain, increasing the probability of retention (Ellis, 1984). Coon (1984) states that, in general, visual images are recalled with greater ease than words alone. Smith and Elliott (1979) suggest the visualization process can be further strengthened by using imagery to create a mental picture that is striking in its absurdity or exaggeration.

In addition to mere visualization, utilizing several senses when learning provides multiple access to the memory, thus increasing the facility of remembering (Ellis, 1984). Mangrum (1983) suggests reciting aloud the information to be learned. If auditory tapes are made from lecture materials or notes and then reviewed, this serves the dual purpose of engaging more than one sensory system and facilitates review (Snider, 1983). Smith (1961) suggests that the writing of notes, reciting the material aloud, drawing sketches or diagrams, and creating exams be used in conjunction with reading.

Similar to Smith and Elliott (1979), Coon (1984) suggests the forming of exaggerated, unusual, or bizarre associations. He believes the more bizarre the association, the more likely it will be remembered. Smith (1961) suggests establishing strong and vivid impressions of the information to be learned. She sees devoting time to learn the materials as a prerequisite to forming intense impressions. Smith also believes the intensity of these impressions are increased by repetition.

Interest in the information and a purpose for reading increases retention of information (Mangrum, 1983). Being aware of personal biases that might interfere with learning is important (Ellis, 1984). If the first reading of the material is performed with strong purpose, this will aid later recall even if the purpose is only to master the information to obtain a good grade when evaluated (Mangrum, 1983). Another way to develop a purpose is to use the imagination to make what is learned meaningful so the learner can appreciate its significance to his/her daily life or future goals (Ellis, 1984). Coon (1984) states that transferring information from short-term memory to long-term memory is facilitated by giving meaning to the information. Mangrum (1983) suggests the student work toward an understanding of the information. The familiarity of the information is increased when it is connected with what is already in the long-term memory (Coon, 1984).

Snider (1983) believes the optimal condition for learning occurs when the relationships among ideas are understood and the ideas are repeated frequently. Associating the ideas or information to be learned is a way to understand the relationships (Mangrum, 1983). If the relationships are not understood, then the learning probably occurs by rote and is not easily manipulated or recalled if the data are requested in a different format. It is best to learn facts by understanding their relationships to other facts and studying these relationships, rather than using memory techniques such as mnemonics (Snider, 1983). Coon (1984) defines mnemonics as "any kind of memory system or aid" (p. 103). Smith (1961) advocates that a "natural, rational association of ideas" is superior to artificial associations such as acronyms and mnemonics (p. 54).

However, if there is not a relationship among facts or the student is having difficulty visualizing one, the student may choose an acronym to help memory retention (Snider, 1983). Coon (1984) suggests creating acronyms by using the first letter of each word in a list to produce a new work (e.g., *W*ide *R*ange *A*chievement *T*est — WRAT). He also states that syllables of words can be used to create a new word (for example, smoke + fog = smog). Also, acronyms can be created by using the first letters of compound word (Woolf, 1974). Special sentences using the acronyms can be created (Snider, 1983). Acronyms or sentences containing acronyms can link key words or concepts together in an organized fashion (Mangrum, 1983). For example, they can connect the items together in a sequence which may be important in some studies (Coon, 1984).

Mnemonic devices are closely related to acronyms. Mnemonics can be used in at least two ways. These devices can be used to associate what is to be remembered by an expression, rhyme, or other means such as "There is a rate in separate" (Ohio Department of Education, 1986). Ellis (1984) suggests mnemonics can be used to make associations between material previously learned and new material. The superiority of mnemonics over simple rote memorization has been demonstrated in several students (Coon, 1984).

Ellis (1984) encourages learners to start viewing material from a general perspective, in an overview, before attempting to know the specific details. Attending to and concentrating on the information without distractions is also important (Mangrum, 1983). Smith (1961) recommends that readers try not to remember isolated facts but rather repeatedly study the materials as a whole. One of the most simplistic aids to the memory is to periodically review and repeat the information. Overlearning the information is a far better strategy than underlearning (Ellis, 1984). Mangrum (1983) also advocates overlearning and reviewing. Frequently reading or hearing the same materials will enhance memorization of the materials (Snider, 1983). Smith (1961) states the immediacy of the recall is important. She recommends the reader space the reading into intervals and attempt to recall important information between readings. At each break, the reader should try to recall the prior facts as well as the new ones. If the idea or fact is elusive, Ellis (1984) suggests reflecting upon related concepts. Often this act of recalling enables the learner to remember the original concept.

Developing Notetaking Skills

Notetaking is the ability to record information into a usable format to enhance understanding, intention, and recall of information. It involves proficient outlining and summarizing skills (ODE, 1986). Notetaking is not simply the exact recording of information; it is the skill of transforming the information into an understandable format. Notetaking is a three-part process involving observation, recording, and review (Ellis, 1984). This study skill is important in most classes as the vehicle for learning new material. Notetaking "is a fairly difficult study skill to master" (ODE, p. 29).

Teachers can perform many tasks to increase the organization of lectures to facilitate notetaking. The teacher may write an outline when lecturing or illustrate the lecture with a model of notetaking (Gettinger & Knopik, 1985). This can be done by using the board, an overhead projector, or distributing written lecture notes. The teacher may want to teach various notetaking strategies and require notetaking as part of the readings (ODE, 1986). The students can be instructed to recognize main ideas and details (Mangrum, 1983).

McAndrew (1983) offers teachers suggestions that may facilitate notetaking from lectures. Pacing the lecture at an appropriate tempo increases coherent notetaking as it allows adequate time to record the notes. Verbal and nonverbal cues can be used to emphasize important points. Writing an outline or writing important points on the board increases the probability that the information will be copied into notebooks by students. Giving information about which type of test will be given for evaluation might improve notetaking. Handouts containing comprehensive notes and space for new notes might be especially helpful to students who are poor notetakers.

Another way to increase effective notetaking skills is for the students to be encouraged to prepare in advance for lectures. Reading the assignments, taking notes or generating an outline of the readings, and completing homework assignments decreases the amount of notetaking in class (Snider, 1983). The notes taken in class are more likely to cover important concepts and details. Scanning the readings and reviewing the notes again just before class also facilitates effective notetaking (Ellis, 1984).

Students should select notetaking formats that they feel most comfortable with and consistently use that format (Gettinger & Knopik, 1985). As in discriminate listening, students should learn to recognize organizational words (Towle, 1982). Key words such as "introducing," "in conclusion," and transition phrases can help organize notes (Ellis, 1984). Towle (1982) points out that knowing how to spell and write are prerequisites for competent notetaking. She also indicates that the vocabulary in presentations and required readings must be equal to or below the student's level of comprehension.

Storing notes in chronological or subject order in a notebook saves time when reviewing the information. The notes should be labeled for easy retrieval (Ellis, 1984; Gettinger & Knopik, 1985). The date, name of class, and page number on each page of the notes is helpful (ODE, 1986). Leaving a wide left margin gives room for adding questions or key information (Ellis, 1984; ODE, 1986). Taking notes on only one side of the paper facilitates review and comparison. Another method is to record the information on index cards (Ellis, 1984).

If notes are written in ink they are less likely to become illegible from smudging (ODE, 1986). Ellis suggests writing notes in an outline format. If this is not possible, he recommends making informal paragraphs. Another format is to write the information in block form, leaving spaces in between blocks for additional information (ODE, 1986).

Notes do not have to be written as complete sentences (Mangrum, 1983; Smith, 1961). They need to be brief yet precise, containing enough key words, phrases, and sentence parts to jog the memory (Ellis, 1984; Gettinger & Knopik, 1985; Smith, 1961; Snider, 1983; Towle, 1982). Using standard abbreviations or abbreviating words by omitting unimportant vowels increases notetaking speed and precision (Ellis, 1984; Snider, 1983). If the information is very important, it may require complete sentences to capture the concepts (Ellis, 1984). A direct quotation from the readings must be written with quotation marks and the appropriate page number from the readings (Mangrum, 1983). Ellis (1984) suggests using diagrams and pictures to highlight important points. Many authors propose that the notes paraphrase the original information. If students put the information in their own words, they are more likely to retain it (Anderson, 1979; Gettinger & Knopik, 1985; Smith, 1961; Towle, 1982).

Notetaking alone does not increase retention of information; research indicates learning is facilitated when the notes are reviewed (Rickards & Friedman, 1978). Revising, reorganizing, and rewriting notes are ways to facilitate review (ODE, 1986; Towle, 1982). Combining notes from different sources on the same subject is another method to organize studying (ODE, 1986). Smith (1961) suggests that practice in recall and review of the notes increases understanding of textual material.

Towle (1982) divides notetaking into two different skills that overlap in many tasks: notetaking from verbal presentations and notetaking from printed materials. Notetaking from lectures may be performed more often by students as they may not take notes on required readings. Notetaking from lectures requires concentrating on the speaker's presentation and attending to what is being said (Ellis, 1984; Snider, 1983). Notes should not be a replication of the entire lecture. They should be a condensation of the material (Gettinger & Knopik, 1985). Repetition in a presentation often underscores an important point. It is best for students to review the notes when the lecture is still fresh in their mind (Gettinger & Knopik, 1985).

The notetaking from required readings needs to be thoughtful and selective (ODE, 1986). Towle (1982) suggests that students identify the main topics and subtopics in the notes. She also indicates that summaries in readings can be used to locate the main points identified in the notes. Developing study questions will increase focus on the notetaking process.

Outlining

The study skill of outlining is used to organize information for papers, in taking lecture notes, or recording important points in reading assignments (Mangrum, 1983). Because outlining is primarily used to condense printed materials, outlining from books and notes will be addressed. It is possible to use outlining when taking notes from auditory presentations; in fact, outlining may be the best way to organize this material (Ellis, 1984). Students may want to write or rewrite notes in outline form.

The most important prerequisite to outlining printed materials is the ability to read and understand the materials (Towle, 1982). If the material is at the student's reading level, the student should read the assignment completely before proceeding with outlining. To be successful in the skill of underlining, the concepts in the assignment and the relationships among them must be understood (ODE, 1986). Outlining is used to demonstrate how ideas or facts fit together (Mangrum, 1983). A solid background in categorizing information and identifying main ideas is a prerequisite for generating good outlines (ODE, 1986). The text typically provides a guide for outlining its headings, subheadings, and opening and summary sentences (Towle, 1982). Smith (1961) suggests that an outline be generated on chapters that are required reading. Outlining can help students discover the organization of the material (ODE, 1986). The student can use the organization to dictate the outline. The students need to be trained to recognize and use the superordinate sentences that organize the materials as this will increase the retention of both subordinate and superordinate sentences (McAndrew, 1983). The outline can be memorized and used as an anchor for recalling details (Smith, 1961).

One way to teach outlining is to present the skills step by step, give examples of outlining, and focus on the utility of outlining. The teacher may want to give the students outlines that are partially completed so that they may practice outlining (Gettinger & Knopik, 1985). Readers interested in teaching outlining may want to refer to Mangrum (1983) or Snider (1983) for organized modules addressing the teaching of outlining skills.

Underlining and Highlighting Materials

The study skill of underlining or highlighting may be one of the most popular skills used when attempting to summarize information from books. Smith (1961) states that underlining seems to be the only skill many students know and use. Often students cannot distinguish important information from trivial, and as a result, underline too much (Smith, 1986). The amount of underlining should be minimal (Gettinger & Knopik, 1985; McAndrew, 1983). If the underlining is not discriminating, the students will not be able to use underlining to organize studying.

To increase effective underlining, reading the assignment completely before underlining decreases the amount of underlining (Gettinger & Knopik, 1985). If students are taught to recognize superordinate sentences that convey general ideas and underline these, they will decrease the amount of study time needed, as well as the amount of underlining, and increase the likelihood that the details contained in the subordinate sentences are remembered (McAndrew, 1983).

The ability to recognize main terms, concepts, and supportive details is important in underlining (Towle, 1982). Also, underlining main ideas, important details, and facts is necessary for effective underlining (Snider, 1983). The underlining can be organized by identifying main ideas using signal words (e.g., headings, subheadings) in the text (Towle, 1982). McAndrew (1983) suggests distributing pre-underlined materials as examples, which can help develop underlining skills.

McAndrew (1983) further believes that underlining can save time in two ways: (a) if only superordinate sentences are underlined, the time spent underlining will be minimal; and (b) using underlined material to organize studying saves time. He also believes that students need to be taught to discriminate, that is, when to use techniques other than underlining. Smith (1961) postulates that underlining could be the first step in preparation for recall, but regards other memory aids as more effective organizers.

Learning Test-Taking Skills

A study skills program must include a component that teaches the student how to study for tests. Teaching the student proper preparation and test-wiseness skills might improve the validity of test results as it minimizes test format problems (Wise, Genshaft, &

Byrley, 1987). Millman, Bishop, and Ebel (1965) define test-wiseness as the ability to understand the different formats and characteristics of tests for the purpose of increasing one's score. A format that can be used on objective and essay tests which addresses both test-wiseness and other strategies is the SCORER system developed by Carmen and Adams (1972). The steps in SCORER are:

S — Schedule your time
C — Clue words, questions should be sought
O — Omit difficult questions
R — Read carefully
E — Estimate your answers
R — Review your work

As with many of the study skills techniques, the research on the SCORER system has been scant (Wise, Genshaft, & Byrley, 1987). Other systems, such as Test-Making Activity (McPhail, 1981), need to be examined by the teacher before selection of one for adoption.

Seven of the basic study skills have been defined and discussed in this section. In the next section, a few of the issues related to study skills will be discussed.

ISSUES AND GUIDELINES

In addition to facilitating the learning of content, Marshak and Burkle (1981) believe study skills can help students develop an awareness of how they learn best. They also state that this awareness can help students assume more responsibility for their own learning. Gettinger and Knopik (1985) suggest that a study skills program involve a component where students learn about how they learn. Marshak and Burkle (1981) and Gettinger and Knopik (1985) appear to be addressing the concept often referred to as metacognition.

Wong and Wong (1986) define metacognition as the knowledge an individual possess about his/her cognitive resources and cognitive states. Metacognition is the ability of a person to consider the way he/she thinks, and recognize how he/she thinks and learn. Just as study skills are part of "an invisible curriculum," metacognition, a large component of study skills, is virtually ignored (Towle, 1982). Students often are not encouraged to seriously consider how they think, and adapt to the demands of the learning environment or, conversely, adapt the environment to fit their needs. Wise, Genshaft, and Byrley (1987) state that students acquire study skills to gain an awareness of how they learn best and take more responsibility for their own learning. In this way students can generalize their knowledge to challenges both within and outside of the school environment.

Students who experience difficulty with their coursework have often been taught that they are not capable of meeting many learning demands. They may have been told and may come to believe they are too inadequate as learners to acquire knowledge. What is important is to create an awareness in these learners of their metacognition. Without this awareness the study skills acquired may not fit into the individual's unique thinking style. Exposure to study skills techniques does not ensure the knowledge will be used or used effectively (Wise, Genshaft, and Byrley, 1987). Robyak (1977) suggests a distinction be made between the use of study skills and the knowledge of study skills. Gettinger and Knopik (1987) propose a two-fold study skills model that addresses the deficit areas and considers the particular styles and needs of the learner.

Individual learning styles is another issue related to study skills. School staff may wish to assess each student's learning style with a tool such as the Swassing-Barbe Modality Index (Zaner-Bloser, Inc., 1979), and then use the student's preferred modality (auditory, kinesthetic, or visual) when teaching study skills. Towle (1982) suggests teachers select learning aids based on the modality strengths of the students. It is hoped that use of materials which address the preferred modality will increase comprehension and volume of information retained. Difficulty may arise if students become too dependent upon presentations to their preferred modalities that they cannot adapt to learning situations which require other modalities. Perhaps students could learn to identify their preferred modality and use this modality to help strengthen the other modalities in their repertoire.

CONCLUSION

Teaching specific study skills as part of the school curriculum occurs infrequently; also, students with special needs are often overlooked. An organized program that addresses these issues can be beneficial to both the students as well as the schools. The students could become more eager and autonomous learners; the district could divert students from becoming labeled unnecessarily.

The purpose of this paper has been to acquaint the reader with study skills instruction and highlight the advantages of developing an integrated study skills program. Although all students should be taught study skills, students who are experiencing difficulty are in even greater need of learning study skills. This paper has reviewed the nature and scope of study skills; briefly summarized seven basic study skill techniques; described how metacognition can enhance learning, and how awareness of modality strengths can facilitate learning. Full scale research focusing on the integration of a study skills program in a school system, clearly is needed so that study skills can be more effectively taught to students.

REFERENCES

Anderson, R. C. (1979). Control of student mediating processes during verbal learning and instruction. *Review of Educational Research, 40*, 349-369.

Archer, J., Jr., & Neubauer, T. (1981). Study skills on a shoestring. *NASPA Journal, 18*(3), 48-52.

Armbruster, B. B., & Anderson, T. H. (1981). Research synthesis on study skills. *Educational Leadership, 39*, 154-156.

Barron, B. G., McCoy, J., Cuevas, P., Cuevas, S., & Rachal, G. (1983). Study skills: A new look. *Reading Improvement, 20*, 329-332.

Berger, N. S., & Perfetti, C. A. (1977). Reading skill and memory for spoken and written discourse. *Journal of Reading Behavior, 9*(1), 7-16.

Bergman, F. L. (1975). TSQUARE for studying. *Journal of Reading, 19*, 167-169.

Brown, A. L., Campoine, J. C., & Day, J. D. (1981). Learning to learn: On training students to learn from texts. *Educational Researcher, 10*, 14-21.

Carmen, R. A., & Adams, W. R. (1972). *Study skills: A student's guide for survival*. New York: Wiley.

Carlson, N. R. (1986). *Physiology of Behavior (3rd ed.)*. Boston: Allyn & Bacon.

Coon, D. (1984). Mnemonics—Memory Magic. In Adams, W. R. *Prep for Better Reading (2nd ed.)*. New York: Holt Rinehart, and Winston, 103-106.

Davenport, E. (1984). Study skills: Tools of the trade to make studying easier and more efficient. *Early Years, 15*(2), 43-44.
Dean, J. (1977). Study skills: Learning how to learn. *Education, 5,* 9-11.
Desiderato, O., & Koskinen, P. (1969). Anxiety, study habits and academic achievement. *Journal of Consulting Psychology, 16,* 162-165.
Eanet, M. G., & Manzo, A. V. (1976). REAP—A strategy for improving reading/writing skills. *Journal of Reading, 19,* 647-652.
Ellis, D. G. (1984). *Becoming a master student (4th ed.).* Rapid City, SD: College Survival, Inc.
Gettinger, M., & Knopik, S. N. (1985). Children and study skills. In A. Thomas and J. Grimes (Eds.), *Children's Needs: Psychological Perspectives.* Washington, DC: NASP.
Harris, A. J. (1968). Research on some aspects of comprehension: Rate, flexibility, and study skills. *Journal of Reading, 12,* 258-260.
Lange, J. T. (1983). Using the S2RAT to improve reading skills in content areas. *The Reading Teacher, 36*(4), 402-404.
Mangrum, C. T. (1983). *Learning to Study Book H: Study skills and strategies.* Providence, RI: Jamestown Publishers.
Markel, G. (1981). Improving test taking skills of LD adolescents. *Academic Therapy, 16*(3), 333-342.
Marshak, D., & Burkle, C. R. (1981). Learning to study: A basic skill. *Principal, 61*(2), 38-40.
McAndrew, D. (1983). Underlining and notetaking: Some suggestions from research. *Journal of Reading, 27*(2), 103-108.
McPhail, I. (1981). Why teach test-wiseness? *Journal of Reading, 25,* 32-38.
Millman, J., Bishop, C. H., & Ebel, R. (1965). An analysis of test-wiseness. *Educational and Psychological Measurement, 24*(3), 707-726.
Ohio Department of Education. (1986). *Study skills: A resource book.* Columbus, OH: Author.
Pauk, W., & Cassell, R. (1971). *Manual for the Cornell Learning and Study Skills Inventory.* Jacksonville, IL: Psychologists and Educators Press.
Rickards, J. P., & Friedman, P. (1978). The encoding versus the external storage hypothesis in notetaking. *Contemporary Educational Psychology, 8,* 136-43.
Robinson, F. P. (1941). *Diagnostic and remedial techniques for effective study.* New York: Harper and Brothers.
Robyak, J. E. (1977). A revised study skills model: Do some of them practice what we teach? *Personnel and Guidance Journal, 56,* 171-175.
Salinger, T. (1983). Study skills: A "basic" in elementary reading instruction. *Reading Improvement, 20*(4), 333-337.
Smith, C. B., & Elliott, P.G. (1979). *Reading activities for middle and secondary schools: A handbook for teachers.* New York: Holt Rinehart, and Winston.
Smith, N. B. (1961). *Be a better reader-book VI.* Englewood Cliffs, NJ: Prentice Hall, Inc.
Snider, J. (1983). *How to Study in High School.* Providence, RI: Jamestown Publishers.

Stahl, N. (1983). A historical analysis of textbook study systems (Doctoral dissertation, University of Pittsburgh). *Dissertation Abstracts International, 45*(2), 480-A.

Thomas, E. L., & Robinson, H. A. (1977). *Improving Reading in every class (2nd ed.)*. Boston: Allyn & Bacon.

Towle, M. (1982). Learning how to be a student when you have a learning disability. *Journal of Learning Disabilities, 15*(2), 90-93.

Walker, J. E. (1986). What to do with 100+ study systems. *Reading Today, 3*(5), 14.

Wise, P., Genshaft, J., & Byrley, M. (1987). Study-skills training: A comprehensive approach. In C. A. Maher & J. E. Zins (Eds.), *Psychoeducational Interventions in the Schools*. New York: Pergamon Press.

Wong, B. Y. L., & Wong, R. (1986). Study behavior as a function of metacognitive knowledge about critical task variables: An investigation of above average, average, and learning disabled readers. *Learning Disabilities Research, 1*(2), 101-111.

Woolf, H. B. (Ed.). (1974). *The Merriam-Webster Dictionary*. New York: Pocket Books.

Zaner-Bloser, Inc. (1979). *The Swassing-Barbe Modality Index: Directions for administration and scoring*. Columbus, OH: Author.

Time Management in the Classroom: Increasing Instructional Time

Cathy Collins
Texas Christian University

SUMMARY. Many special services providers want to assist classroom teachers in using instructional time more wisely. Unfortunately, prior to this publication, few aids were available to assist in this effort.

The purpose of this paper is to inform special services providers about time management so that they can assist classroom teachers and other special service personnel to increase student success. In the course of this discussion, I will explore: (a) means of diagnosing teachers with time-management problems, (b) procedures that build their time-use skills, and (c) methods of teaching students to use their time more effectively.

NATURE AND SCOPE OF THE RELATIONSHIP BETWEEN STUDENT FAILURE AND TEACHERS' MISUSE OF TIME

Classroom teachers can misuse time in the following ways and thereby reduce at-risk students' chances for success.

1. They can be ineffective monitors of in-class time, lacking skills of simultaneously managing time, resources, and students, which are needed to provide the security base at-risk students need to begin to grow.

Requests for reprints should be directed to: Cathy Collins, School of Education, Texas Christian University, P.O. Box 32925, Fort Worth, TX 76129.

© 1990 by The Haworth Press, Inc. All rights reserved.

2. They can have weak organizational skills which, in turn, decrease the quality of time and time given to instruction.
3. They schedule improperly so that the time allocated, both within and between lessons, does not match that which most at-risk students need to achieve at their maximum rate.
4. They can be ineffective in managing their time, which limits their availability to meet individual student needs.

More importantly, most classroom teachers do not know that they are having difficulty managing time. They attribute classroom problems to other causes (Collins, 1987). Because this inability is an almost "natural blindness," called *betriesblind*, special services providers can become valuable partners to regular education teachers. Special services providers can help teachers reach a goal they feel they need but, if left unaided, may not be able to achieve themselves. This goal is eliminating ways in which their decisions and behavior in managing the class are limiting their students' success. In the next section, several methods of managing classroom time will be identified.

Helping Classroom Teachers Use Time to Create a Security Base for Learning

In the course of careers, teachers enter school buildings that are new to them. Yet, as they walk down the hall for the first time and gaze at the activities in the classes, they can discern which teachers are among the best in the building and which are not. Prior to the study of time management, one could have justified these candid evaluations (as well as the unexplained ability to make such rapid distinctions) to the statement, "Good teachers are just born, not made; good teaching is an innate ability."

Recent work in time management, however, has illuminated the criterion upon which a distinction could be made: *effective teachers have the ability to simultaneously and continuously manage individuals, resources, course content, and time* (Collins, 1987; Wiggers, Forney, & Wallace-Schutzman, 1983). This ability establishes an environment in which students can more confidently engage in purposeful activities. One might be able to detect this involvement in observing the effective teachers' rooms.

What time management skills are needed to establish such a secure, nurturing environment? Recent work (McGraw, 1987) has revealed that most at-risk students need to know that: (a) their day will begin with a well-established procedure; (b) their lessons create new opportunities for learning and are monitored so as to end with enough time to make a stress-free transition to the next class or subject; (c) their learning objectives are attainable yet challenging; and (d) their teacher has planned instructional alternatives in case their learning needs are greater than the teacher originally judged.

Special services providers can present Table 1 to teachers needing information in achieving (a) and (b) above. Such teachers can study the table (a description of the procedures most successful teachers use to open and close their classes), and adapt the procedures to match their own personal teaching styles (Tschudin, 1978).

Clearly, it is very important to establish lessons with appropriate objectives. Regular classroom educators, however, may not fully realize that such objectives rely upon the use of effective time-use skills. Further, they might benefit from discussions of how appropriate objectives increase students' learning time.

Specifically, when students are able to repeatedly complete their learning objectives within the time allowed, they begin to trust themselves to be successful. Some also begin to trust that their teacher has the expertise to create a lesson that they can complete in the allotted time. With such skilled and effective teachers, at-risk students focus more attention upon learning, that is, they do not pay as much attention to the amount of time they will need to complete the task or how much time they have left. They are assured that their teacher has accurately judged time (and it is sufficient) so they can pursue their part in learning, which is "putting that time to good use."

If special services providers begin to suspect that a regular classroom teacher has difficulty in establishing time-effective objectives, they can help by having an informal discussion and by asking some of the following questions:

TABLE 1. Opening Class Procedures

ATTENDANCE CHECK METHODS

1. Check orally from grade book.
2. Check silently from seating chart.
3. Have classroom officer or adult volunteer aide check the attendance.
4. Give each student a number and have each call out his or her number or raise his or her hand as you or classroom officer calls out the number.

   Your procedure:_____
   _____

ADMINISTRATIVE DUTIES

1. Have a standard procedure in place so students know what they are expected to do while you have administrative duties; they should not sit idle.
2. Have a timer and as soon as students walk in, set it and then tell them that they have 3 (or 5, etc.) minutes to finish_____ _____. When time is up, you could have finished the administrative duties, and will grade the student papers, forming a 100 percent club or other incentive program for perfect or 80 percent plus work.
3. Have students write in a daily log, diary type format, for a six-week reward that the class values.
4. Display brief assignments on overhead projector screen or blackboard before students arrive and let them work the mini-lessons as soon as they walk in; these lessons could be reviews of yesterday's work, introductions to the lesson of the day, brainteasers, crossword puzzles for vocabulary development, or logic problems.

   Your procedure:_____
   _____

GIVING CLEAR DIRECTIONS FOR ASSIGNMENTS

1. Give oral explanations of mental set, rationale, objective, but also give visual outline of key points on board, handout, or overhead.
2. Specify standards of form and level of neatness for each assignment, or give a general standard that students are expected to use always; tell students which standard you are using. Include what heading you prefer, whether students are to write on back of paper, use pen or pencil, erase or draw lines through, how to number, and what are the due dates; and remind students of policy if work is late (e.g., points subtracted, staying after school, turning in assignments on time even if incomplete).
3. Post a sample heading of an assignment and remind students several times in the early weeks of school to refer to it and use it.

   Your procedure:_____
   _____

TABLE 1 (continued)

STUDENTS WHO ARE ABSENT

1. Post weekly assignment lists on bulletin board.
2. Each time a handout is given, place five extra copies in an ongoing folder for absentees, put the date on each handout (or have classroom officer responsible for handing out papers, stamp dates and file handouts); absentees know where tp get information on missed work so that it can be completed before their makeup deadline has ended.
3. Decide how much time will be allowed for makeup work and stick to it, for example, students have a specific amount of time after their return to school to complete assignments and one day absent means work is done day after student returns to school.
4. Decide if there will be a penalty and how much it will be for missed work and/or any paper turned in late.
5. Set a place where the students can turn in makeup work and where they can pick it up after it's been graded (e.g., trays/folders labeled "absent in"/"absent out") and allow slower learners to grade and write explanations on each incorrect answer as to why it was incorrect. If anyone aside from the teacher grades makeup papers or if the teacher decides to grade once each week, then a system to verify that the papers were turned in within the time period allowed will be needed.
6. Set a time before or after when the teacher, volunteer older students, or class officer will be available to help students with makeup work.
7. Establish a procedure whereby class officers or monitors can use the teacher's edition of the class text to help classmates with makeup work.

Your Procedure:_____

STUDENTS WHO ARE TARDY

1. Initiate a school wide policy and encourage all teachers to never make exceptions for tardiness. For example, letting a few students slip in late at the beginning of the period might cause the procedures to break down.
2. Assign detention unless the student has a legitimate excuse for tardiness.
3. Place a "t" in the grade book (or classroom officer places "t") each time a student is tardy and the tardiness results in some type of action on the student's part.
4. Put clipboard by the door and students who are tardy sign in when they arrive each period and at the end of the day; the teacher or a classroom monitor changes the absences to tardies in the grade book.

Your Procedure:_____

1. What objectives were explained to students at the beginning of the learning period?
2. Do student(s) know what activity is to be used to meet that objective, in advance of beginning the activity?
3. Are the student(s) clear as to what they should feel, see, or

experience as a result of successfully completing the objective?

Through this communication the teacher might not only develop better classroom time-use skills but at-risk students might be better able to use their own time management skills to learn.

Last of all, classroom teachers might create a more secure environment by considering alternatives that can be built into a daily lesson plan. Consideration of alternatives might be facilitated by teachers routinely asking the following questions about each lesson:

1. Can I use time during this lesson to vary the size of the group in which students will work, vary the room arrangement, spend more time using concrete objects, or enhance the learning experience by taking time to move to another location such as outdoors or the cafeteria?
2. Have I allocated time to meet auditory, visual, tactile, and kinesthetic learning needs? Have I incorporated the option of using more than one modality in demonstrating mastery of the learning objective?
3. What method of grading will give the fastest and most direct feedback to students?
4. What amount, depth, and variety of coverage is expected as a maximum and minimum learning?
5. What are the attention span demands of this lesson and do these demands match the time of day and point in the year in which the lesson will be delivered?

Another time-efficient way to provide for personal learning needs is to use a notebook, or space in the lesson plan book, to list individual student needs. In this way, after each lesson, time will be scheduled to reteach the concept. This procedure should become standard. That is, it must be practiced consistently before most at-risk students feel secure enough to take learning risks in a heterogeneously grouped classroom.

Facilitating Classroom Teachers' Organizational Skills so as to Impact the Quality of Their Instruction

Research has demonstrated that most time-efficient teachers, "in the process of becoming," developed time-use skills and use a master lesson plan (Collins, 1987; Green & Rasinski, 1985; O'Neal, 1984; and Wyne & Stuck, 1982). Eight of the time-use skills of time-efficient teachers are listed below.

1. Time-efficient teachers spend more time thinking about the plan they are making for students and less time writing elaborate, detailed lesson plans than do less efficient teachers.
2. Students of time-efficient teachers are more prepared for their lessons because the teacher has provided them with long-range calendars of assignments and posted assignments in the classroom.
3. These teachers give more interesting introductions to lessons because they have the time to find new materials, plan how to explain the rationale for each lesson, and design ways to frequently review the rules and procedures in activities.
4. They explain concepts in concrete terms, using examples, non-examples, analogies, and personal experiences.
5. They guide students in practicing the concepts before they allow them to work independently.
6. They reteach the concepts several times, using samples to stimulate different modalities in the first two days of instruction.
7. They provide new information more frequently than less successful teachers, that is, their organizational skills enable them to implement more objectives.
8. They divide complex tasks into simpler tasks with greater ease than less successful teachers. They also give step-by-step directions for new learning tasks.

In addition, these teachers deliver lessons that do not interfere with the pace of slower learning students. Specifically, these successful teachers have overcome five problems in lesson delivery. These problems, as well as the methods they used to overcome them are cited in Table 2.

TABLE 2. Problems/Solutions in Lesson Delivery

Problems	Solutions
1. Moving from one topic to another too rapidly or putting in too much trivial or extraneous information.	1. Make an outline of content and stick to it; hold back complexities until main points are developed.
2. Giving too many directions or presenting too much too quickly.	2. Give everything in steps, for example, step 1, step 2; check for understanding before proceeding.
3. Being ambiguous or indefinite such as saying "maybe", "more or less", "you know", "not always", "sort of".	3. Refer to concrete objects or examples; state what is correct and what is not correct and why.
4. Moving too rapidly to next topic because no student asks a question.	4a. Ask one or two students to summarize the main points or to make up a question to ask the remainder of the class to see if the class is understanding the main points being covered.
	4b. As you write the lesson plan, write in the left margin of each lesson plan approximately how many minutes each section will take.

Working with Teachers to Improve Schedules so as to Better Accommodate At-Risk Students' Learning Needs

Student success is dependent upon teachers' skills in scheduling classroom time. These skills apply to schedules followed within single classes, schedules followed in consecutive classes, and weekly/yearly timetables. As much as 80 percent of the difference in student achievement can be explained by the degree of teacher skill in scheduling time to teach (Barr, 1980; Everston, Emmer, Sanford, Clements, & Worsham, 1984; and Sanford, 1983). For example, in one study (Davidson & Holly, 1979), teachers learned how to make better schedules. When these schedules were followed, these teachers increased their students' instructional time by 23 to 34 minutes a day. This gave their students a total of 10-16 more days of learning time a year. This increase appeared to occur solely through the teachers' more effective use of classroom time.

How Can Regular Classroom Teachers Schedule and Pace Activities, Shift Topics, Decide When (and How) to Change Activities, Signal Correct Behaviors, and Make Transitions to Enhance Learning for At-Risk Students

Some of the effective, time-use scheduling skills are:

1. Keeping the daily schedule visible at all times.
2. Keeping the desk clear except for the lesson plan book, which is opened.
3. Posting the week's objectives and learning plans in the classroom.
4. Placing the teachers' manuals and lesson plans for different subjects in separate places in the room.
5. Following a consistent procedure for students to leave the room that does not allow students to interrupt small group or one-on-one instruction.
6. Using a consistent signal to end the class, such as "It's time to stop working now," or "Let's stop work and review as we prepare for the next lesson."

7. Allowing class monitors to set up materials and distribute papers, while the teacher meets with individual students.
8. During the first week of school, the students are kept in large group activities and practice procedures for moving to small groups, to the locker, etc., until each procedure is automatic and orderly.
9. Detecting and correcting student behavior problems immediately (see Collins, 1987, and Collins, 1988b for a description of methods).
10. Allowing no more than 30 seconds for transitions between lessons by the fourth week of school.
11. Making the yearly plan in consideration of special events, such as Halloween and school sports, which impact the lives of all students.

ASSISTING TEACHERS IN BETTER MANAGING THEIR OWN TIME

Classroom teachers' awareness of their own time-management weaknesses can help keep at-risk students on task. To increase this awareness, the most common classroom time wasters are cited in Table 3. Although the scope of this discussion does not include methods by which special services providers can assist teachers in eliminating specific time-wasting habits, special services providers can provide these teachers with a copy of Table 3 and direct them to a resource of methods to eliminate time-wasters (see, e.g., Collins, 1987). Such assistance might benefit at-risk students. That is, every time a regular education teacher learns to more appropriately use classroom time, the learning time for at-risk students can increase.

How Special Service Providers Can Assist Teachers to Maximize Classroom Learning Time

Although there are many ways that special services providers can help teachers identify their time-management difficulties (Collins, 1987), I will discuss only two. These two can be implemented after only one meeting with the teacher.

First, special services providers can help teachers by assisting

TABLE 3. Most Common Time Wasters

1. Being bothered and frustrated by the clutter on the desk.
2. Having to overcome an "obstacle course" each time a piece of paper is needed from the files.
3. Not being skilled in the art of "wastebasketry" (Douglass, 1980, p. 153).
4. Being excessively motivated tends to encourage a teacher to channel energy into excessively narrow thought patterns. On the other hand, limited motivation will not stimulate the persistence that will be vital to complete a task.
5. Attempting to do too much at the time or overcommitting.
6. Acting on biases.
7. Being unable to overcome betriebsblind ("company blindness"), one is so familiar with one's surroundings that the waste and unproductive movements are not noticed.
8. Participating in ineffective or too many meetings of limited value.
9. Being unable to say "no."
10. Having to contend with alot of "red tape."
11. Spending too much time on the telephone.
12. Entertaining too many drop-in visitors.
13. Doing too much paperwork.
14. Making agreements with others about time that results in negative payoffs or allowing others to set personal priorities for another person.
15. Being unable to self-discipline.
16. Being unable to take responsibility for time.
17. Being unaware or unable to distinguish what is truly important and most valuable in a situation.
18. Wishing to be well liked.
19. Enjoying the feelings of being busy.
20. Having bad habits in personal working style.
21. Exhibiting disorganized behavior.
22. Making tasks too complex when they could be done simply.
23. Being unable to make decisions as well as one would like.
24. Using procrastination.
25. Lacking the strength or skills to select key activities, projects, and people with who one wants to spend time.
26. Socializing and/or participating in idle conversation.
27. Lacking good planning skills
28. Communicating ineffectively or receiving poor/infrequent communications.
29. Being unable to listen actively or to receive as much as one would like from the time spent listening.
30. Having ineffective delegating skills that leave one taking on more tasks than one is capable of handling.
31. Leaving tasks unfinished or jumping from one task to another; constantly switching priorities.
32. Attending to too many details or being a perfectionist.
33. Waiting.
34. Traveling.
35. Commuting.
36. Inability to establish self-imposed deadlines.
37. Having confused chains of command or multiple sources of immediate authority/responsibility.

TABLE 3 (continued)

38. Inability to maximize changes and to capitalize upon the opportunity of the moment.
39. Making frequent mistakes or giving ineffective performances.
40. Having no standards or standards that do not maximize your capabilities and capacity.
41. Being unable to detect progress or to maintain achievement records.
42. Experiencing wondering attention.
43. Exhibiting poor handwritting.
44. Misplacing items.
45. Failing to listen.
46. Overdoing routine tasks.
47. Brooding over difficult assignment.

their introspection. By asking which of the following experiences they most often have, special services providers can direct the teachers' thinking toward the problem. Teachers can be asked if they often: (a) feel overwhelmed; (b) feel as if their activities lack a clear focus; (c) seem overcommitted; (d) feel powerless to change forces, outside the classroom, that impact time in the classroom; (e) feel dissatisfied with themselves or their profession; (f) sense a tension between themselves and one or more students in the room; (g) feel as if they are not receiving adequate rewards for their work; and/or (h) notice that they are not routinely providing enough work for students, and students are wasting time.

These feelings and actions might arise from different time-wasting decisions. Each time-wasting decision may require a different method to overcome misused time. Time-wasting decisions might be reduced by using one or more of the time-management methods listed in the next section of this paper. Special services providers can assist teachers to know which types of time-wasting activities they use. For example, teachers can be asked to think about the time of day, type of student, time of week and/or time of month in which loss of time is most evident. These questions can focus attention on when and with whom teachers should use the time management methods described in the next section.

The second method that can assist teachers to maximize classroom learning time is the use of Teachers' Time-Use Journal (Table 4). To be most effective, the teacher should keep the journal, faithfully, at the end of each day for one full work week. On Friday, the

TABLE 4

TEACHER'S TIME USE JOURNAL

Date _____ Day of Week _____
Name _____

Today:
1. I felt good doing/completing/beginning _____
   _____.
2. I was not pleased with _____.
3. I said "yes" when I could and should have said "no" when _____
   _____.
4. I said "no" when I could and should have said "yes" when _____
   _____.
5. I felt that I was wasting time or using it inappropriately when ____
   _____.
6. The high points of my day were: _____
   _____.
7. The low points of my day were: _____
   _____.
8. I was unable to do or did not complete these tasks: _____
   _____.
9. I spent too much time doing _____.
10. Agreements made with myself that impacted my time positively were: ___
    _____.
11. Agreements made with others that impacted my time positively were: ___
    _____.
12. Agreements made with others that impacted my time negatively were ___
    _____.
13. Insights I gained today about using my time were _____
    _____.
14. Things I could, should, and would have done today if I had managed my time more efficiently were: _____
    _____.
15. Ideas and thoughts I had today were: _____
    _____.
16. In the time I allowed for myself today, I _____
    _____.
17. The three most time-consuming tasks or goals that I cannot control the amount of time they take are: _____
    _____.
18. Analysis of the day's activities in light of talents used and enjoyment/outputs gained reveals that: _____
    _____.

Tomorrow spend 10 minutes completing another copy of this form. Keep separate notes without referring back to this worksheet.

Revised from Time Dialogue Journal in R.D. Rutherford's *Administrative Time Power* (Austin, Tex.: Learning Concepts, 1978) and Daily Time Record Log, in Merrill and Donna Douglass's *Manage Your Time, Manage Your Work, Manage Yourself* (New York: Amacon, 1980).

special services provider can meet with the teacher to discuss the insights that evolved.

Assisting Teachers and Students to Maximize Their Instructional Time

There are ten methods of managing classroom time more effectively.

Method 1: Becoming aware of tendencies that cause teachers to misuse time. Method 1 can be used when one exercises introspection and develops plans to use time more productively. (Tendencies that cause teachers to misuse time are cited in Table 5.) Teachers could ask their school principals to distribute Table 5 or ask if they could share them in a faculty meeting. After each tendency is introduced, teachers can select a method they will use to overcome it. They can then develop a plan to familiarize their students with the tendency. Through these means, teachers might minimize their own (and their students) misuse of time.

Method 2: Begin with familiar sections of difficult tasks. Secondly, teachers and students can learn that whenever they dread doing a task, they might complete it more rapidly if they begin: (a) at a point that is interesting or clearly understood, (b) with something they have done before, and/or (c) with a part that calls upon one or more of their talents. If they begin in this way, rather than trying to work in the order the tasks will appear in the finished assignment, teachers and students can complete several tasks that will create many small successes without having to risk failing.

Method 3: Leave some tasks in view. The third method was first presented by Alan Lakelin (1973) and Speed Leas (1978). Lakelin, a leading time management consultant, discovered that certain tasks have to be "seen often" before we will commit to complete them. Thus, Method 3 is to *leave some types of tasks in view*. As Leas points out, however, only five percent of all tasks pass the "qualifiying test" to use Method 3 of time management. That is, before a task can be most efficiently completed by being left in view, it must be: (a) a task the teacher is motivated to complete, (b) a task that is enjoyed, (c) a task that holds high value and/or is a priority in the learning objectives, (d) a task capable of being neatly and attrac-

TABLE 5. Tendencies That Influence the Way Teachers Allocate Time

1. Teachers will do what they like to do before they do what they do not like to do (e.g., "I find that I like jobs better when my friends work with me or when I push a little harder and do the difficult things in order.") Tell how the tendency can be overcome in a statement similar to the one just given. _____

2. Teachers do the things they know how to do faster than the things they do not know how to do, and they do things for which the resources are available. _____

3. Teachers do the things that are easiest before doing things that are difficult. They tackle small jobs before tackling large jobs, and things are done that provide the most immediate closure. One easy thing can be done as a "priming of the pump" to get a big task going.

4. Teachers do things that require little time before the things that require a large amount of time. The things that are urgent are done before things that are important. _____

5. Teachers perform scheduled activities before nonscheduled ones. ____

6. Teachers respond to demands of others before demands from themselves. Teachers work on the basis of the consequences of the group. _____

7. Teachers will readily respond to crises and emergencies, and wait until a deadline approaches before they get moving. _____

8. Teachers do interesting things before uninteresting ones. _____
   (It could only take a very small and simple thing, like using a new mechanical pencil to make an uninteresting task more appealing.)

9. Teachers respond to duties in the order of personal objectives and to the consequences of doing or not doing something. _____

10. Teachers work on things in order of their arrival. Things are done that present themselves as most important by the suggestion of others or by the nature of the task itself. _____

tively arranged in the space available, and (e) a task one feels slight pressure to complete.

Method 4: Learn to set aside time to work on deadlines. The fourth method is to *learn to establish appropriate deadlines*. Many teachers believe that their time-stresses are a result of having too many deadlines and that their administrators do not give enough time to complete the tasks. However, most teachers have not been educated how to: (a) assess the amount of time needed to complete tasks, and (b) increase their flexibility of thinking so as to create more time to reach deadlines.

To begin, teachers and students must learn to factor time for Murphy's Laws (the problems for which they have no control and for which they can not predict). Then, they must practice beginning some part of each task as soon as it is assigned. For example, students can begin work on their first homework problem while the teacher is writing something on the board.

Teachers and students might reduce the amount of time tasks take. Deadlines might give teachers and students two added reasons to work diligently. That is, with deadlines they not only work to complete the task but they work hard to prove their competence and avoid disappointing others. Deadlines also can increase the timeliness of the task. This occurs because teachers and students invest less time in avoiding work and in putting off more difficult decisions.

Method 5: Do it better. This method was developed as a "marriage" of two conflicting quotations about time: "If anything is worth doing, it's worth doing well" and "Do something now, even if it's wrong." The *do-it-better method* refers to doing one's best on everything and doing everything within the time allowed. This may mean that teachers will begin to use a new procedure with routine tasks. For example, one day, a teacher had only ten minutes to record math grades. Normally, this teacher spends about 30 minutes recording grades because students just turn in their papers as they leave. By using the *do-it-better method*, this teacher was able to record all grades in the 10 minutes available. This was accomplished because students turned in their papers in alphabetical order.

Method 6: Use "7 and 11" on monotonous tasks. The "7 and 11" method is based on the principle that proficiency increases if attention is given to repetitive tasks for relatively brief as compared to extended periods of time (Lakelin, 1973). Teachers and students should learn to allocate only a few minutes, during at least two periods of the day, to boring yet required tasks. To illustrate, teachers can learn to use the *"7 and 11 minute method"* to increase at-risk students' ability to learn multiplication facts. They should schedule practice sessions for a few minutes at the beginning of the class and a few minutes at the end of the class rather than to schedule one large block of time for the activity.

Method 7: Make an assembly-line as often as possible. As implied in the title, this time management principle is best used with tasks that: (a) have several sub-tasks requiring the same action, (b) can be easily divided into sequential sub-tasks, (c) require different skills or tools, and/or (d) have a wide variety of sub-tasks to complete before the end is reached. With this method, all sub-tasks that require the same decision, skill or tool will be done before moving to the next sub-task of each unit's work.

The success of this method is based on the principle that our capabilities and efficiency are increased by doing one activity repeatedly. Further, boredom and tedium are reduced. To illustrate, when the assembly-line method is used when papers are graded, teachers do not have to continually ask themselves: (a) "Did I grade # 3 on this paper?," (b) "What part of question # 7 did I want everyone to mention?," (c) "Was I too lenient with Susan's answers?," and (d) "What am I going to do now? I've graded almost all the papers and given several A's. Now I come to George's paper and it is superior to all the others." In conclusion, the assembly-line method can reduce indecision, eliminate wasted time, and increase quality.

Method 8: Build a set of training wheels. Whenever a teacher or student sets a goal a little beyond their level of unassisted ability, you can point out how their goal challenges them to grow and compliment them for setting it. Then you lend support so they can rise to the demands of the task by "building a set of training wheels for them."

One means of building this support is to suggest that teachers learn to work in the same room when they have something difficult to complete. The presence of their colleagues can motivate teachers to persevere. Special services providers can model Method 8 by asking a regular classroom teacher to work with them. For example, a special services provider and classroom teacher can work at the back of a classroom, during the next four planning periods "taking turns" buying the cold drinks or snacks for each other, until the difficult work is completed.

Method 9: Change the procedure to suit the task and the teacher's or student's working style. There are times when it's not the job that caused the teacher or student to waste time but, rather, the way they did it. The procedures teachers and students follow in the classroom are most often selected because of tradition. One indicator that a classroom procedure is wasting time for at-risk students is that the quality of their work decreases. A second indicator is that the students begin to justify why their work quality is decreasing. For example, students may report that their tasks aren't very important.

Special services providers can assist regular classroom teachers by asking them to examine how many materials and activities can be combined. Specifically, teachers' thinking can be expanded so that they can use other teachers or students to increase or decrease the intensity of the learning process and better match teaching styles with students' learning styles.

Method 10: Spending less time grading papers and doing paperwork. Lastly, special services providers can help teachers spend less time grading papers without reducing the quality of their feedback to students. Although a recent publication, *Grading Made Easy* (Collins, 1988c) describes 43 time-effective techniques of grading, the seven listed below might help teachers begin to spend less time with paperwork and grading.

1. Teachers can use more oral drill whereby each student writes his/her answer on an individual, hand-held blackboard so they can observe each student's response to each item.
2. Teachers can ask oral, extended-thinking questions that require two or more days of work before answering. Also, they can give written assignments that require two weeks of work.
3. Each afternoon before they leave, teachers can ask each student to give an oral example of the major concepts taught that day.

4. Teachers can use charts and checklists so students can record and graph their own progress scores for 3 weeks or more.
5. Teachers can grade one major paper per week. This paper could involve a synthesis and evaluation of lower-level thinking tasks done during the week.
6. Teachers can grade every fourth item on a practice exercise. In this way, teachers can memorize the answers and grade each paper rapidly without losing the diagnostic value of the practice work.
7. Teachers can carry a clipboard around the room as they monitor students' work. They can place checkmarks in columns and make notes at the bottom of the page. Essentially, teachers grade students as they work and teachers save considerable time in writing notes on papers. Teachers discuss the problems as they develop instead of trying to recapture these points by grading papers at home.

Teaching Time Management Principles to Students

There are many possible benefits of teaching time-management principles to students. One of the most significant is that teachers can increase their own time-use skills through preparing examples to use in teaching these principles to students.

To begin, teachers introduce to students the specific time management-skills found in Tables 6 and 7. After these have been learned, time-management methods described in this paper are simplified and taught to students.

One of the most difficult time problems students have is learning to use materials effectively. By posting specific instructions at the location where materials will be used, procedures will be less difficult and time consuming for students.

Table 6 contains a form that can help students establish goals that can be achieved. Table 7 contains a form teachers can use in structuring student input in lesson planning. Specifically, teachers are to list the most important topics they wish to address in a lesson or unit. The second section of Table 7 is used for students to suggest either additional important topics, or methods of learning the topics of greatest interest to them. Finally, the last section of Table 7 is

TABLE 6. Setting Goals with Students

1. What parts of this subject are the most interesting to you?

2. What skill would you like to be able to do in this class by the end of the semester? This year?

3. You think you could best learn this skill if we did _____ (e.g., an experiment, small-group work, reading about it, interviewing an authority on the topic, taking a field trip, working in class, practicing at home)?

4. What kinds of work do you like to do in groups?

   With a partner?

   Alone?

5. What reward would you like to receive when you reach the goal of this project?

6. What keeps you from doing as well as you would like to in this subject?

7. How can you learn best in this class?

used to record when topics will be completed so that students, parents, and teachers have a written document of the lessons planned.

Table 8 is a form to be used by students as they transfer their new planning skills to projects they direct themselves. Students set their own deadlines. Teachers check them. The student then selects the methods by which the project will be completed. Additional notes can be attached to this form so the student learns to write goals clearly.

Another means of assisting students is to solicit the aid of their parents. India Podsen (1984), has many suggestions about how this can be accomplished.

SUGGESTIONS FOR FUTURE PRACTICES AND APPLIED RESEARCH

There is much to be learned before we can use classroom time more effectively. Implementing the suggestions in this paper is a first step. Specifically, by analyzing the presumed effects these suggestions have upon at-risk students' success, we can refine classroom

TABLE 7. Student Involvement in Planning

Lesson_____

Topics that will be covered

1.
2.
3.
4.
5.
6.
7.
8.
9.
10.

Students Choices of Other Topics or Methods of Study

1.
2.
3.
4.
5.
6.
7.
8.
9.
10.

Dates That Topics Will Be Completed

1.
2.
3.
4.
5.
6.
7.
8.
9.
10.

procedures, monitor systems, schedule deliveries, and strengthen at-risk students' own time-management skills more effectively. Because initial research (Collins, 1988d) has demonstrated the significant impact time-management skill has upon student success, controlled studies with divergent student populations would be advantageous. With the time-use methods currently available, our

TABLE 8

STUDENT-PLANNED PROJECTS

Name _____

	Due Date	Check
Part 1	_____	_____
Part 2	_____	_____
Part 3	_____	_____
Part 4	_____	_____
Final Due Date	_____	_____
Reward	_____	_____

Task:			
Differentiated Task:			
Setting:			
	Lecture	Learning center	Role playing
	Film	Community mentor	Independent study
	Task card	Simulation	Worksheet
	Game	Peer group (committee)	Library
	Tutor	Small group teacher-directed lesson	Programmed textbook

task as educators is to adapt them most appropriately to the classroom setting. Regrettably, there is considerable research to be done before maximum instructional time is available to all at-risk students. It was the intent of this paper to assist special services providers to improve present practices and influence the direction of future research.

REFERENCES

Barr, R. (1980, April). *School, Class, Group, and Pace Effects on Learning.* Paper presented at the annual meeting of the American Educational Research Association, Boston, MA.

Collins, C. (1987). *Time management for teachers*. Englewood Cliffs, NJ: Prentice-Hall, Inc.

Collins, C. (1988a). *How to become a more distinguished teacher*. Fort Worth, TX: Educational Research Dissemination.

Collins, C. (1988b). *The acting out child*. Fort Worth, TX: Educational Research Dissemination.

Collins, C. (1988c). *Grading made easy*. Fort Worth, TX: Educational Research Dissemination.

Collins, C. (1988d). Principals: Taking the lead in thinking skills. In B. Garrington (Ed.) *Realistic educational achievement can happen: Vol. 3*. Austin, TX: Texas Educational Agency.

Davidson, J. L., & Holly, F. M. (1979). Are you providing half-time instruction?, *The American School Board Journal, 166* (3), 40-42.

Douglass, M., & Douglass, D. (1980). *Manage your time, manage your work, manage yourself*. New York: Amacon.

Everston, C. M., Emmer, E., Sanford, J., Clements, B., & Worsham, M. (1984). *Classroom management for secondary teachers*. Englewood Cliffs, NJ: Prentice-Hall, Inc.

Green, J. L. & Rasinski, T. (1985, April). *Teacher style and classroom management: Stability and variation across instructional events*. Paper presented at the annual convention of the American Educational Research Association, Chicago.

Leas, S. B. (1978). *Time management: A working guide for church leaders*. Nashville, TN: Abingdon.

Lakelin, A. (1973). *How to get control of your time and your life*. New York: American Library.

McGraw, K. (1987). *Developmental Psychology*. New York: Harcourt, Brace Jovanovich Publishers.

O'Neal, S. (1984). Staff development strategy for improving teacher practice (one plan does not fit all). *R&DCTE Review: The Newsletter of the Research and Development Center for Teacher Education, 2* (3), 3-5.

Podsen, I. (1984). My child has poor study habits: Academic excellence begins at home. *American Education, 20* (7), 28-32.

Sanford, J. P. (1983). Time use and activities in junior high classes. *Journal of Educational Research, 76*, 140-7.

Tschudin, R. (1978). Secrets of A+ teaching. *Instructor, 88*, 65-74.

Wiggers, T., Forney, D., & Wallace-Schutzman, F. (1983). Burnout is not necessary: Prevention and recovery. *NASPA Journal, 29*, (7), 23-7.

Wyne, M. D. & Stuck, B. G. (1982). Time and learning: Implications for the classroom teacher, *Elementary School Journal, 83*, (1), 67-75.

Providing Opportunities for Student Success Through Cooperative Learning and Peer Tutoring

David W. Peterson
Janice A. Miller

La Grange (IL) Area Department of Special Education

SUMMARY. Peer tutoring and cooperative learning are both peer-influenced academic intervention methods that involve carefully structuring interactions between students either in dyads or groups to promote academic achievement. This paper provides an overview of these interventions and highlights the need for special services providers to be knowledgeable about these potentially powerful interventions. Similarities and differences between the two categories of interventions are presented and research supporting their effectiveness with a wide range of students is reviewed. Specific guidelines for development and implementation are provided, and issues to be considered when evaluating student progress are discussed.

The American educational system, in many respects, seems to be caught "between the devil and the deep blue sea." On the one hand, there are those who lament the failures of the current system. For example, Madeline Will (1986), Assistant Secretary for Special Education and Rehabilitative Services, calls for closer collaboration between regular and special educators and describes some of the problems that have not been addressed through the provision of specialized services. These problems include the number of high school drop-outs, high rates of adult illiteracy, inadequate prepara-

---

Requests for reprints should be directed to: David W. Peterson, La Grange Area Department of Special Education, 1301 W. Cossitt, La Grange, IL 60525. Both authors contributed equally to the preparation of this paper.

© 1990 by The Haworth Press, Inc. All rights reserved.

tion for the demands of college, and the need for many remedial services at the elementary level. In addition to Will's list of problems, there is also the need to provide effective instruction to a growing population of culturally different students.

On the other hand, there are social and political pressures impinging on the schools that make resolution of many of these problems even more difficult. Emphasis on teaching basic skills, comparison of the American educational system to the educational systems of other countries, notably that of Japan's, and diminishing fiscal resources all contribute to the tension between the need to provide effective instruction for all students and the ability of the schools to do so.

The purpose of this paper is to provide a description of educational interventions that can be applied with currently available resources within elementary and secondary classrooms to meet the academic and social needs of a diverse student population. The term peer-influenced academic interventions is used to describe interventions which include cross- and same-age peer tutoring and cooperative learning.

Individualization of instruction, maximization of allocated learning time, increased opportunity to respond and high rates of success on academic tasks have all been correlated with increased achievement (Fisher, Felby, Marleave, Cohen, Dishaw, Moore, & Berliner 1978; Greenwood & Delquadri, 1982; Rosenshine & Berliner, 1978). However, without either additional resources or the implementation of alternative instructional technologies the likelihood that these effective teaching strategies will be found within classrooms is decreased (Kauffman, Gerber, & Semmel, 1988). Peer-influenced academic interventions are alternative instructional technologies that allow for increased opportunities for student responding and for appropriate instruction at the student's level.

In addition to addressing the instructional needs of a diverse group of students within the classroom, peer-influenced interventions can also facilitate cross-cultural and interracial friendships (Cooper, Johnson, Johnson, & Wilderson, 1977; Weigel, Wiser, & Cook, 1975). Increased acceptance of heterogeneity of handicapped peers has been found as well (Johnson & Johnson, 1980b).

Peer-influenced academic interventions are compatible with a prereferral or preventive support system. Special services providers, such as resource teachers, school psychologists, school social workers, and counselors, can consult with regular education teachers on the implementation of peer-influenced interventions. These interventions can contribute to prereferral intervention systems that have been shown to reduce the number of students who are referred for special education or remedial services (Graden, Casey, & Christensen, 1985).

This paper defines peer tutoring and cooperative learning methods, and highlights the similarities and differences between the two categories of peer-influenced interventions. Research supporting the effectiveness of peer-influenced interventions is provided. Finally, guidelines for developing, implementing, and evaluating peer-influenced interventions are discussed.

DEFINING PEER-INFLUENCED ACADEMIC INTERVENTIONS

The term peer-influenced academic intervention refers to a continuum of methods for structuring interactions between students to achieve primarily academic goals (see Table 1). Although a central goal of all peer-influenced interventions is to have students learn a specified academic task, there may be additional outcomes that are achieved in terms of social-emotional goals. These may relate to self-esteem, locus of control, liking of class or school, feelings about classmates, and perspective-taking (Slavin, 1980a, 1983).

In addition to structuring interactions between students, peer-influenced interventions also require a different role for the teacher. No longer the sole source of instruction, the teacher's new role is to arrange the classroom environment in a way that will systematically enhance the exchange of information between and among peers.

Peer Tutoring

Same- and cross-age peer tutoring is defined as instructional opportunities in which students work on academic tasks in dyads, where one student serves as the tutor and one student as the tutee. The interaction is regularly scheduled, often daily, and the content

Table 1
Summary Description of Peer-Influenced Academic Interventions

Peer Tutoring

Students work in pairs on academic tasks carefully prescribed by the teacher. One student is the tutor and the other is the tutee. May involve students of the same age or grade, or the tutor may be older.

Classwide Peer Tutoring (CWPT)   (Delquadri, Greenwood, Whorton, Carta, & Hall, 1986)

Within a classroom, students are assigned to dyads by the teacher and are also randomly assigned to one of two teams. Pairs take turns as tutor and tutee and follow a prescribed instructional procedure to practice basic skills content. Students earn points for their team number of responses as tutee, for appropriate dyad behavior, and for performance on weekly individual quizzes.

Classwide Student Tutoring Teams (CSTT)   (Maheady, Sacca, & Harper, 1988)

Combines procedures of Classwide Peer Tutoring, in terms of structured teaching procedures, daily point earning and public performance display, and aspects of cooperative learning, in terms of assignment to teams by rank.

Jigsaw   (Aronson, 1978)

Students are assigned to six-member teams and each team member is given one section of a five-part academic unit. Two students share a section as a precaution in case of absenteeism. Expert groups are composed of team members from different teams who share the same academic material. They meet to discuss their material before returning to teach it to their respective team members. After being taught each section by the team members, students take individual quizzes and are graded on their performance on the quiz.

Circles of Learning   (Johnson, Johnson, Holubec, & Roy, 1984)

Students work in 2-6 member heterogenous teams on a project or assignment. A single product from the group is expected and the group members may self-evaluate how well they worked together as a group at the end of the session. The teacher's role is to monitor the groups and praise the students when they demonstrate cooperative behavior. Individual tests and grades are given, but group grades/rewards may also be given.

TABLE 1 (continued)

Group-Investigation (GI)   (Sharan and Sharan, 1976)

In this method, students self-select their cooperative group of 2-6 members. The group chooses a topic from a unit being studied by the class and then decides who will study and prepare information on subtopics of the unit for a final report. Students are encouraged to use a variety of materials, engage in discussion with each other, and seek information from many sources. The groups present their projects to the class and evaluation of the group and/or individuals is completed.

Co-op Co-op (Kagan, 1985)

Similar to Group Investigation in intent, but the procedures for implementation are more prescribed. Students may choose groups based on interest. Team building skills are taught. Student contributions to the team's efforts as well as individual papers are the basis of evaluation.

Small-Group Learning and Teaching in Mathematics   (Davidson, 1985)

The focus is on the solution of mathematics problems through group discussion. Student input into team selection is considered. Evaluation is based on many sources -- individual and group performance.

Student Teams - Achievement Division (STAD)   (Slavin, 1978)

Four to five students are assigned to heterogenous learning teams. The teacher introduces the material to be learned and then provides study worksheets to team members. Students study the material with their team members until everyone understands the material. Next, students take individual quizzes, but the scores are used to compute a team score. The contribution each student can make to the team score is based on improvement as compared to past quiz averages. High-scoring teams and high-performing students are recognized in a weekly class newsletter.

Teams-Games-Tournaments (TGT)   (DeVries, Slavin, Fennessey, Edwards, & Lombardo, 1980)

This method of cooperative learning uses the same team structure and instructional format as in STAD. In addition, students play in weekly tournament games with students of comparable ability from other teams in the classroom. Assignments are changed every week with the high and low scorers of each table moved to the next highest or lowest table respectively in order to maintain fair competition. Students can contribute to their team score based on their performance in the weekly tournaments. Again, a class newsletter is used to recognize high scoring teams and individual tournament winners.

TABLE 1 (continued)

Team Assisted Individualization (TAI) (Slavin, Madden, and Leavy, 1982)

In TAI, the focus is on mathematics instruction. Heterogenous teams of 4-5 students are formed. Based on a diagnostic test, each student is given an individually prescribed set of materials. For each unit, students read an instruction sheet, complete skillsheets, take checkouts, and finally a test. Working in pairs, students check each others worksheets and checkouts. When a checkout has been passed with a score of 80% or better, the student takes the test and the results are scored by a student monitor. Teams receive certificates for exceeding preset standards on the tests and for completing units.

Jigsaw II (Slavin, 1980b)

In this modification of Jigsaw, students are formed into 4-5 member heterogenous teams. Every student studies all of the material, but is given a section in which to become an expert. As in the original Jigsaw, students meet in expert groups, teach their fellow team members, and take individual quizzes. However, individual scores are computed based on improvements and these become a group score. A class newsletter is used to recognize high scoring teams and individuals.

Cooperative Integrated Reading and Composition (CIRC) (Slavin, Stevens, Madden, 1988)

The focus is on teaching reading, writing, and language arts in heterogeneous intermediate classrooms using mixed-ability cooperative learning teams and same-ability reading groups. Student read aloud with their same ability partner and practice reading comprehension and process writing skills in their mixed-ability teams. Students earn points toward their team score.

and materials of the lesson are prescribed by the teacher or other professional staff member (e.g., school psychologist, resource teacher). Professional staff train the tutors, carefully supervise tutoring sessions, and frequently measure tutees' progress to ensure that they achieve academic goals.

Cooperative Learning

In cooperative learning groups, the focus is on the learning of all students within the group through either the sharing of information or through the attainment of a group goal. It is often easier to understand cooperative learning methods by differentiating them from individualistic and competitive learning methods (Johnson & Johnson, 1975). In an individualistic learning situation, the student works on an academic task alone and is evaluated and rewarded based on a preset criterion. For example, the teacher may give students five minutes free time if they complete 95% of their independent seatwork each day. In a competitive learning situation the student is evaluated and rewarded based on comparisons of the student's performance to other students in the class. If only the student with the most accurately completed work, for example, were given five minutes free time each day, the teacher would be creating a competitive learning situation.

In both individualistic and competitive learning situations students generally work alone and the motivation to assist one another is either absent (in individualistic situations) or is discouraged by competition for rewards (in competitive situations). Cooperative learning groups, by contrast, promote "positive interdependence" (Johnson & Johnson, 1978), that is, the establishment of a group goal or the necessity to share information to encourage collaboration among students.

Distinctions among different cooperative learning methods can be made in relation to the following variables:

1. Cognitive complexity of the task: Are the skills being taught less complex, rote skills or ones that will develop higher-level thinking skills?
2. Group goal or product: Is there a clearly established goal for the group, such as producing a single report or product?
3. Task specialization: Do students become "experts" on a topic and then share their expertise with group members?
4. Intergroup competition: Do groups compete against each other for rewards or recognition?
5. Equal opportunity scoring: Are all students of varying ability levels in the group equally able to contribute to the group's total score?
6. Reward/recognition: Is recognition given to a group based on an evaluation of the group's final product or is it based on the evaluation of individual group members' learning?
7. Subject areas: Is the method limited to a specific subject area or can it be used in all areas?

8. Peer tutoring: Is explicit peer tutoring an inherent part of the cooperative learning structure?
9. Group process: Does the method focus on the way that group members interact with each other?

COMPARISON OF PEER TUTORING AND COOPERATIVE LEARNING METHODS

Nature of the Learning Task

All peer-influenced academic interventions are designed to promote student achievement through peer interaction. However, in peer tutoring the emphasis is usually on the acquisition of basic skills or knowledge (e.g., math facts, spelling, improving oral reading). Cooperative learning methods are designed to teach either basic skills (e.g., Student-Teams-Achievement Division, Teams-Games-Tournaments, Team Assisted Individualization) or to enhance higher-level and creative thinking skills (e.g., Group-Investigation, Small-Group Mathematics).

Social Organization and Interaction

Although peer interaction is a cornerstone of both peer tutoring and cooperative learning methods, the organization and nature of the interactions between and among peers differ. In peer tutoring groups, pupils are organized into dyads. The tutor has a higher status and directs information and knowledge to the tutee and the tutee's role is to accept this direction. In cooperative learning, the size of the group varies from two to usually no more than five or six and group members are of equal status and have equal responsibility to exchange information.

The way in which interdependence among students is established also differentiates peer tutoring and cooperative learning methods. In peer tutoring, the structure of the learning situation and the clear specification of roles promote interdependence between the tutor and the tutee. In contrast, interdependence among group members in cooperative learning groups is based on the sharing of information, as in Jigsaw, or results from the establishment of a group goal or a group reward system, as in Circles of Learning and Team Assisted Individualization.

The extent of peer interaction may also differ between peer tutoring and cooperative learning methods. Whereas there is usually little interaction between peer tutoring dyads, there may be considerable interaction of either a competitive nature (Teams-Games-Tournaments) or of a collaborative nature (Group-Investigation) between cooperative groups within a classroom.

Outcomes

The success of both these methods is judged by gains in student achievement. In peer tutoring, the emphasis is on the evaluation of the performance of the tutee. Although there is evidence to suggest that tutors also may benefit academically from participating in the peer tutoring sessions (Cohen, Kulik, & Kulik, 1982), the primary target for increased achievement is the tutee. In cooperative learning groups, however, the evaluation of the learning may be based on either the performance of the group (e.g., completion of a group worksheet) or on the performance of individual students (e.g., quizzes, tournaments). Similar differences between peer tutoring and cooperative learning methods apply to the distribution of rewards. Tutors and tutees in peer tutoring groups may be rewarded for their individual efforts in the sessions—the tutees for their performance and tutors for their implementation of the lessons. In contrast, in cooperative learning groups rewards are given based on the accomplishments of the group or the aggregation of individual team members' efforts.

RESEARCH ON COOPERATIVE LEARNING

Research has examined the effects of cooperative learning methods on achievement and on social-emotional outcomes. In comparison to individualistic or competitive learning methods, cooperative learning methods are clearly as effective or more effective in enhancing student learning. These results apply to the learning of many types of students at varying age levels and in many different subject areas. This conclusion is supported by a meta-analysis of

122 studies (Johnson, Maruyama, Johnson, Nelson, & Skon, 1981) that compared the effects of cooperative, competitive, and individualistic instruction on student achievement and productivity. The only tasks that were not positively affected by cooperative learning were those requiring rote decoding and correcting skills. In addition, the achievement of Blacks and Hispanics was found to be more positively affected by the implementation of cooperative learning groups than that of Anglos. Results from this meta-anaylsis should be interpreted cautiously because it was not restricted to studies that involved achievement in the natural classroom environment (Slavin, 1980a, 1988). In addition, measures of achievement were based upon performance on a group task rather than individual learning. Slavin (1988) cites two essential conditions that must be present to maximize achievement. First, there must be a method for ensuring individual accountability to prevent the group from relying excessively on the efforts of one or two group members. Second, the group must have a goal that the members value as important. It is hypothesized that this group goal motivates students to both ask for help and give help to others in the group.

In order to support his assertions about these two conditions Slavin (1988) reviewed cooperative learning studies to determine whether group goals and individual accountability were incorporated and to determine their effects on achievement. Students in studies that incorporated both group goals and individual accountability achieved more than students in studies in which neither condition was incorporated in the cooperative learning method.

Although individual accountability and the establishment of a group goal may have impact upon achievement in cooperative groups, student interaction may also be an important variable to consider. Giving and getting help are two interactions that have been studied in relation to student achievement. If giving help and getting help occur in response to a request for assistance, then they are positively correlated with achievement. Students who are given answers without explanation or who do not receive help after asking for it do not achieve more in cooperative groups (Webb, 1982).

Research findings have consistently revealed that handicapped and racial minority members of heterogeneous groups of students, who work cooperatively with each other, have more frequent cross-racial and cross-handicap friendship choices and increased self-esteem and liking of school (Johnson & Johnson, 1980a; Madden & Slavin, 1983; Sharan, 1980). Group competition and the lack of success of the cooperative group may negatively influence cross-handicap and cross-racial friendships and the self-esteem of lower performing students (Ames, 1981; Johnson & Johnson, 1984). However, if lower performing or racially/culturally different students have equal opportunity to contribute to the success of the group such negative impacts may be avoided.

RESEARCH ON PEER TUTORING

Numerous studies have established the efficacy of a variety of peer tutoring interventions in promoting student achievement and have evaluated the relative effects of differing tutor and tutee characteristics (e.g., handicapping conditions, age, sex differences within dyads). A meta-analysis of 65 studies (Cohen, Kulik, and Kulik, 1982) revealed that peer tutoring programs have significant positive effects on tutor and tutee achievement and attitude toward subject matter. Achievement effects were more pronounced in math than in reading and this analysis did not reveal significant changes in self-concept among either tutors or tutees. Devin-Sheehan, Feldman, and Allen (1976) conducted a review of both structured and unstructured tutoring programs and found that tutees made significant academic gains and that tutors made more modest gains.

Despite attempts to evaluate the impact of a variety of tutor-tutee characteristics on intervention effectiveness, findings regarding skill disparities, sex differences, and age within tutoring dyads have not been consistent across studies (Devin-Sheehan et al., 1976). However, Linton (1973) reported that tutors who are older and more advanced academically may be more effective tutors.

Strong positive achievement effects have also been reported with populations of students with handicaps. A review of studies using students with disabilities as both tutors and tutees demonstrated significant achievement gains but again found inconclusive evidence for affective outcomes (Scruggs & Richter, 1985). More recently, Maheady, Sacca, and Harper (1988) reported similar achievement gains among students with mild handicaps.

The degree of structure (i.e., the extent to which tutors use controlled teaching strategies and elicit consistent response patterns across learning trials) incorporated within tutoring programs has been shown to be an important variable in designing tutoring programs. The meta-analysis conducted by Cohen et al. (1982) and another review (Rosenshine & Furst, 1969) have both confirmed greater academic gains within tutoring programs employing greater structure.

Finally, although few studies have compared peer tutoring with other instructional methodologies, Jenkins, Mayhall, Peschka, and Jenkins (1974) reported that some peer tutoring programs produced greater achievement gains than instruction by classroom teachers.

Although the academic benefits of peer and cross-age tutoring are clearly established, research on a variety of important program design elements is needed. Methodological problems hamper many studies (Devin-Sheehan et al., 1976) and data regarding the specific variables which contribute the most to successful programs needs to be gathered (Feldman, Devin-Sheehan, & Allen, 1976). Scruggs and Richter (1985) cite the need for more conclusive data on the effects of tutoring programs on affective functioning and more data are needed regarding specific aspects of tutor/tutee interactions (Kalfus, 1984). System and organizational components which foster effective programs also need to be identified (Maher, 1986). Furthermore, Miller and Peterson (1987) suggest the need to examine the effectiveness of peer tutoring interventions in relation to other interventions, to evaluate other mediating variables, and perhaps most important, to evaluate differing methods for encouraging the adoption of these interventions within the regular classroom.

DEVELOPING AND IMPLEMENTING COOPERATIVE LEARNING PROGRAMS

The development and implementation of cooperative learning groups in a classroom requires changes in both the role of the teacher and the role of the student. Consultation from support staff may be particularly useful to facilitate these changes.

The implementation of cooperative groups requires that teachers delegate some responsibility for instruction and that the teacher becomes a facilitator and monitor of effective group interaction. Some teachers may have difficulty making such a role shift (Moskowitz, Malvin, Schaeffer, & Schaps, 1983) and may change cooperative learning procedures in a manner that negates the positive effects. Those responsible for implementation must also encourage students to help each other. Helping behaviors can be built into cooperative structures through task specialization in which each member of the group is responsible for mastering one aspect of the task (e.g., Jigsaw, Co-Op) and for teaching the other members that aspect. Another strategy for encouraging cooperative behavior involves assigning specific roles to each group member (e.g., recorder, checker) and reinforcing students for demonstrating effective group functioning (Johnson & Johnson, 1978). Finally, another strategy that can be used to encourage helping behaviors and promote interdependence involves requiring the group to solve any interactional problems it may have without direct intervention from an adult. This can result in groups developing problem-solving skills and solutions that are not imposed by the adult. This strategy may be one of the most difficult for teachers to use because it requires facilitation skills that teachers may not possess or be comfortable using in the classroom.

Implementors of cooperative learning groups must not only promote effective interaction among group members but also must promote a group norm toward individual accountability. This norm can be achieved by making individual contributions visible to group members and can be incorporated into the determination of the group reward. However, it is important that every member of the group has an equal chance to contribute to the team's score, and it is for this reason that individual improvement scores are often used.

In deciding which cooperative method to implement, professional staff need to consider the goals of the instruction and the age of the students. Some cooperative methods have been more frequently used to teach basic skills and help students acquire discrete or prescribed information (e.g., Student-Teams Achievement Division, Team Assisted Individualization), whereas others that are more open-ended have generally been used in content areas such as social studies or science (e.g., Group Investigation, Co-Op). Some methods have been used to teach both prescribed skills and to develop higher-level thinking tasks (e.g., Circles of Learning, Cooperative Integrated Reading and Composition). Cooperative learning methods in which the task is less prescribed and more open-ended may be more appropriate for more mature learners.

The number of students that can comprise a cooperative learning group is variable and teachers may determine the size of the group based on the age and maturity level of the students. Younger or less experienced students probably should initially be in smaller groups, even dyads, because larger groups are more complicated social entities in which to function.

DEVELOPING AND IMPLEMENTING PEER TUTORING PROGRAMS

Successful development and implementation of peer tutoring programs involves careful planning in regard to tutor training, establishing compatible tutoring dyads, selecting the format and content of lessons, and program supervision and scheduling.

Tutor Training

Tutor training has been shown to be related to the overall effectiveness of peer tutoring programs (Harrison, 1976; Osguthorpe & Harrison, 1976) and numerous authors have described specific elements of effective tutor training programs (Deterline, 1970; Ehly, 1986; Ehly & Larsen, 1980; Jenkins & Jenkins, 1981, 1985; Lippit, 1976; Pierce, Stahlbrand, & Armstrong, 1984). Analysis of these various recommendations suggest that training programs should include the following components:

1. Using and allocating time effectively during sessions.
2. Securing and maintaining tutee attention during sessions.
3. Locating, organizing, and effectively using materials.
4. Establishing clear expectations for learning during sessions.
5. Providing clear directions on how tutees are expected to respond.

6. Using teaching techniques which avoid the punishment of tutees.
7. Praising correct verbal responses and using tangible reinforcers on an intermittent schedule.
8. Using empirically validated error correction procedures (i.e., model, lead, test).
9. Using cues and prompting to shape successive approximations of correct responses.
10. Measuring tutee progress at the conclusion of a lesson or unit.
11. Maintaining accurate records of tutee progress.

Miller and Peterson (1987) stress the importance of structured training programs that teach effective instructional methods and discourage tutor behaviors that may impede positive interactions during tutoring sessions. Modeling, role playing and feedback during tutor training sessions will also help ensure that tutors acquire effective teaching competencies.

Establishing Dyads and Selecting Tutors and Tutees

Ehly (1986) suggests that the student's interest in tutoring and social skills are of primary importance in selecting tutors. Professional staff may wish to select tutors who demonstrate prerequisite social skills and on-task behavior. However, the success of programs using tutors lacking such skills would suggest that tutors of varying pretraining skill can be used as long as training is highly structured and feedback can be provided on a formative basis during the implementation of the tutoring program (Miller & Peterson, 1987). Research regarding the academic skills of tutors is also equivocal. Though it has been suggested that tutors be older than tutees (Ely, 1986; Jenkins & Jenkins, 1981) and possess at least average academic skills, the success of learning disabled tutors (Scruggs & Osguthorpe, 1986) suggests that training procedures and cross-age dyads (pairing older tutors with skill deficiencies with younger tutees) can overcome specific skill deficits among tutors.

Whereas Scruggs and Osguthorpe (1986) suggest that students with poor attentional skills may be less successful, the wide range of programs demonstrating success with a variety of tutees suggest that the instructional needs of the students should be the primary determinant in selecting tutees. More specifically, tutees should be selected based upon a close match between target students' instructional needs and the specific objectives of the planned program.

Establishing Lesson Content and Format

The content of tutoring lessons should be consistent with the program's objectives and closely related to the curriculum used within the students' regular classroom. Jenkins and Jenkins (1985) suggest that selection of content directly from classroom materials will promote generalization of skills and increase the effectiveness of tutoring. Tutoring should provide repetition and practice that will reinforce ongoing instruction and provide additional opportunities for student responses (Hawryluk & Smallwood, 1988).

Lessons should be clearly structured and prepared well in advance of tutoring sessions. Whenever possible, the format of lessons should be structured so that both tutoring techniques and formats for tutee responding are consistent across sessions. Provisions for consultation and feedback to tutors following sessions should be made to assure that tutors have an opportunity to discuss specific concerns or problems.

Logistical and Management Issues

Tutoring sessions should be scheduled to accommodate existing classroom schedules and efforts should be made to minimize disruption to other instructional programs. Mayhall and Jenkins (1977) found that daily tutoring sessions of moderate duration (approximately 30 minutes) were more effective than less frequent sessions. Even younger primary students can benefit from brief daily sessions.

Management responsibilities should be clearly specified, clearly assigned to available personnel and involve both daily tutor supervision and program maintenance tasks (Miller & Peterson, 1987). Structured, daily supervision has been shown to be important to program success (Mayhall et al., 1975) and supervisors can provide specific praise, model teaching behaviors, assist in data collection and recording, and circulate among tutoring dyads to provide general assistance.

GENERAL ISSUES IN PLANNING AND EVALUATING PEER-INFLUENCED ACADEMIC INTERVENTIONS

Program Planning

The extent to which peer-influenced academic interventions are successful may well be dependent upon conducting thorough assessments of students' instructional needs and carefully evaluating teacher and administrator readiness for such programs (Hawryluk & Smallwood, 1988). Those planning and evaluating peer-influenced interventions must then design interventions that address specific student needs and provide sufficient preparation for the school staff and administrators who will be involved in implementing the programs.

Interviews with teachers, analysis of students' daily work, and reviews of standardized tests can be used to assess student needs and determine: (a) the number, age, and grade levels of students requiring specific instruction; (b) specific academic deficits within target classes; (c) affective and social needs; (d) and previous intervention efforts and their results. Once student needs are pinpointed, specific program goals and objectives can be established, enabling consultants and teachers to select peer-influenced interventions which address specific student needs.

The readiness of the educational organization in which the interventions are to be developed should also be assessed (Hawryluk & Smallwood, 1988; Miller & Peterson, 1987). Maher and Bennett (1984) describe a model for assessing the readiness of a variety of organizational variables and their impact on program planning. Such assessments should include administrators, teachers, and parents and should focus on determining potential obstacles to implementation and to the identification of system resources that can be enlisted for support. The results of these assessments will determine the type and amount of information that should be provided to these various groups through inservice training and ongoing consultation.

Selecting a Peer-Influenced Intervention

The selection of either a peer tutoring or cooperative learning intervention should be influenced by the specific goals and objectives established during program needs assessments. Factors which should be included in decision making include: (a) the type and content of the academic tasks to be taught, (b) specific skill levels and needs of the students to be included in the intervention, (c) affective and social needs, and (d) and the number of students to be involved.

For example, complex tasks involving higher order cognitive skills may be more readily adapted to cooperative learning programs, whereas tasks involving drill and practice (e.g., math facts) may be better suited to peer tutoring paradigms. Larger groups of students may be better suited to cooperative learning or class-wide peer tutoring programs, whereas small groups may be better suited to more traditional peer tutoring strategies. Little research is available on the comparative benefits of either type of intervention and it behooves the program consultant to carefully assess organizational and student needs in order to select an intervention that will be effectively implemented given the resources available in a particular setting.

Evaluating the Impact of the Intervention

Careful evaluation of peer-influenced academic interventions is needed to determine if program goals and objectives have been attained and to assist program staff and consultants in the modification of programs. The focus of evaluation activities should be determined by the goals and scope of the program as well as the evaluation/accountability needs of the system in which the intervention has been implemented.

Given the primarily academic nature of these peer-influenced interventions, evaluation should minimally include an assessment of academic gains by participating students. We strongly recommend the use of curriculum based academic measures (Deno, 1985; Gickling & Havertape, 1981) or daily performance measures (Jenkins & Jenkins, 1981) that directly assess the particular academic skills being taught. Although more traditional norm-referenced tests have been used to assess student progress, such measures are relatively insensitive to academic growth (Carver, 1974; Jenkins & Pany, 1978) and are ill-suited to formative evaluation needs. Classroom test scores can also be used to assess intervention efficacy and generalization (Maheady, Sacca, & Harper, 1988).

Depending upon specific program goals, evaluations may include affective variables including attitudes toward subject matter or self-concept. Questionnaires, interviews of participating students, or published instruments can be used to assess affective outcomes. Miller and Peterson (1987) also suggest collection of direct observational data to assess on-task behavior during intervention periods. Maher (1986) describes a comprehensive approach to evaluating one peer-influenced academic program.

CONCLUSION

Peer-influenced academic interventions offer bright promise in assisting special service providers and regular educators in meeting the challenge to improve the quality and effectiveness of instruction available to all students. This paper has outlined research documenting the effectiveness of both cooperative learning and peer tutoring, and has provided guidelines for the development, implementation, and evaluation of these interventions. Given the apparent effectiveness and low cost of these interventions, it is puzzling to find that they have not been widely implemented. If greater numbers of students are to benefit from cooperative learning and peer tutoring interventions, special services providers must develop training programs and support systems that will increase implementation in our schools and demonstrate the effectiveness of these interventions to policy makers.

REFERENCES

Ames, C. (1981). Competitive versus cooperative reward structures: The influence of individual and group performance factors on achievement attributions and affect. *American Educational Research Journal, 18*, 273-287.

Aronson, E. (1978). *The jigsaw classroom*. Beverly Hills, CA: Sage.

Carver, R. (1974). Two dimensions of tests: Psychometric and edumetric. *American Psychologist, 29*, 512-518.

Cohen, P. A., Kulik, J. A., & Kulik, C. C. (1982). Educational outcomes of tutoring: A meta-analysis of findings. *American Educational Research Journal, 19,* 237-248.

Cooper, L., Johnson, D. W., Johnson, R., & Wilderson, F. (1977). Effects of cooperative, competitive, and individualistic experiences on interpersonal attraction among heterogeneous peers. *Journal of Social Psychology, 111,* 243-252.

Davidson, N. (1985). Small-group learning and teaching in mathematics: A selected review of the research. In Slavin, R., Sharon, S., Kagan, S., Hertz-Lazarowitz, R., Webb, C., & Schmuck, R. (Eds.), *Learning to cooperate, cooperating to learn* (pp. 211-230). New York: Plenum Press.

Delquadri, J., Greenwood, C., Whorton, D., Carta, J., & Hall, R. (1986). Classwide Peer Tutoring. *Exceptional Children, 52,* 535-542.

Deno, S. L. (1985). Curriculum-based measurement: The emerging alternative. *Exceptional Children, 52,* 219-232.

Deterline, W. A. (1970). *Training and management of student tutors: Final report.* (ERIC Document Reproduction No. ED 048-133).

Devin-Sheehan, L., Feldman, R., & Allen, V. (1976). Research on children tutoring children: A critical review. *Review of Educational Research, 46,* 355-385.

DeVries, D., Slavin, R., Fennessey, G., Edwards, K., & Lombardo, M. (1980). *Teams-games-tournaments: The team learning approach.* Englewood Cliffs, NJ: Educational Technology Publications.

Ehly, S. (1986). *Peer tutoring: A guide for school psychologists.* Kent, OH: National Association of School Psychologists.

Ehly, S. W., & Larsen, S. C. (1980). *Peer tutoring for individualized instruction.* Boston: Allyn and Bacon, Inc.

Feldman, R. S., Devin-Sheehan, L., & Allen, V. L. (1976). Children tutoring children: A critical review of research. In V. A. Allen (Ed.), *Children as teachers: Theory and research on tutoring* (pp. 235-252). New York, Academic Press.

Fisher, C., Felby, N., Marleave, R., Cohen, L., Dishaw, M., Moore, J., & Berliner, D. (1978). *Teaching and learning in the elementary school: A summary of the beginning teacher evaluation study.* San Francisco: Far West Laboratory.

Gickling, E. E., & Havertape, J. F. (1981). Curriculum-based assessment. In J. A. Tucker (Ed.), *Non-test based assessment* (pp. S1-S23). Minneapolis, MN: The National School Psychology Inservice Training Network, University of Minnesota.

Graden, J. L., Casey, A., & Christensen, S. L. (1985). Implementing a prereferral intervention system: Part I. The model. *Exceptional Children, 51,* 377-384.

Greenwood, C., & Delquadri, J. (1982, September). *The opportunity to respond and student academic performance in school.* Paper presented at the Conference on Behavior Analysis in Education, Ohio State University, Columbus, OH.

Harrison, G. V. (1976). Structured tutoring: Antidote for low achievement. In V. A. Allen (Ed.), *Children as teachers: Theory and research on tutoring* (pp. 169-177). New York: Academic Press.

Hawryluk, M., & Smallwood, D. (1988). Using peers as instructional agents: Peer tutoring and cooperative learning. In Graden, J., Zins, J., & Curtis, M. (Eds.), *Alternative educational delivery systems* (pp. 371-390). Washington DC: National Association of School Psychologists.

Jenkins, J. R., & Jenkins, L. M. (1981). *Cross age and peer tutoring: Help for children with learning problems*. Reston, VA: Council for Exceptional Children.

Jenkins, J., & Jenkins, L. (1985). Peer tutoring in elementary and secondary programs. *Focus on Exceptional Children, 17*, 1-12.

Jenkins, J. R., Mayhall, W. F., Peschka, C., & Jenkins, L. M. (1974). Comparing small group and tutorial instruction in resource rooms. *Exceptional Children, 40*, 245-250.

Jenkins, J., & Pany D. (1978). Standardized achievement tests: How useful for education? *Exceptional Children, 34*, 448-453.

Johnson, D., & Johnson, R. (1975). *Learning together and alone*. Englewood Cliffs, NJ: Prentice-Hall.

Johnson, D., & Johnson, R. (1978). Cooperative, competitive and individualistic learning. *Journal of Research and Development in Education, 12* (1), 3-15.

Johnson, D., & Johnson, R. (1980a). Effects of intergroup cooperation and intergroup competition on ingroup and outgroup cross-handicap relationships. *Journal of Social Psychology, 124*, 85-94.

Johnson, D., & Johnson, R. (1980b). Integrating handicapped students into the mainstream. *Exceptional Children, 47*, 90-98.

Johnson, D., & Johnson, R. (1984). Effects of intergroup cooperation and intergroup competition on ingroup and outgroup cross-handicap relationships. *Journal of Social Psychology, 124*, 85-94.

Johnson, D., Johnson, R., Holubec, E., & Roy, P. (1984). *Circles of learning*. Alexandria, VA: Association for Supervision and Curriculum Development.

Johnson, D., Maruyama, G., Johnson, R., Nelson, D., & Skon, L. (1981). The effects of cooperative, competitive and individualistic goal structures on achievement: A meta-analysis. *Psychological Bulletin, 89*, 47-62.

Kagan, S. (1985). Co-op Co-op. A flexible cooperative learning technique. In Slavin, R., Sharan, S., Kagan, S., Hertz-Lazarowitz, R., Webb, C., & Schmuck, R. (Eds.), *Learning to cooperate, cooperating to learn* (pp. 437-462). New York: Plenum Press.

Kalfus, G. (1984). Peer mediated interventions: A critical review. *Child and Family Behavior Therapy, 6*, 17-43.

Kauffman, J., Gerber, M., & Semmel, M. (1988). Arguable assumptions underlying the regular education initiative. *Journal of Learning Disabilities, 21* (1), 6-11.

Linton, T. (1973). The effects of grade displacement between student tutors and students tutored. *Dissertation Abstracts International, 33,* 4091-A. (University Microfilms No. 72-32, 034.)

Lippitt, P. (1976). Learning through cross-age helping: Why and how. In V. A. Allen (Ed.), *Children as teachers: Theory and research on tutoring* (pp. 157-168). New York: Academic Press.

Madden, N., & Slavin, R. (1983). Effects of cooperative learning on the social acceptance of mainstreamed academically handicapped students. *Journal of Special Education, 17,* 171-182.

Maheady, L., Sacca, M., & Harper, G. (1988). Classwide peer tutoring with mildly handicapped high school students. *Exceptional Children, 55,* 52-59.

Maher, C. A. (1986). Direct replication of a cross age tutoring program involving handicapped adolescents and children. *School Psychology Review, 15,* 100-118.

Maher, C. A., & Bennett, R. R. (1984). *Planning and evaluating special education services.* Englewood Cliffs, NJ: Prentice-Hall.

Mayhall, W. R., & Jenkins, J. R. (1977). Scheduling daily or less-than-daily instruction: Implications for resource programs. *Journal of Learning Disabilities, 10,* 3, 159-163.

Mayhall, W. R., Jenkins, J. R., Chestnut, N., Rose, F., Schroeder, K., & Jordan, B. (1975). Supervision and site of instruction as factors in tutorial programs. *Exceptional Children, 42,* 151-154.

Miller, J., & Peterson, D. (1987). Peer influenced academic interventions. In Maher, C., & Zins, J. (Eds.), *Psychoeducational interventions in the schools: Methods and procedures for enhancing student competence* (pp. 81-100). New York: Pergamon.

Moskowitz, J., Malvin, J., Schaeffer, G., & Schaps, E. (1983). Evaluation of a cooperative learning strategy. *American Educational Research Journal, 20,* 687-696.

Osguthorpe, R. T., & Harrison, G. V. (1976). Training parents in a personalized system of reading instruction. *Improving Human Performance Quarterly, 5,* 62-68.

Pierce, M. M., Stahlbrand, K., & Armstrong, S. B. (1984). *Increasing student productivity through peer tutoring programs.* Austin, TX: Pro-Ed.

Rosenshine, B. V., & Berliner D. C. (1978). Academic engaged time. *British Journal of Teacher Education, 4,* 3-16.

Rosenshine, B., & Furst, N. (1969). *The effects of tutoring upon pupil achievement: A research review.* Washington, DC: Office of Education. (ERIC Document Reproduction Service No. ED 064-462).

Scruggs, T. E., & Osguthorpe, R. T. (1986). Tutoring interventions within special education settings: A comparison of cross-age and peer tutoring. *Psychology in the Schools, 23,* 187-193.

Scruggs, T. E., & Richter, L. (1985). Tutoring learning disabled students: A critical review. *Learning Disability Quarterly, 8,* 286-298.

Sharan, S. (1980). Cooperative learning in small groups: Recent methods and effects on achievement, attitudes, and ethnic relations. *Review of Educational Research, 50,* (2), 241-271.

Sharan, S., & Sharan, Y. (1976). *Small-group teaching.* Englewood Cliffs, NJ: Educational Technology Publications.

Slavin, R. (1978). Student teams and achievement divisions. *Journal of Research and Development in Education, 12,* 39-49.

Slavin, R. (1980a). Cooperative learning. *Review of Educational Research, 50,* 315-342.

Slavin, R. (1980b). *Using student team learning: Revised edition.* Baltimore, MD: Center for Social Organization of Schools, The Johns Hopkins University.

Slavin, R. (1983). *Cooperative learning.* London: Longman.

Slavin, R. (1988). Cooperative learning and student achievement. *Educational Leadership, 46,* (2), 31-33.

Slavin, R. E., Madden, N. A., & Leavey, M. (1982). Effects of student teams and individualized instruction on student mathematics achievement, attitudes, and behaviors. Paper presented at the annual convention of the American Educational Research Association, New York.

Slavin, R., Stevens, R., & Madden, N. (1988). Accommodating student diversity in reading and writing instruction: A cooperative learning approach. *Remedial & Special Education, 9,* (1), 60-66.

Webb, N. (1982). Student interaction and learning in small groups. *Review of Educational Research, 52,* 421-445.

Weigel, R., Wiser, P., & Cook, S. (1975). The impact of cooperative learning experiences on cross ethnic relations and attitudes. *Journal of Social Issues, 31,* (1), 219-245.

Will, M. (1986). *Educating students with learning problems: A shared responsibility.* Washington, DC: U.S. Department of Education, Office of Special Education and Rehabilitation Services.

PART III:
SCHOOL-WIDE APPROACHES IN PROMOTING STUDENT SUCCESS

Keeping Students in School: Academic and Affective Strategies

Gary Natriello
Aaron M. Pallas

Teachers College, Columbia University

Edward L. McDill
James M. McPartland

Johns Hopkins University

SUMMARY. This paper examines strategies for the development of programs to prevent students from dropping out of school before graduation. The first set of strategies involves increasing the opportunities for students to succeed in school. This may be accomplished by setting standards that are challenging but within reach of students, by providing students with appropriate support to meet those standards, and by making the school curriculum relevant to the current and future lives of students. The second set of strategies in-

---

Requests for reprints should be directed to: Gary Natriello, Teachers College, Columbia University, New York, NY 10027.

© 1990 by The Haworth Press, Inc. All rights reserved.

volves increasing the opportunities for students to develop positive relationships in school. Such relationships may be with adult staff members, with other students, or with the school as an institution.

The renewed vigor with which both the public and the education community are examining the high school dropout problem has led to a proliferation of dropout prevention programs. Many schools and school districts have initiated such programs in recent years, and larger systems and schools often have several programs operating simultaneously. The sheer volume of these programs is overwhelming.

But behind the clever acronyms and catchy names lies a nagging uncertainty: what do we know about programs and strategies that work in dropout prevention? School personnel have to make choices about how to deploy the scarce human and fiscal resources available to combat the dropout problem. Yet most of what has been written about dropout prevention provides only minimal guidance to school-based personnel about concrete strategies or the reasoning and evidence behind them. Several compendia of program descriptions have been released recently (Clifford, 1986; Council of Great City Schools, 1987; Hahn & Danzberger, 1987; OERI Urban Superintendents Network, 1987; Orr, 1987) but most of these "laundry lists" of programs are not organized in ways that help practitioners understand the distinct categories or contrasting perspectives that may underlie different approaches to dropout prevention.

Similarly, most scientific research on the school dropout has focused on the personal characteristics which lead students to drop out, rather than on the programs that may reduce the risk of dropping out. For example, many studies have examined aspects of students' family backgrounds or personal experiences that are correlated with the probability of leaving high school before graduation, but few studies have evaluated the impact of interventions intended to reduce the school dropout problem.

Our recent review of dropout prevention program descriptions and evaluations highlighted four groups of programmatic strategies: increasing academic success in school, promoting positive interpersonal relationships in school, making schooling seem more relevant to the economic futures of students, and ameliorating outside factors which interfere with school success (Natriello, Pallas, McDill, McPartland, & Royster, 1988). In this paper, we examine the first two of these strategies designed to reduce the number of students leaving school prior to graduation.

We focus on these two major types for two reasons. First, they are most directly linked to what both the conventional wisdom and research evidence say about the causes of dropping out. The most likely candidates for dropping out of high school are (a) students who have serious difficulties in passing their school's courses and tests (McDill, Natriello, & Pallas, 1985), and (b) students who do not believe that adults in their school personally care about their welfare (Fine, 1987). These program strategies are designed explicitly to affect students at risk of dropping out of school for these reasons.

Second, these strategies involve school practices and policies which school service providers can formulate and implement. Academic success in school is related to students' opportunities for success in school. Whether students experience positive interpersonal relationships in school is related to the nature of adult-student relations established by adults in the school. Both the structuring of opportunities for school success and the establishment of positive interpersonal relations between adults and students are areas in which teachers, special services providers, and administrators can make a difference.

ACADEMIC SUCCESS IN SCHOOL

One of the strongest correlates of dropping out found in research on students is the lack of academic success in school (McDill, Natriello, & Pallas, 1985, 1986; Wagenaar, 1987). Students who more often obtain low grades, fail subjects, and are retained in grade have a much higher chance of leaving school before high school graduation. Simply put, many students who have trouble meeting the academic demands of school will leave rather than persist in the face of the frustration they often experience trying to pass their courses. However, student difficulties with school work can derive from different aspects of the academic criteria set by the school, the student's own current abilities in each subject area, and his or her willingness to direct efforts toward learning and performance on academic tasks. Moreover, studies of the sequence of events relating to dropping out indicate that the mismatch between school demands and student behaviors can grow over time; thus opportunities for success become more remote and motivation to remain in school becomes weaker (Grant Foundation Commission, 1988; Natriello, 1982). It is useful to examine the different aspects of the match between school demands and student behavior in considering the points for possible intervention in dropout prevention programs.

One of the most often noted reasons for the high dropout rate in American schools is the lack of an appropriate match between the academic program of the school and the skills and interests of students. Indeed, the failure of the academic program of the school to meet the needs of students is often cited as a major cause of the dropout problem (Fine, 1987; Wehlage and Rutter, 1987). Accounts of the problems with the academic program specify three dimensions connected with dropping out. First, for many students the academic program is too difficult and overwhelming. Second, for other students the academic program is not sufficiently challenging and engaging. Third, for substantial numbers of students the academic program is simply not an important part of their lives; that is, it is not salient in their thinking about their priorities. Each of these failures to engage students with the school program can be instrumental in causing them to leave school.

For many students who eventually drop out of school, the problem with the academic program is that the curriculum presented is too difficult for them to achieve respectable grades. In the nationally representative sample of students in the High School and Beyond Study, 30% of the ones who dropped out of high school between the tenth and twelfth grades reported that poor grades were a reason for leaving (Ekstrom, Goertz, Pollack, & Rock, 1987). These students could not achieve success with the school program presented to them.

There are two aspects to the problem of lack of success in school. Students whose every effort fails to elicit a positive response from the school come to view its organization as non-responsive to them and beyond their control. It is interesting to note that students who drop out do not seem to fare any worse in the development of self-esteem or internal locus of control than students who remain in school (Wehlage & Rutter, 1987).

While many students leave school because they find the academic program too difficult or overwhelming, others leave because they find it insufficiently challenging. Sometimes students encounter teachers whose expectations for them are too low. For example, Natriello and Dornbusch (1984), in a study of the standards for student academic performance in classrooms, report that students were less likely to attend in those classrooms where teachers' standards for student performance were lower than in classrooms where the standards were high. They conclude that students were less likely to attend classes with low standards because they knew that they would miss relatively less academic content.

Schools may fail to engage students for a third reason. For many, the curriculum of the schools seems irrelevant. Some students see the school curriculum as not useful for their current and future endeavors. Others, particularly those who are not members of the white middle class, see the school curriculum as alien to the culture in which they are growing up (Fine, 1987; Grant Foundation Commission, 1988). For example, for some black students, to participate actively in the school curriculum means renouncing their black community and "acting white" (Fordham & Ogbu, 1986).

STRENGTHENING THE CONNECTION OF STUDENTS TO THE ACADEMIC PROGRAM OF THE SCHOOL

In light of these reasons that students become disengaged from the school program, we posit three basic strategies which can be used to counteract the lack of match between the school program and the needs of students. First, it is possible to modify the academic standards of the school curriculum to accommodate students more effectively. Second, students' skills and abilities might be strengthened to permit them to meet the expectations inherent in the school curriculum. Finally, the school academic program can be made more salient to the lives of students. Each of these basic strategies might strengthen the connection of students to the school program, and each of these has taken different forms in attempts to ameliorate the dropout problem in U.S. schools.

Programmatic Strategies for Adjusting Academic Standards to Fit Students

If students become disengaged from school because they find the standards too difficult or too easy, then one strategy to minimize disengagement is to develop standards that meet the needs of students, that is, standards that are challenging but attainable. A number of methods have been suggested and implemented for meeting the needs of students.

Perhaps the most widely discussed and used strategy is that of individualizing the curriculum so that it is tailored to each student's ability. An individual curriculum and instructional strategy are designed to present each student with attainable standards for academic performance (Hahn & Danzberger, 1987; McDill et al., 1980). In so doing, students might experience both academic success with its attendant benefits to their self-esteem and a more responsive school organization in reaction to their efforts. Special services providers could work with classroom teachers to develop such individual instructional approaches.

Of course, the matching of the level of difficulty of the school curriculum, whether individualized or not, to the ability levels of students requires improved diagnostic strategies. In the absence of adequate diagnostic information it is impossible to tailor the curriculum to the students' abilities. At the very least, such diagnostic techniques should be used to determine when students are ready to move on to a new grade level. Such a program is in operation in Minneapolis where criterion-referenced tests are administered each year to students in kindergarten through the ninth grade ". . . to track students' academic progress and to judge whether they have mastered the knowledge required to proceed to the next grade" (OERI Urban Superintendents Network, 1987). Specialists with expertise in student assessment could work with classroom teachers to design assessment strategies and interpret the results.

One key strategy for addressing the lack of school responsiveness to academic performance for students with records of consistently poor performance is an alteration in the process for evaluating student work. Natriello and McPartland (1987) have shown that teachers make use of four evaluation or grading techniques in their classrooms: evaluation on the basis of pre-determined external standards, evaluation based on the relative performance of the class, evaluation based on student effort, and evaluation based on the growth or change in student performance level. Only the last two strategies provide low performing students with an opportunity to obtain positive evaluations (Natriello & McPartland, 1987). Thus, the evaluation of students' performance in terms of their effort and/or progress may be effective in keeping students in school.

Another approach to providing opportunities for success for students, who would otherwise experience consistent failure in the classroom, involves a restructuring of the tasks of the classroom so that they draw on a wider range of ability dimensions. Such multiple-ability classrooms (Cohen, 1986; Rosenholtz, 1977) attempt to move beyond the narrow range of academic tasks, all of which rely upon reading skills, so that every student can experience some success. In the multiple-ability classroom, the intention is for all students to find some task at which they can experience a sense of competence. Classroom teachers will require special assistance in developing such multiple-ability approaches to classroom instruction and task organization.

To combat the low standards which lead to students not being sufficiently challenged in school, there are strategies which seek to raise standards in a demonstrable way. Whether it is the "high standards" of the effective schools movement (Edmonds, 1979), the high aspirations of Operation PUSH (Murray, Murray, Gragg, & Kumi, 1982), the accelerated schooling model of Levin (1987), or the "Success for All" project (Madden & Slavin, in press), the attempt is to be explicit about having high standards that are worth achieving.

Programmatic Strategies for Enhancing Student Abilities and Skills to Meet the Demands of the School Curriculum

Adjusting the standards of the school program may go only so far in closing the gap between the demands of the curriculum and the abilities and skills of students. A second basic strategy to improve the match between students and schools involves techniques for strengthening the skills and abilities of students in order that they are more able to meet whatever demands the school program may entail. Various programmatic approaches to enhancing student abilities and skills have been developed.

Remedial instruction in one form or another has often been used in an attempt to raise student skills to the level demanded by the school curriculum. Such remedial services take a variety of forms from special classes such as those offered under the provisions of Chapter 1 (Kennedy, Birman, & Demaline, 1986) to programs which involve a total alteration of the entire school curriculum with the provision of additional resources throughout the program. Such an approach is envisioned as part of Levin's (1987) proposed accelerated school where the goal is to accelerate students' academic growth.

Remediation also occurs in special programs in addition to the regular school program. For example, the Comprehensive Competency Program (CCP) of Washington, D.C. is a self-paced, individualized, competency-based program which packages the best available educational technologies developed in Job Corps and other basic and vocational skills programs and makes them available to public schools and other institutions. Students in CCP attend learning centers where they work at their own pace on academic skills, life skill competencies such as reading the newspaper and calculating overtime pay, and pre-employment skills such as job seeking (Hahn & Danzberger, 1987).

The provision of opportunities for learning during the summer months is another remediation strategy. For example, the Summer Training and Education Program (STEP) developed by Public/Private Ventures of Philadelphia with support from the Ford Foundation is designed to respond to a number of problems that lead low-income youth to drop out of school before graduation.

> The STEP model aims to increase basic skills and lower dropout and teen pregnancy rates by providing poor and underperforming youth with remediation, life skills and work experience during two consecutive and intensive summer programs,

with ongoing support and personal contact during the intervening school year. (Sipe, Grossman, & Milliner, 1987, p. i)

Early results indicate that students in the program achieved gains in math and held their own in reading, whereas students in a control group suffered losses in both areas (Sipe, Grossman, & Milliner, 1987).

A particularly interesting approach to providing students with additional assistance when instructional resources are limited is the use of peer tutors to help students experiencing difficulty with the school curriculum. Both the tutors and the students being tutored have reported improved attitudes toward school as a result of participation in peer tutoring programs (Ashley, Jones, Zahniser, & Inks, 1986). Bloom (1984) has noted that students (both tutors and tutees) in effective peer tutoring programs achieve at higher levels than students in conventional learning or those in mastery learning situations. Teachers could utilize the assistance of special services providers to organize such tutoring programs.

Programmatic Strategies for Increasing the Salience of the School Curriculum

Whether students have sufficient skills to meet the standards of the school program may be unimportant if they are not initially motivated to try to perform in school. For many students the curriculum is simply not perceived as sufficiently important or salient to motivate them to devote the required effort to succeed. A variety of approaches have been used to make schools more salient to students.

Some programs have made use of a multi-ethnic curriculum to appeal to minority students who view the dominant white culture as foreign. Such curricular approaches attempt to relate the subject matter of the school to the lives of the students and their communities and cultures. For example, the Indian Heritage Middle/High School in Seattle enrolls native American students. In addition to the basic skills the school program includes work in native American culture and ethnic background (OERI Urban Superintendents' Network, 1987).

Other programs have incorporated some form of career education to communicate explicitly how the school curriculum can be connected to future careers for those who are successful. An example of a contemporary career education program is the New York City Job and Career Center. Using facilities and counselors provided by the New York State Department of Labor, the Center sponsors field trips, exhibits, visual displays and discussions from the City's major employers. The services of the Center are available to students in public and private schools, to dropouts, and to unemployed adults (Grant Foundation Commission, 1988).

Another approach to making the program of the school more meaningful to students is to attach some type of incentive to school performance. The Cleveland Public Schools have adopted a program which relies on cash as an incentive. With funding from corporations and local foundations, the Cleveland program pays students in grades 7 to 12 $40 for each A grade, $20 for each B, and $10 for each C. This money is usable for postsecondary education (Grant Foundation Commission, 1988).

POSITIVE RELATIONSHIPS IN SCHOOL

Although quantitative evidence is scarce, several qualitative studies of student dropouts strongly suggest that many of them feel that no one at school pays attention to them or cares about their progress (Fine, 1987). Even beyond feeling ignored or unimportant at school, many dropouts seem to have a sense that the goal of school officials is to rate and sort them rather than to find ways to help them be successful. Students who have a weak attachment to the school are likely to drift away, and eventually drop out. Students who maintain a strong bond with the school are likely to continue to attend school regularly, and hence are more likely to graduate (Gottfredson, 1987).

Strengthening the Affective Attachments of Students to the School

There are several ways in which young people interact with their school environments. Students maintain relationships with peers, teachers, and the school itself. Schools have developed strategies to strengthen these attachments, both separately and in combination.

We have identified three ways in which school staffs can attempt to strengthen students' bonds to school by influencing the students': (a) associations with adults in the schools, (b) associations with their school peers, and (c) attachment to the school as an institution.

Programmatic Strategies for Strengthening the Connections to Adults in the School

The first strategy involves creating a "mentor" relationship linking students to adults in the school. Most secondary schools are large relatively impersonal institutions. High schools are designed and organized to process large batches of students. They also are highly differentiated — to the extent that a student may have a different teacher for every period of the school day. Conversely, a given student may be one of 150 or more to be taught by a particular math teacher or English teacher. The end result is that students rarely have sustained and in-depth social contact with their teachers.

The quality and quantity of contact that students have with other school staff also typically are inadequate. Although a student usually is assigned to a single guidance counselor, student-counselor ratios are frequently as high as 500 to 1. Although some students demand less attention than others, it still is highly unlikely that at-risk students can gain sufficient access to their counselors to forge strong social bonds. Under these circumstances, students may well come to the conclusion that no one at the school cares about their welfare. To counteract this trend and its likely consequences, the school must reorganize the daily schedule to allow students to have more close contact with adults in the school, and ensure that this contact has a positive valence.

Programmatic Strategies for Strengthening the Connection of Students to Peers in School

The second strategy to strengthen students' attachment to school operates through students' relations with their peers. Both surveys of students and ethnographic studies of schools have long suggested that adolescents are not opposed to the *idea* of school; and many of them like school (Epstein, 1981; Epstein & McPartland, 1976). There are, of course, components of these attitudes which are consistently counter to the intentions of the school; no one enjoys failing in his or her classes, for example, and some students find it difficult to negotiate the authority relations of the classroom (Natriello, 1984). In spite of these problems, the school plays a central role in the adolescent social structure. Adolescents spend more than 40% of their waking hours in school during the school year. It is not surprising, then, that the school becomes a locus of social activity for youth.

As some youth drop out of school, however, the balance of in-school social contact to out-of-school contact begins to shift. Adolescents want to spend time with their friends. If most of a student's friends are no longer attending school, the student may withdraw to keep contact with his or her peers. After all, most secondary schools are not organized to facilitate social interaction among students. Students rarely spend much of their school day with their friends, and classroom instruction typically constrains peer contact.

For school personnel to hold such students in schools, they must develop ways to promote peer networks which provide support and attachment. The major vehicle for this is a program of extracurricular activities which allows students to interact with their peers in the school setting. These before- and after-school activities include sports, recreation, and school clubs, some of which double as academic enrichment programs. Although these activities may be intrinsically interesting to adolescents, they mainly serve to allow teens to socialize in a setting officially sanctioned by the school.

Another way to strengthen peer attachments in the school context is to socialize new students into the life of the high school. This strategy uses orientation programs as an in-service socialization mechanism. In some settings, new students are paired with students who have been in the school for some time. The more experienced student can then act as a mentor to the new student, providing information about the school and lending social support (Grant Foundations Commission, 1988). Students are thus guaranteed to know someone in the high school, thereby reducing its impersonal and alienating character and helping to forge a social bond between the new students and those already in the school.

Mentoring programs like this can have positive consequences for the mentor as well. Acting as a mentor provides a student with a sense of responsibility and of being needed. The mentor is aware that the school is depending on him or her to perform a valuable function and that the new student is relying on the help of the mentor. This sense of being needed may be related to better attendance among at-risk youth who serve as mentors. This strategy also has been used for purposes other than school orientation, such as academic instruction. There are several examples of cross-age remedial peer tutoring, for instance, which show positive academic effects (Madden & Slavin, in press).

Programmatic Strategies for Strengthening the Connection of Students to the School as an Institution

The third strategy for strengthening attachment to schools is based on linking the student to the school as an institution. The goal here is to foster student interest in the school. We have already noted that the size of most secondary schools renders them impersonal, and many students can pass through a high school with the sense that the school has had little effect on them, and they have had little impact on the school. Schools must take active steps to integrate the student into the school environment.

The recognition of poor integration into the school is not unique to dropout prevention efforts, and in fact is integral to the well-known effective schools model (Edmonds, 1979). The effective schools model is predicated on the premise that students confronting clear and consistent goals in a safe, orderly environment will succeed in school. In addition, Newmann (1981), writing on student alienation in high schools, has hypothesized that student participation in school policy and management may help prevent dropping out.

One possible way to promote this linkage is to convince students that they will receive fair and equitable treatment in school. This involves making the school rules explicit so that all students know them; making them appear fair; and applying them consistently to students. Gottfredson and Gottfredson (1985) found that schools whose students reported that the rules were fair and clear, experienced less disruption than schools where students reported inconsistent and unfair applications of rules. They did not conclude, though, that student participation in rule-making was related to levels of school disruption.

It is plausible that students will be more attached to settings where they can exercise some control over their environment. This might take the form of student control over which school to attend (Perpich, 1988), or course selection, or being able to choose a desired school-related extracurricular activity. Among at-risk middle school students in New York City, for example, those reporting greater control over planning their programs tend to like school more than those reporting less control (though there is no evidence of a net effect on attendance rates) (Grannis, Reihl, Pallas, Lerer, & Randolph, 1988).

Another way of linking students to the school involves anticipatory socialization, that is, providing junior high school students opportunities to learn what the high school is like and what is to be expected of them, in order that when they do go on to high school the setting is not mysterious or foreboding. In New York City, this strategy is implemented under the rubric of linkage programs, involving collaborative efforts between junior high schools and high schools. Large numbers of at risk middle school students report listening to students or adults from a high school describe high school life, but far fewer students report having gone to a high school for a special event or after-school activity, or with a class. Moreover, there is little evidence of sustained efforts at linking middle school students to high schools; most attempts are one-shot efforts. This may account for why linkage activities seem so ineffective in promoting positive student outcomes in New York City (Grannis et al., 1988). Special services providers at the middle school level could assume responsibility for conducting linkage activities over a period of time to attempt to achieve more positive outcomes.

CONCLUSION

As this brief review suggests, there is no shortage of programmatic strategies for attempting to hold students in school until graduation. Our examination of the existing research on dropout prevention programs suggests that there is no single approach that has a dramatic impact in reducing the dropout rate. A variety of programs based upon somewhat different assumptions as to the cause of early school leaving might be expected to have a small effect.

The implications for practitioners concerned with ameliorating the dropout problem are several. First, dropping out of school is a multifaceted problem, and solving it will require multiple approaches. For example, in this paper we have examined both academic and affective approaches. Clearly, neither approach alone will be sufficient. Providing social support alone to students who cannot meet the academic demands of the school or academic support alone to students who feel unconnected to the school will probably both produce disappointing results.

Second, the appropriate configuration of programs and resources will depend upon local circumstances, particularly the needs of the students at-risk. Too many schools and districts appear to have adopted dropout prevention programs without first developing an understanding of the needs of their students. The programs noted above appeared to be effective in their own settings; they may not be effective in a different environment.

Third, the most prominently mentioned method of addressing the needs of at-risk youth is through the development of new programs, but it is important not to overlook opportunities to incorporate changes to benefit such students in the routine operation of schools. For example, staff members should not need a special program to make an extra effort to develop congenial relationships with students. Similarly, teachers and special services providers can make themselves more available to provide academic assistance when necessary.

The problems presented by at-risk youth did not develop quickly, and they are not likely to be solved in the immediate future. However, with sustained attention from competent and concerned educators, it should be possible to provide all students with a fair chance of completing their high school education.

REFERENCES

Ashely, W., Jones, J., Zahniser, G., & Inks, L. (1986). *Peer Tutoring: A Guide to Program Design*. Research and Development Series, No. 260. Columbus, OH: Ohio State University Center for Research in Vocational Education.

Bloom, B. (1984). The search for methods of group instruction as effective as one-to-one tutoring. *Educational Leadership, 41*, 4-17.

Clifford, J.C. (1986). A Taxonomy of Dropout Prevention Strategies in Selected School Districts. Unpublished Doctoral Dissertation. Teachers College, Columbia University.

Cohen, E.G. (1986). *Designing Groupwork: Strategies for the heterogeneous classroom*. New York: Teachers College Press.

Council of Great City Schools (1987). *Challenge to urban education: Results in the making*. Washington, DC: Council of Great City Schools.

Edmonds, R.R. (1979). Effective schools for the urban poor. *Educational Leadership, 37*, 15-24.

Ekstrom, R.B., Goertz, M.E., Pollack, J.M., & Rock, D.A. (1987). Who drops out of high school and why: Findings from a national study. In G. Natriello (Ed.), *School dropouts: Patterns and policies* (pp. 52-69). New York: Teachers College Press.

Epstein, J.L. (Ed.) (1981). *The quality of school life*. Lexington, MA: Lexington Books.

Epstein, J.L. & McPartland, J.M. (1976). The concept and measurement of the quality of school life. *American Educational Research Journal, 13*, 15-30.

Fine, M. (1987). Why urban adolescents drop into and out of public high schools. In G. Natriello (Ed.), *School dropouts: Patterns and policies* (pp. 89-105). New York: Teachers College Press.

Fordham, S. & Ogbu, J. (1986). Black students' school success: Coping with the burden of "acting white." *The Urban Review, 18*, 176-206.

Gottfredson, G.D. (1987). American education—American delinquency. *Today's Delinquent, 6*, 5-70.

Gottfredson, G.D. & Gottfredson, D.C. (1985). *Victimization in schools*. New York: Plenum Press.

Grannis, J., Riehl, C., Pallas, A., Lerer, N., & Randolph, S. (1988). *Evaluation of the New York City dropout prevention initiative: Final report on the middle schools for year 2, 1986-87*. New York: Teachers College, Columbia University.

Grant Foundation Commission on Work, Family, and Citizenship (1988). *The forgotten half: Non-College youth in America*. Washington, DC: The William T. Grant Foundation.

Hahn, A. & Danzberger, J. (1987). *Dropouts in America: Enough is known for action*. Washington, DC: Institute for Educational Leadership.

Kennedy, M.M., Birman, B.F., & Demaline, R.E. (1986). *The Effectiveness of Chapter 1 services*. Washington, DC: U.S. Government Printing Office.

Levin, H. (1987). *Toward accelerated schools*. New Brunswick, NJ: Rutgers University, Center for Policy Research in Education.

Madden, N.A. & Slavin, R.F. (in press). Effective pullout programs for students at risk. In R.E. Slavin, N.L. Karweit, & N.A. Madden (Eds.), *Effective programs for students at risk*. Needham Heights, MA: Allyn and Bacon.

McDill, E.L., Natriello, G., & Pallas, A.M. (1985). Raising standards and retaining students: The impact of the reform recommendations on dropouts. *Review of Educational Research, 55*, 415-433.

McDill, E.L., Natriello, G., & Pallas, A.M. (1986). A population at risk: Potential consequences of tougher school standards for student dropouts. *American Journal of Education*, *94*, 135-181.

Murray, S.R., Murray, C., Gragg, F.E., & Kumi, L.M. (1982). *National evaluation of the PUSH for excellence project: Final Report*. Washington, DC: American Institutes for Research.

Natriello, G. (1982). *Organizational evaluation systems and student disengagement in secondary schools*. Final Report Submitted to the National Institute of Education. St. Louis: Washington University.

Natriello, G. (1984). Problems in the evaluation of students and student disengagement from secondary schools. *Journal of Research and Development in Education*, *17*, 14-24.

Natriello, G. & Dornbusch, S.M. (1984). *Teacher evaluative standards and student effort*. New York: Longman.

Natriello, G. & McPartland, J. (1987). *Adjustments in high school teachers' grading criteria: Accommodation or motivation*. Paper presented at the annual meeting of the American Educational Research Association, Washington, DC.

Natriello, G., Pallas, A.M., McDill, E.L., McPartland, J.M., & Royster, D. (1988, April). *An examination of the assumptions and evidence for alternative drop-out prevention programs in high schools*. Paper presented at the annual meeting of the American Educational Research Association, New Orleans, LA.

Newmann, F. (1981). Reducing student alienation in high schools: Implications of theory. *Harvard Educational Review*, *51*, 546-564.

OERI Urban Superintendents Network (1987). *Dealing with dropouts: The urban superintendents' call to action*. Washington, DC.: U.S. Government Printing Office.

Orr, M.T. (1987). *Keeping students in school*. San Francisco: Jossey-Bass.

Perpich, R. (1988). Minnesota plan expands options for public school students. *State Education Leader*, 7, 2, 5.

Rosenholtz, S.J. (1987). The multiple ability curriculum: An intervention against the self-fulfilling prophecy. Unpublished doctoral dissertation. Stanford University.

Sipe, C.L., Grossman, J.B., & Milliner, J.A. (1987). *Summer training and education program (STEP) Report on the 1986 experience—executive summary*. Philadelphia, PA: Public/Private Ventures.

Wagenaar, T. (1987). What do we know about dropping out of high school? In R.G. Corwin, (Ed.), *Research in Sociology of Education and Socialization* vol. 7 (pp. 161-190). Grenwich, CT: JAI Press.

Wehlage, G.G. & Rutter, R.A. (1987). Dropping out: How much do schools contribute to the problem? In G. Natriello (Ed.), *School dropouts: Patterns and policies* (pp. 70-88). New York: Teachers College Press.

Promoting Parent Involvement in Schools to Serve At-Risk Students

Diane L. Smallwood

South Brunswick (NJ) Public Schools

Mary Katherine Hawryluk
Ellen Pierson

Rutgers University

SUMMARY. The recent educational literature and popular media reflect growing concern about deficient student achievement in the regular education system, a problem that has resulted in inappropriate classification of students as handicapped, as well as resulted in increased dropout rates. A wide range of variables contribute to school failure, including a complex interaction of home and school characteristics. For this reason, efforts to intervene with students who are at-risk for school failure must include attention to the relationship between parents and school professionals. This paper reviews the literature on parent involvement, which shows that increased participation by parents in educational programs has a positive relationship to student achievement. Specific roles for parents are examined, followed by guidelines for promoting parent involvement.

In finding solutions to current educational problems, special services providers and other professionals can draw upon resources that are both cost-effective and readily available within the local community. Parents of school-aged children represent an underutilized resource that can be used to serve a range of educational

---

Requests for reprints should be directed to: Diane L. Smallwood, South Brunswick Public Schools, South Brunswick, NJ 08852.

© 1990 by The Haworth Press, Inc. All rights reserved.

concerns. Research on effective schools (e.g., Moles, 1982; Newcombe, 1982) documenting a positive relationship between increased parent involvement and student achievement highlights the importance of collaborative home-school relationships. The purpose of this paper is twofold: (a) to familiarize readers with roles for parents in the education of their children, and (b) to present guidelines for practice that may be used by school professionals to work effectively with parents and to promote parent involvement in children's education.

EDUCATIONAL ROLES FOR PARENTS

Even a cursory review of the literature reveals diverse meanings for the term "parent involvement." Although some authors seem to equate involvement with a fairly limited range of activities, such as attendance at parent-teacher conferences (e.g., Stevenson & Baker, 1987), others have outlined a wide variety of educational roles for parents (e.g., Lillie, 1981). In this paper, parent involvement will be considered as inclusion or participation of parents or other primary caregivers in the educational process, both as service providers and as service recipients. As service providers, parents interact with their own children in ways specifically designed to enhance school performance. As service recipients, parents receive from school personnel information or support designed to enhance their ability to assist their own children with learning. A broader view of parent involvement would encompass efforts to intervene with other students or with the school program as a whole, but such extended roles are beyond the scope of this paper.

The following sections, which review the literature on parent involvement, are organized according to roles that parents might take to facilitate student success in regular education. Specific forms of parent involvement examined include: (a) communicating with teachers and other school personnel, (b) teaching academic and/or behavioral skills, (c) acting as home-based reinforcement agents or behavior managers, and (d) becoming involved in counseling programs.

Parent-School Communication

A central form of parent involvement is communication with classroom teachers. Research in this area suggests that frequency of contacts between home and school often correlates positively with school performance.

Iverson, Brownlee, and Walberg (1981) studied a group of elementary school students with measured reading levels of one to two years below grade level, from economically disadvantaged homes. Contact between each child's reading teacher and parent were recorded monthly, with "contact" defined as an in-person conference, telephone call, or written communication. Results indicated that frequency of contacts was positively correlated with academic achievement for children in grades one through three.

Grimmet and McCoy (1980) reported gains in reading achievement of third-grade students whose parents had received information regarding the reading program and a form for communicating with the reading teacher. Moreover, parents who had received a detailed description of the reading program were more likely to communicate with the teacher than those parents who were uninformed.

Home-school communication also may affect dropout rates and school alienation problems. Marockie and Jones (1987) reported on a program that targeted at-risk youngsters for intervention. One aspect of this comprehensive home-school communication project was a "Care-Call" component, staffed by retired teaching professionals. The school staff's response to any student's absence was a telephone call to the home, to express concern about the absence and to offer the school's help in returning the student to school as quickly as possible. Program data showed a significant reduction in the dropout rate throughout the duration of the project.

Parents As Teachers

Parents may contribute to their children's education through a variety of teaching activities. Research in this area suggests that significant gains in reading achievement are derived from both highly structured parent-child activities, such as paired reading methods (Morgan, 1976), and more informal approaches, such as reading to children or listening to children read (Becher, 1985).

American schools and researchers appear to have made less systematic use of parent-professional relationships than British educators, particularly in the area of direct involvement in teaching academic skills. Considerable research on parents as teachers comes from institutions in England, and demonstrates that parents can be trained to be effective teachers of their own children.

Reading to children is probably the most convenient and frequently recommended parental activity shown to have a positive relationship to reading attitudes and achievement (Becher, 1985). In general, children whose parents read to them at least four times a week achieve higher levels in reading and are more positive about reading activities than children whose parents do not read to them on a regular basis. Discussion between parent and child while reading a story also may enhance the child's reading achievement. For a concise review of specific benefits of reading to children, the reader is referred to Becher (1985).

Closely related to reading to children is the practice of listening to children read. Numerous studies have reported significant improvement in reading skills among children whose parents listened to them read at home (Crawford, 1985; Hewison & Tizard, 1980; Shuttleworth, 1986; Tizard, Schofield, & Hewison, 1982). Moreover, a two-year study by Tizard, Schofield, and Hewison (1982) of children in multiracial inner city schools in England suggested that home-based practice yielded greater benefits than school-based remedial help, a finding that lends strong support to the use of parents as teachers.

A highly structured form of parent involvement is found in the paired reading technique described initially by Morgan (1976) and utilized in more recent studies by other researchers (Bushell, Miller, & Robson, 1982; Miller, Robson, & Bushell, 1986). Essentially, in paired reading, the parent and child read simultaneously from a book chosen by the child. The child attempts to read every word, with the parent providing correction as needed. In a study with failing readers and their parents, Miller et al. (1986) found significant gains in accuracy of oral reading among children who participated in a paired reading approach.

Benefits of structured tutoring by parents also have been documented. Searls, Lewis, and Morrow (1982) found that when parents of first-graders provided daily tutoring designed to supplement classroom lessons, students showed significantly greater gains in reading and mathematics than a nontreatment control group. Positive changes in parental attitudes toward school also were found. Unfortunately, because similar improvement was not found in a sample of second-graders, these results must be viewed as preliminary.

Home-Based Reinforcement

When students experience difficulty meeting behavioral or academic demands, modification of the contingencies surrounding school performance is usually essential to change. Although classroom-based reinforcement programs can be effective in this regard, teachers often are frustrated by the limited range of meaningful consequences for student behavior and achievement available in school settings. By contrast, parents have access to a wide array of reinforcers and punishments that may be used to modify school performance, including privileges, material items, and perhaps most important, parental approval and recognition. Recently, therefore, considerable attention has been given to home-school contingency (HSC) programs in which parents provide consequences for selected aspects of their children's school performance.

Research lends substantial support to HSC programs as vehicles for enhancing school performance of unsuccessful students. Positive results have been achieved with students in the early and middle elementary grades (Allyon, Garber, & Pisor, 1975; Drew, Evans, Bostow, Gieger, & Drash, 1982) and at the junior high school level (Leach & Byrne, 1986; Schumaker, Hovell, & Sherman, 1977). Although goals, format, and procedures of such programs vary from one application to the next, they typically consist of regular feedback from the teacher to parents about student performance. Based upon the feedback, the parent provides a specific, agreed upon, consequence to the student.

A frequent goal of HSC programs with at-risk students is reduction of disruptive or inappropriate classroom behavior. In a classic study by Allyon et al. (1975), third-grade students received a "Good Behavior" note to bring home to their parents on days when they behaved appropriately in school. Parents were encouraged to show pleasure and to provide appropriate positive reinforcers when their child earned the note. Results showed a dramatic reduction in classroom disruption. Moreover, the HSC program yielded greater maintenance of gains than did a classroom-based incentive system.

HSC programs also seem successful in reducing the disruptive behavior of older students. Fairchild (1983) reported substantial improvement in a 13-year old's classroom behavior and effort in response to a daily report card system that involved parental withdrawal of privileges based upon negative teacher ratings. Additionally, a gradual increase in the student's grade point average occurred over the course of the intervention. Similarly, Leach and Byrne (1986) determined that a home reinforcement system yielded increased compliance with classroom rules and completion of classwork on the part of disruptive secondary school students.

Enhancement of classroom productivity and work quality is another frequent aim of HSC programs with at-risk students. Daily school-home notes in conjunction with parent implemented consequences appeared effective in increasing the amount and accuracy of seatwork completed by young elementary students in both reading (Imber, Imber, & Rothstein, 1979) and math (Blechman, Taylor, & Schrader, 1981; Drew et al., 1982). Junior high school students showed substantial gains in assignment completion and semester grades when they received home privileges for improved performance (Schumaker et al., 1977). Classroom behavior also was enhanced.

A common assumption among educators and parents is that television viewing may interfere with homework completion. In a study by Wolfe, Mendes, and Factor (1984), parents were trained to use behavior management strategies to reduce their children's viewing time. Youngsters received tokens that could be exchanged for television time and earned positive reinforcers for complying with family rules regarding television (i.e., amount of time, shows to be watched, etc.). Results revealed a dramatic reduction in the amount of time students spent watching television, although it was unclear to what extent time spent on homework was increased.

Parent and Family Counseling

Family conflict or stress is considered a frequent contributor to school problems (Carlson, 1987; Paget, 1987). Moreover, a student's academic or behavioral difficulties in school can have a negative impact on family functioning, and especially on interaction patterns between the student and parents (Anesko & O'Leary, 1983). A vicious cycle may emerge in which school problems and family difficulties escalate in response to one another. Hence, supportive services for parents, such as training/education and counseling may be as important as the more direct forms of involvement discussed in the preceding sections.

Although the literature on family therapy and parent training is rapidly expanding, school-based or school-focused interventions in these domains have not been well documented. With the exception of programs for families of handicapped children, most education and counseling services to parents have been targeted at home behavior (Broughton, Barton, & Owen, 1981). It is hoped that the studies reviewed here represent a trend toward expanded efforts with parents aimed at alleviating school difficulties of at-risk students.

Anesko and O'Leary (1983) implemented a training program designed to help parents of elementary school children reduce parent-child conflict and manage interactions concerning homework. Parents were instructed in principles of positive and negative reinforcement, goal setting, and behavioral contracting and then applied these concepts to homework problems with their own children. Outcome data revealed a modest reduction in parent-child conflict regarding homework, although long-term benefits of the program were less evident.

Family systems approaches to student performance problems are reflected in recent reports by Conoley (1987) and Carlson (1987). As a consulting psychologist in a public school district, Conoley applied strategic family therapy interventions with parents of students experiencing academic and behavior problems in school. Using case studies, she noted the importance of modifying family interaction patterns pertaining to school performance problems, illustrating the use of strategies such as paradox and reframing to induce change. Also evident in these cases was juxtaposition of cognitive-behavioral strategies with strategic family therapy techniques.

Carlson (1987) described the use of a structural family therapy approach in addressing school adjustment difficulties. In her case examples, she illustrated applications of restructuring and redefining boundaries with two families of youngsters evidencing significant classroom behavior problems. Carlson emphasized the appropriateness of family systems interventions in school settings, but highlighted the importance of sufficient financial and human resources, administrative support, and adequate training of school professionals in theory and techniques associated with this approach.

PROMOTING PARENT INVOLVEMENT: GUIDELINES FOR SCHOOL PROFESSIONALS

The foregoing review indicated that parents can intervene with their youngsters in a variety of ways to facilitate improvement in academic achievement and school behavior. Moreover, psychological and educational support to parents may enable them to establish home routines and interaction patterns that are conducive to students' school success. In order for parents to participate successfully in the educational process, however, procedures for parent involvement must be integrated into the existing structure of school programs. Parent involvement should not be treated as a luxury, but needs be viewed as an essential element of efforts to enhance achievement among failing students. Similarly, it is important that sufficient flexibility exists in expectations and options for involvement to allow for individual differences among parents and students. In this section, several key issues are examined that should be considered by school professionals in their efforts to promote involvement among parents of students with school performance deficits, including: (a) readiness for parent involvement, (b) child and family development, and (c) impact of involvement on family relationships.

A central premise of this discussion is that special services providers, including special education teachers, school psychologists, social workers, speech pathologists, and learning disabilities specialists, can work collaboratively with regular educators to promote parent involvement. Roles for special services professionals may entail direct service to parents (e.g., counseling, training) and indirect service such as consultation to regular education personnel or assistance with program development and evaluation. Issues covered in this section are pertinent to special and regular educators, in both direct and indirect service efforts with parents.

Readiness for Parent Involvement

The likelihood that parents will become involved in beneficial ways in their youngsters' education may well be determined by school and parent "readiness" for involvement. The notion of readiness, as it pertains to parent involvement, refers both to attitudinal factors, such as views concerning appropriate roles for parents, and to availability of resources such as time and physical space needed for successful parent participation (Maher & Bennett, 1984).

School Readiness

A major barrier to parent involvement is reluctance on the part of teachers and other professionals to include parents as active, co-equal members of the educational "team." Professionals may believe that they are the experts on education, and that parents have little to offer that could enhance efforts to help at-risk students. Alternatively, some school personnel may feel threatened by parents who wish to take an active role in decision making or in working with their child on educational tasks. Concern that parents may be critical of the child's educational program or of teacher competence may impede professionals' willingness to share information with parents. Although the majority of parents hold very positive views of their children's teachers (Harris & Associates, Inc., 1987), conflict between parents and teachers does occur, especially when a youngster is having difficulty in school. In order for school personnel to become more receptive to parent involvement, they need to feel confident of their ability to explain educational programs and practices to parents and to handle disagreements that do arise. Because training in communication skills and conflict management with parents is not included in most teacher preparation programs, in-service education in these areas seems a logical first step in establishing readiness for parent involvement.

Even when teachers hold very positive attitudes toward parents, involvement may be limited if time for meeting and working with parents is not adequate. A frequent barrier to parents' participation is the mismatch between their time availability and that of school personnel (Harris & Associates, Inc., 1987). Parents who are employed may be most available to meet in the evenings, but teachers who spend time with parents after school hours typically do so voluntarily, at their own expense. Even within the school day, time for collaborating with parents is limited and is likely to occur during teachers' class preparation time or lunch period. When a student is having serious difficulties in school, a half-hour meeting often is insufficient for problem solving or training parents in strategies for helping the youngster at home. Time limitations not only present a practical barrier to parent involvement, but may, over time, exacerbate attitudinal impediments. If working with parents must always be done at the expense of other professional or personal commitments, school personnel are likely to view such efforts as more burdensome than beneficial. Although only a partial solution, it would seem that financial remuneration or compensatory time for evening hours with parents, as well as modification of school day schedules to allocate time for parent contact, are essential if meaningful involvement is to become a reality.

Other resource constraints also can limit parent involvement. Space for meeting with parents is often difficult to find in a school. It is not uncommon for school personnel and parents to convene in rooms that are too small or do not afford the privacy that may be needed for productive, comfortable discussion. Failure to allocate space specifically for contact with parents gives the message to parents and professionals alike that involvement is not deemed truly important. In a similar vein, limited financial resources may make phone calls or even written correspondence between school and home difficult.

Resource availability for parent involvement is determined by those responsible for school policy making and administration, including the school board, superintendent, and principals. In many ways, then, administrative support is at the heart of school readiness for parent involvement. Administrators can sanction compensation to staff for time spent with parents and can work to ensure that space, materials, and finances are allocated in ways that allow personnel to spend time with and offer service to parents. Administrators also pave the way for positive attitudes toward involvement, both by their own examples and by providing the training and supervision that staff need to work successfully and comfortably with parents.

Parent Readiness

Parent interest in becoming involved in their youngster's education and parent comfort in working with school personnel are clearly essential to successful involvement. Although research indicates that most parents want to take an active part in the schooling process, they are not always at ease in approaching teachers with concerns about their children (Harris & Associates, Inc., 1987). Parents' own school experiences are likely to influence their attitudes toward school personnel. If they experienced problems or were intimidated by teachers, they may be reluctant to assume an active or assertive stance with regard to their youngsters' teachers. One solution to parents' discomfort with involvement, clearly, is enhanced attitudes and skill on the part of school staff, as discussed above. Equally important, though, is skill development on the part of parents. Kohr, Parrish, Neef, Driessen, and Hallinan (1988) developed a program to train parents of handicapped children to communicate more effectively with professionals. They found that parents were able to learn the designated communication skills and to apply them in their interactions with professionals. This program illustrates one way in which parent interaction with school personnel can be enhanced. It is important to bear in mind, however, that there are parents who prefer, for a variety of reasons, to limit their involvement (MacMillan & Turnbull, 1983). This is a legitimate choice and one that should be respected.

Like school professionals, parents also have time constraints that influence their involvement in schools. The need for more flexible scheduling of meetings with parents has already been noted. Other solutions may include developing babysitting options and encouraging local employers to provide release time for parents to attend school activities. Telephone "hot lines" to provide parents with advice on helping their children with schoolwork may also be useful in addressing time constraints that impede parents' participation in the schooling process.

Just as school readiness for parent involvement is shaped by administrators, parent readiness is likely to be influenced by other parents and the community. Parent-teacher associations may play an especially useful role in promoting involvement, through public relations efforts, training opportunities, and development of special interest subgroups (e.g., parents of youngsters with learning disabilities). A parent liaison system for each class, grade level, or school building also may be useful in establishing the norm of involvement and making parents feel more comfortable taking an active role in the schooling process.

A Developmental Perspective

Recent research indicates that the frequency of parent contacts with the school decreases as the student gets older (Harris & Associates, Inc., 1987; Stevenson & Baker, 1987). Moreover, it seems that parents and teachers alike are more satisfied with extent of parent involvement at the elementary level than they are at the secondary level (Harris & Associates, Inc., 1987). These findings underscore the importance of a developmental perspective in efforts to engage parents in schools. Needs of children and roles of parents vis-à-vis the educational process evolve over time. So too, the demands and structure of educational programs are substantially different at the elementary, intermediate, and secondary levels. The task of school professionals, in conjunction with parents, is to tailor options for involvement to the developmental characteristics of students, their families, and the school program.

During the early school years (preschool through early elementary), for example, forms of involvement that entail direct, daily support to the child with school-related tasks and frequent communication with teachers are likely to be both appropriate and feasible. Young children are very dependent upon their parents and generally receptive to parental input and guidance. Furthermore, school programs for young children typically are structured so that only one to two teachers work with the student and hence can readily collaborate with parents in fostering the youngster's learning and development.

In the later elementary, junior high, and high school years, a different set of developmental needs should shape the nature and extent of parent involvement. As children grow older, they are expected to assume increasing responsibility for performance of school-related tasks. Whereas fairly extensive and intensive parental assistance with school tasks is reasonable with the young child, such support with a secondary school student not only conflicts with progress toward greater independence, but may be annoying to the young adolescent. Too, as children get older, parents are likely to expand work-related and community commitments outside the home, thus limiting time availability for direct involvement in the school process. Forms of involvement that are feasible and appropriate are likely to entail less direct and perhaps less frequent interaction with the child and with the school. Parents of older at-risk students might, for instance, implement an HSC program but not provide daily tutoring in school subjects. Moreover, contacts with school personnel may become less frequent, both because the youngster is expected to inform the parent about school matters and because there are now several teachers working with the student.

Clearly, there is no formula for the types of involvement suited to parents of different age students. But, as school professionals assess current practices of involving parents and plan new efforts, developmental issues should be taken into account. The success of parent involvement may hinge upon an affirmative answer to two questions: (a) "Is this activity likely to be attractive and feasible for parents at this age level?" and (b) "Is this form of involvement consistent with the demands and structure of the educational program at this grade level?"

Parent Involvement and Family Relationships

When parents become more actively involved in school programs, they undertake new roles and ways of interacting both with their children and with school personnel. Although the desired consequence of such change is enhanced school performance, it is important not to overlook other outcomes, especially those pertaining to the parent-child relationship, as well as the parents' own adjustment and relationships with other family members. Recent discussion in the special education literature (Foster, Berger, & McLean, 1981; Turnbull & Turnbull, 1982) suggest that extensive parental involvement in the educational program of a handicapped child can, at times, have problematic side effects. Specifically, parents may experience increased stress as they assume additional responsibilities and time commitments. In addition, existing relationships and role assignments within the family can be disrupted. Finally, the parent can become so focused on promoting the child's educational progress that the nurturing and playful dimensions of the parenting role may diminish.

If parent involvement can have detrimental effects for some families with handicapped youngsters, similar problems may occur when parents of at-risk students become more involved in the schooling process. Although empirical evidence on this issue is lacking, it seems plausible that in some families, certain forms of involvement could change relationships and roles in undesirable ways. In the context of HSC programs, for instance, the parent-child relationship centers at least in part on the provision of positive reinforcers for school performance. Drew et al. (1982) noted that in the initial stages of such a program, there was considerable conflict between parent and child when the reinforcer was not earned, a situation that parents found highly stressful. In Fairchild's (1983) intervention with an adolescent boy, the parents were unwilling to implement a contingency system that involved positive reinforcement because their use of such approaches in the past had resulted in the youngster expecting rewards for compliance with any parental request. Teaching roles for parents could also become problematic for some families, especially if the parent becomes frustrated by a youngster's slow progress and interactions around school work become increasingly conflictual. Moreover, time spent on daily tutoring activities may reduce the parents' availability to other family members.

The purpose of the above discussion is not to discourage professionals from involving parents in school programs. In most situations, it seems likely that the benefits of increased involvement will outweigh negative outcomes. The task of school personnel, however, is to monitor the ways in which parental involvement is affecting personal adjustment and interpersonal relationships, and to provide support in helping families avoid problems that could arise.

CONCLUSIONS

A substantial body of research indicates that children are likely to show improved school performance when their parents communicate regularly with school personnel and engage in home-based activities specifically designed to address learning or behavior problems. Thus, increased parent involvement in educational programs can be viewed as a critical component of efforts to enhance the academic functioning of at-risk students.

In seeking to establish effective home-school partnerships, educators are faced with a twofold challenge. First, it is important to design and offer a varied range of options for parent involvement that can be tailored to the individual characteristics and needs of parents and students. Opportunities for parent involvement should be developmentally appropriate and consistent with the structure, routine, and resources of the school program. Strong administrative support is needed to ensure that adequate resources are allocated for work with parents and that staff are recognized and reinforced for positive interactions with parents.

A second challenge for school professionals is inherent in the task of developing effective working relationships with parents. Optimally, parent-professional interactions should be founded upon mutual respect, placing a consistent emphasis on the ultimate goal of enhancing student adjustment and performance. Toward this end, both parents and educators need to be skilled in interpersonal communication, problem solving, and conflict resolution. Ongoing training and education for both parents and school personnel, supported by appropriate administrative policies, is essential in this regard.

It is important to recognize that productive home-school relationships are unlikely to occur without systematic program planning and evaluation. Therefore, the guidelines for parent involvement presented in this paper should be integrated with general principles of program planning and evaluation (Maher & Bennett, 1984) to ensure development and maintenance of appropriate programs for maximizing student success.

REFERENCES

Allyon, T., Garber, S., & Pisor, K. (1975). The elimination of discipline problems through a combined school-home motivational system. *Behavior Therapy, 6,* 616-626.

Anesko, K. M., & O'Leary, S. G. (1983). The effectiveness of brief parent training for the management of children's homework problems. *Child & Family Behavior Therapy, 4,* 113-126.

Becher, R. M. (1985). Parent involvement and reading achievement: A review of research and implications for practice. *Childhood Education, 62*(1), 44-50.

Blechman, E. A., Taylor, C. J., & Schrader, S. M. (1981). Family problem solving versus home notes as early intervention with high-risk children. *Journal of Consulting and Clinical Psychology, 49,* 919-926.

Broughton, S. F., Barton, E. S., & Owen, P. R. (1981). Home-based contingency systems for school problems. *School Psychology Review, 10,* 27-35.

Bushell, R., Miller, A., & Robson, D. (1982). Parents as remedial teachers: An account of a paired reading project with junior school failing readers and their parents. *Journal of the Association of Educational Psychologists, 5*(9), 7-13.

Carlson, C. I. (1987). Resolving school problems with structural family therapy. *School Psychology Review, 16,* 457-468.

Conoley, J. C. (1987). Strategic family intervention: Three cases of school-aged children. *School Psychology Review, 16,* 469-486.

Crawford, A. (1985). Parental involvement and reading attainment. *Educational and Child Psychology, 2,* 17-25.

Drew, B. M., Evans, J. H., Bostow, D. E., Geiger, G., & Drash, P. W. (1982). Increasing daily assignment completion and accuracy using a daily report card procedure. *Psychology in the Schools, 19,* 540-547.

Fairchild, T. N. (1983). Effects of a daily report card system on an eighth-grader exhibiting behavioral and motivational problems. *School Counselor, 31*(1), 83-86.

Foster, M., Berger, M., & McLean, M. (1981). Rethinking a good idea: A reassessment of parent involvement. *Topics in Early Childhood Special Education, 1*(3), 55-65.

Grimmet, S. A., & McCoy, M. (1980). Effects of parental communication on reading performance of third grade children. *Reading Teacher, 34,* 303-308.

Harris, L., & Associates, Inc. (1987). *Metropolitan Life survey of the American teacher, 1987: Strengthening links between home and school.* New York: Metropolitan Life Insurance Company.

Hewison, J., & Tizard, J. (1980). Parental involvement and reading attainment. *British Journal of Educational Psychology, 50,* 209-215.

Imber, S. C., Imber, R. B., & Rothstein, C. (1979). Modifying independent work habits: An effective teacher-parent communication program. *Exceptional Children, 46,* 218-221.

Iverson, B. K., Brownlee, G. D., & Walberg, H. J. (1981). Parent-teacher contacts and student learning. *Journal of Educational Research, 74,* 394-396.

Kohr, M. A., Parrish, J. M., Neef, N. A., Driessen, J. R., & Hallinan, P. C. (1988). Communications skills training for parents: Experimental and social validation. *Journal of Applied Behavior Analysis, 21,* 21-30.

Leach, D. J., & Byrne, M. K. (1986). "Spill-over" effects of a home-based reinforcement programme in a secondary school. *Educational Psychology, 6,* 265-276.

Lillie, D. (1981). Educational and psychological strategies for working with parents. In J. L. Paul (Ed.), *Understanding and working with parents of children with special needs* (pp. 89-117). New York: Holt, Rinehart, & Winston.

MacMillan, D. L., & Turnbull, A. P. (1983). Parent involvement with special education: Respecting individual preferences. *Education and Training of the Mentally Retarded, 18,* 5-10.

Maher, C. A., & Bennett, R. E. (1984). *Planning and evaluating special education services.* Englewood Cliffs, NJ: Prentice-Hall.

Marockie, H., & Jones, H. L. (1987). Reducing dropout rates through home-school communication. *Education and Urban Society, 19,* 200-205.

Miller, A., Robson, D., & Bushell, R. (1986). Parental participation in paired reading: A controlled study. *Educational Psychology, 6,* 277-284.

Moles, O. C. (1982). Synthesis of recent research on parent participation in children's education. *Educational Leadership, 40*(2), 44-45.

Morgan, R. T. T. (1976). Paired reading tuition: A preliminary report on a technique for cases of reading deficit. *Child Care, Health and Development, 2,* 13-28.

Newcombe, E. (1982). *Parent involvement in education: Highlights form the literature.* Philadelphia: Research for Better Schools.

Paget, K. D. (1987). Systematic family assessment: Concepts and strategies for school psychologists. *School Psychology Review, 16,* 429-442.

Schumaker, J. B., Hovell, M. F., & Sherman, J. A. (1977). An analysis of daily report cards and parent-managed privileges in the improvement of adolescents' classroom performance. *Journal of Applied Behavior Analysis, 10,* 449-464.

Shuttleworth, D. (1986). Parents as partners. *Education Canada, 26*(2), 41-43.

Searls, E. F., Lewis, M. B., & Morrow, Y. B. (1982). Parents as tutors—It works! *Reading Psychology: An International Quarterly, 3,* 117-129.

Stevenson, D. L., & Baker, D. P. (1987). The family-school relation and the child's school performance. *Child Development, 58*, 1348-1357.

Tizard, J., Schofield, W. N., & Hewison, J. (1982). Collaboration between teachers and parents in assisting children's reading. *British Journal of Educational Psychology, 52*, 1-15.

Turnbull, A. P., & Turnbull, H. R. (1982). Parent involvement in the education of handicapped children: A critique. *Mental Retardation, 20*, 115-122.

Wolfe, D. A., Mendes, M. G., & Factor, D. (1984). A parent-administered program to reduce children's television viewing. *Journal of Applied Behavior Analysis, 17*, 267-272.

Preventing Classroom Discipline Problems: Promoting Student Success Through Effective Schools and Schooling

Howard M. Knoff

University of South Florida

SUMMARY. This paper focuses on the effective schools and schooling literature as a basis for promoting student success and preventing classroom misbehavior and discipline problems. By facilitating such success, it is suggested that many discipline problems can be avoided and that school staffs will be able to focus even more of their attention to quality, effective education and instruction. System-wide, school building, classroom, teacher, and student-specific practices are all discussed as they relate to effective schools and schooling and to the prevention of student discipline problems. The conclusion notes that successful prevention programs save time, money, and effort, but that they must be systematically planned to meet the needs of the students, school district, and community alike.

Misbehaving or behaviorally disrupting students in the classroom represent one of the most prevalent and frustrating problems in all

---

Requests for reprints should be directed to: Howard M. Knoff, Director, School Psychology Program, Department of Psychological Foundations, FAO 268, University of South Florida, Tampa, FL 33620.

Sections of this paper have been adapted from [Knoff, H. M. (1987). School-based interventions for discipline problems. In C. A. Maher and J. E. Zins (Eds.), *Psychoeducational interventions in the schools: Methods and procedures for enhancing student competence* (pp. 118-140). New York: Pergamon] and [Knoff, H. M. (1988). Effective social interventions. In J. L. Graden, J. E. Zins, and M. J. Curtis (Eds.), *Alternative educational delivery systems: Enhancing instructional options for all students* (pp. 431-453). Washington, DC: National Association of School Psychologists].

© 1990 by The Haworth Press, Inc. All rights reserved.

of teaching, often disrupting both the educational process and the educational progress of teachers and students alike (Jones & Tanner, 1981). Whereas systematic incidence data specifying the number of discipline-related events, referrals, and interventions is rarely kept except at a local level, a 1981 survey by the National Education Association suggests that discipline problems are widespread in our regular education classrooms and that they interfere with student learning and achievement. Discipline problems decrease the academic engagement time of students in the classroom, the instructional pace of the classroom, and they often are symptomatic of ineffective school and classroom processes. From a parental/public perspective, classroom discipline has been consistently rated as one of the most critical problems in our schools over the past two decades (e.g., Elam, 1983; Gallup, 1983). And, as community-based problems (e.g., physical and sexual abuse, drugs, divorce, violence) increasingly enter and impact on our schools, the need to systematically and effectively address school discipline problems from a systems (i.e., school *and* community) perspective becomes increasingly important (Knoff, 1984, 1987).

At the forefront of these systematic interventions are and should be the school district's special services providers (e.g., special education teachers, school psychologists, school counselors), those individuals who are best-trained to address the behavioral and mental health issues that typically coexist and/or cause individual student's classroom discipline problems. These providers' knowledge of psychology, child and adolescent normal and abnormal development, instruction, and education make them natural leaders in the pursuit of the effective schooling processes, positive classroom practices, achievement-oriented activities, and student-focused strategies that prevent classroom discipline problems. It is this pursuit of these four prevention areas that may go furthest to nurture students' appropriate, prosocial behavior and to ensure that most discipline problems never have an opportunity to surface. Indeed, the prevention literature has clearly described numerous comprehensive programs in these areas and their ability to help teachers and administrators to focus on teaching, the primary goal of the educational process (Baker, Swisher, Nadenichek, & Popowicz, 1984; Gelfand, Ficula, & Zarbatany, 1986; Gesten & Jason, 1987; Jason, Durlak,

& Holton-Walker, 1984). This paper will describe these four prevention areas, discuss their impact on the prevention of classroom discipline problems, and address how special services providers can best facilitate their consideration so that students can be taught as effectively as possible in the regular classroom setting. Prior to this discussion, however, some definitions related to classroom discipline and some background on prevention will be provided.

DEFINITIONS

Classroom discipline interventions relate primarily to student misbehavior. Misbehavior may be defined as an observable action which is judged by another individual (e.g., a teacher or administrator), usually in an authority position, to be inappropriate to a given school context, time, or setting (Charles, 1985). Children who are discipline problems, then, are students who are not emotionally disturbed or so behaviorally disordered that a special education placement is warranted (these special education students, nonetheless, still may manifest discipline problems at times). Thus, the concern here is with the *disturbing* as opposed to the *disturbed* child; the child who consciously or not exhibits the behaviors—talking without permission, daydreaming, wandering around the classroom or school hallways, swearing, disobeying the requests of school staff, insolence and rudeness, not being prepared for class—that comprise the vast majority of school discipline problems (Jones, 1979).

Conceptually, misbehavior is often defined by the unique, ecological characteristics of one's society, community, school, and classroom. Often, the philosophies and values of individuals in each of these ecological systems influence which students are referred for possible intervention, what discipline interventions are deemed appropriate or acceptable, when they are considered necessary, how they are chosen and used, and who implements them. Taking this a step further, school discipline problems must be analyzed in the ecology where they exist. Among the ecological components available for analysis are, for example: (a) the identified, misbehaving school children; (b) their classmates, teachers, principals, and other administrators; (c) their classroom, school, and home/school processes and interactions; (d) their parents and *their* parents' child-rearing beliefs, attitudes, expectations, and practices; (e) their siblings, others in the nuclear or extended family unit, and other out-of-school peers and acquaintances; (f) their community, its resources and deficiencies, and *its* child-rearing beliefs, attitudes, expectations, and so forth; and (g) their society, however is it defined and whatever it truly is. Students behave or misbehave within an ecological context. Prevention programs need to focus on the common denominators that exist across all students' ecologies; they also need to be flexible so that unique ecological characteristics also can be addressed.

A PREVENTION PERSPECTIVE FOR SCHOOL DISCIPLINE PROBLEMS

One of the major assumptions of this paper is that most discipline or classroom management problems in the school or classroom can be prevented. In most cases, this occurs by organizing effective schools and by using effective schooling practices for and with all school children. However, prevention also must occur in the home by having parents teach their children appropriate, prosocial behavior and respect for authority figures and societal institutions even before they enter school. Thus, many prevention programs have attempted to identify school (or district-wide) *and* community social, mental health, and/or educational concerns, as they relate to discipline problems, and to organize and implement broad, systemic community-home-school interventions. In addition, because of a collective goal to prevent misbehavior before it or its precursors occur, these programs have necessarily focused on the correlates of misbehavior, ultimately teaching, nurturing, and encouraging behaviors, attitudes, and values that are contrary to and incompatible with misbehavior, while extinguishing, punishing, and discouraging those that lead to misbehavior.

From this community-home-school perspective, the comprehensive, Connecticut-based primary mental health project described by Allen, Chinsky, Larcen, Lochman, and Selinger (1976) and the Rochester (New York) Primary Prevention Project (Cowen, Pederson, Babigian, Izzo, & Trost, 1973) have both addressed preventive services. The Connecticut program's prevention focus concentrated on: (a) helping all families to attend to those early childhood interactions that teach and reinforce the prosocial behaviors necessary for appropriate school behavior, and (b) changing and facilitating positive home-school interactions so they could support the broad educational process. Relative to discipline, then, one of this program's prevention interventions involved teaching school children to successfully use independent problem-solving skills in the classroom, and teaching every parent and home to use and reinforce these skills in the community. The Rochester program focused its community, family, *and* school prevention programs on children's socialization and problem-solving skills by teaching parents and others how to nurture and generalize these skills with preschool and elementary school children so as to prevent the inappropriate behaviors that often later become discipline problems. This program has also done a superb job of building strong home-school relationships, through various volunteer and paraprofessional aide activities, which reinforce its critical prevention elements and characteristics. *Both* programs have documented that the community-home-school perspective can coordinate and implement successful, comprehensive programs which decrease school discipline problems, and that these programs can provide the critical foundation for additional remedial programming when that becomes necessary.

Although the specific skills and strategies that prevent or help to prevent student misbehavior are discussed below, it is important to note that the teaching and reinforcement of these skills in the home have numerous distractors that need to be addressed by other facets of prevention programming. For example, of every 100 children born today, 20 will be born out of wedlock, 15 will be born into households where no parent is employed, 15 will be born into households with a working parent earning a below-poverty wage, 13 will be born to teenage mothers, and 12 will be born to parents who will divorce before the child reaches age 18. Of the teenage girls that have babies, 40% drop out of school and only half graduate from high school by their mid-twenties (Children's Defense Fund, 1988). Thus, an alarming percentage of households with children are beset with the child care, financial, nutritional, and basic needs problems that interfere with these children's academic, social, and emotional readiness to enter school. And, many of these children are being raised by parents who, themselves, are academically, socially, and emotionally unprepared for independent living, much less raising a child. The net result of this is a vicious cycle of students who enter school already at-risk for educational and behavioral problems, who drop-out or finish school with minimal survival and vocational skills, and who then may parent a new generation of similar children such that the cycle continues.

With preventive programs, such as Head Start, reaching only 16 percent of the more than 2.5 million children who need its services, the complexities of developing preventive programs focused in the home for preschool children and their parents are apparent. However, these prevention programs *must* be developed. Financially, for every dollar that we spend on early childhood programs like Head Start, the long-term savings are at least $4.75 (Children's Defense Fund, 1988). Educationally, every prevention program coordinating home, school, and community resources maximizes the potential that the schooling process will be effective and that all school children will receive the best possible educational experience.

To summarize, prevention programs address discipline problems by reinforcing those community, family, school, and individual values, attitudes, skills, and behaviors which nurture positive, appropriate social behaviors and deter inappropriate, disruptive misbehavior. Although integrated community-home-school prevention programs can be extremely effective at the preschool level (and beyond) to prepare students and parents for successful school experiences, there are numerous school-specific programs and strategies that can prepare school systems and staffs to deal preventively with all children, but especially at-risk children, such that discipline problems are minimized and educational success and progress are facilitated. In this respect, the saying "the best defense is a good offense" applies. To the extent that we can maintain student motivation, academic engagement, perceptions of academic and social success, and positive student-teacher interactions, we can minimize the off-task, inappropriate, and disruptive behaviors that add up to discipline problems.

EFFECTIVE SCHOOLS AND SCHOOLING APPROACHES: A FOCUS ON PREVENTION

From a comprehensive school perspective, a great deal of research has identified interventions which can prevent the misbehavior of most school children. As noted above, many of these interventions involve "effective schools or schooling" techniques or approaches which are taught *to administrative or teaching personnel*. That is, the children are secondary beneficiaries of these interventions. The effective schools research has investigated the characteristics and activities that result in student achievement and successful instruction. Although a number of books (e.g., Graden, Zins, & Curtis, 1988; Paine, Radicchi, Rosellini, Deutchman, & Darch, 1983) and a number of inventories (e.g., Ysseldyke & Christenson, 1987) are available to summarize this literature in depth, a brief overview is presented below as relevant to discipline and classroom management problems. This overview is organized into system-wide or school building, classroom, teacher-specific, and student-specific effective schooling practices.

System-Wide or School Building Practices Toward Effective Schooling

Numerous system and/or building-level practices have been consistently and empirically correlated with student achievement, and thus, might prevent student misbehavior (Anderson & Snyder, 1982). In most cases, system and/or building administrators (e.g., superintendents and principals) are most responsible for these preventive practices; indeed, these individuals, their policies, and their actions are often most predictive of a district or building's educational atmosphere and the degree to which student achievement occurs. In effective districts and buildings, then:

1. Administrators and teachers identify their collective concerns about building and classroom discipline, agree upon specific behavioral and achievement-oriented school improvement goals, and create working teams to address different facets of those goals such that realistic implementation plans are developed. Perhaps most important here is the collaborative decision-making process between teachers and administrators such that a proactive climate of profes-

sional development is developed and the preventive nature of the school improvement plans is reinforced.

2. Clear system, building, and classroom expectations for student discipline are publicized for administrators, teachers, and students alike to follow. Just as students are held accountable for their behavior, so too are teachers and administrators held accountable for how they teach, encourage, and reinforce appropriate student behavior. Beyond public expectations, effective systems and buildings have a written and workable student discipline code which specifies the negative *and positive* consequences of student behavior. Students must recognize that they are responsible for appropriate behavior and for the resulting consequences. School staffs must recognize that they are responsible for facilitating student success, and that they ultimately share in a student's success or non-success.

3. Staff development programs that are organized, systematic, effective, school-based, and linked to identified school improvement goals are provided such that administrators and teachers have the knowledge, skill, confidence, and objectivity with which to choose appropriate misbehavior-preventing strategies and techniques. These staff development programs should be cooperatively planned by both administrators and teachers so that there will be a commitment both to the program's content and activities and to its transference into the school and classroom setting.

4. Teachers and administrators regularly meet in joint problem-solving sessions to ensure that preventive discipline programs and approaches are being effectively implemented, and to trouble-shoot in areas where specific system, building, classroom, teacher, or individual student problems or potential problems are arising. So that this process does not focus on solving already-existing student problems, participants will need to make sure that these problems are addressed from the perspective of analyzing inefficient system or building procedures or activities. Furthermore, staff need to recommend system- or building-level adaptations or additions thereby preventing discipline and related problems from occurring with other students in the future.

5. Financial and personnel resources are organized and distributed, to an appropriate degree, as to critical needs, programs, and goals in the area of both school discipline and prevention. For

schools that have developed and implemented preventive programs (e.g., a home-school intervention program in a low SES magnet school with high parental unemployment and high student discipline problems; a teacher-intensive training program in effective instruction), appropriate resources need to be designated and released, as part of a district-wide needs assessment and implementation program. Among these resources should be consultation support services from special services providers so that they can utilize their problem-solving skills and intervention expertise and facilitate program success and long-term student achievement and success.

6. There is significant parent and community involvement in the academic, behavioral, and socialization goals of the school. High levels of parent and community involvement increase their understanding of the goals and activities of the school system and building, their commitment and participation in these goals and activities, their satisfaction with the school and its programs, and the achievement and appropriate behavior of their children.

Classroom-Based Practices Toward Effective Schooling

Beyond the classroom-based extensions of the system- and building-level recommendations above (e.g., analyzing classroom practices and developing achievement-oriented improvement goals; publicizing and reinforcing clear behavioral expectations for students; ensuring that teachers are capable of effective instruction and classroom management, skilled in problem-solving, and supported with appropriate resources and support personnel), a number of specific classroom-based practices have been empirically recognized as facilitating students' academic achievement and appropriate classroom behavior, including:

1. The importance of environmentally-supportive conditions. Student achievement and appropriate classroom behavior are clearly related to such conditions as class size, teacher-pupil ratio, time allocated to academic activities, physical plant, classroom organization (Ysseldyke & Christenson, 1987). Although there is no magic formula that will ensure a student's academic and behavioral success, special services providers must analyze these conditions' influence

on success, while recognizing their interdependence and their relationship to other variables such as those discussed below.

2. The importance of heterogeneous grouping. Although still not definitive, most research in regular education classrooms suggests that heterogeneous groupings maximize student achievement (Dawson, 1987; Slavin, 1987). Such groupings allow for shared responsibility among students, the potential for inter-student modeling and positive peer interaction, a decrease in group stereotyping and stigmatization, the possibility for cooperative group activities and goal structuring, the recognition of individual differences across both behavior and achievement. Heterogeneous grouping does require that individual students receive education programs that address their individual academic needs and learning objectives, yet it does generally result in greater academic gains for students and fewer behavioral problems and disruptions.

3. The importance of curricular alignment or student-curriculum matching. Many classrooms are structured by the specific curriculum being used to teach a specific subject (e.g., Macmillan in reading, Scott-Foresman in math) and by the pressure felt by the teacher to accomplish a certain amount of material over the course of the school year. Sometimes, this results in students who: (a) are "left behind" in an instructional process that does not focus on mastery learning and can not individualize when necessary, and (b) are frustrated and act out that frustration through classroom disruption. Students deserve the right to academically succeed in their coursework, and this success may be most readily achieved through an appropriate match between a student's current progress and the academic material being presented (Berliner, 1988). Such a match increases both the probability of student achievement, the ultimate goal of education, and the accouterments to achievement (e.g., motivation, attention to task, academic engagement) that decrease the incidents of student disruption.

4. The importance of continuous and appropriate evaluations of student progress and success. Along with explicit, high academic and behavioral expectations in the regular classroom, student achievement also is maximized through ongoing evaluations against specific criteria and through feedback that identifies and reinforces successes, and critiques and remediates shortcomings. Students in

effective classrooms demonstrate greater self-reliance and academic self-assurance. They also exhibit fewer discipline problems, because appropriate behavior is continuously reinforced and inappropriate behavior is systematically evaluated and addressed.

Teacher-Specific Practices Toward Effective Schooling

There are numerous practices that teachers use *every day* to facilitate students' academic achievement and to discourage or prevent classroom discipline problems. Most of these fall in the "effective teaching" domain which many assume is taught during a teacher's undergraduate or graduate pre-certification training. Unfortunately, this may not be the case, or if it is, this domain includes teacher behaviors that need continual supervision, reinforcement, and transfer of training attention. Below is a summary of the empirically-derived teacher practices which help to prevent student discipline problems:

1. Rule specification, clarification, practice, and monitoring (Greenwood, Hops, Delquardi, & Guild, 1974; Herman & Traymontana, 1971). When classroom rules are explicitly outlined for students, modeled and practiced for and by them, strengthened by providing positive reinforcement for compliance and specific feedback for non-compliance, then misbehavior generally decreases while on-task behavior and academic achievement increases. Similarly, when teachers structure academic lessons—by previewing and reviewing the critical material, using advanced organizers, providing directions and specifying objectives and expectations, and by explaining the rationale for why things are done—academic achievement and attention to task is increased and the potential for misbehavior is decreased.

2. Teacher "with-it-ness" (Borg, 1975; Brophy & Everston, 1976; Kounin, 1977). This involves the teacher's continual awareness of student behavior and learning such that on-task behavior can be reinforced and off-task or inappropriate behavior can be identified as it begins. When teachers identify the precursors and initial incidences of misbehavior, intervene with the most critical elements of that misbehavior, prevent its exacerbation and spread to other

students, and provide alternatives that are acceptable and incompatible, then misbehavior generally decreases.

3. Teacher attentiveness and intervention preparedness (Kounin, 1977; O'Leary, Kaufman, Kass, & Drabman, 1970). This involves the teacher's ability to monitor concurrent situations, where one situation potentially involves a student misbehavior, and to intervene when necessary without affecting the other, ongoing activity or situation. When intervention is necessary, the teacher is able to identify misbehaving students, to specify the inappropriate behaviors or circumstances and why they are unacceptable, and to suggest acceptable behaviors using quiet reprimands and proximity control. This entire process is intended to decrease misbehavior and prevents other students from increasing their agitation and subsequent disruptiveness.

4. Teacher interaction: facilitating participation/performance and maintaining teaching pace (Berliner, 1985; Brophy & Good, 1986). Teachers, who keep students actively involved in learning activities (e.g., using advanced organizers, preparing them with questions before calling on them for answers, alerting them that requirements for participation may occur at any time) and who avoid irrelevant interruptions, content redundancies, and unnecessary small group activities, typically maintain a level of instructional pace which decreases student opportunities for misbehavior. This optimal level of instructional pace is critical for sound instruction and learning, and its benefits can be generalized, for example, to facilitate student and teacher time management, transitions from one curricular activity to a new one, and/or students' *self-pacing* during independent work or homework (Paine et al., 1983).

5. Effective praise (Becker & Armstrong, 1968; Brophy, 1981). General and noncontingent teacher praise effectively increases primary grade students' appropriate behavior. For older students, however, praise should be specific, low key, sincere, and contingent upon appropriate behavior. Overall, the most effective praise has these latter characteristics, plus its delivery is varied over time, it specifies and positively reinforces performance, it provides students with feedback about their competence or the value of their accomplishments, and it relates current acceptable performance with past performance.

These effective teaching practices influence two important dimensions that are critical for both academic achievement and the maintenance of appropriate classroom behavior, academic engaged time and allocated time (Berliner, 1988; Brophy & Good, 1986; Denham & Lieberman, 1980). Academic engaged time involves the amount of time that a student is on-task relative to a specific assignment. Although academic engaged time has been shown to vary from classroom to classroom, it seems logical to suggest that on-task time is incompatible with misbehavior, and that the teacher whose preventive approach is to maximize academic engagement time will minimize classroom management problems at the same time. Academic allocated time, meanwhile, involves the amount of time that a teacher actually spends in instructional time for a specific subject or curricular area. Due to classroom discipline problems, some teachers lose as much as 50% of their academic allocated time for some subject areas. This construct, then, can become a measure of teacher effectiveness and impact: as academic allocated time increases, classroom disruptions and teacher inefficiencies necessarily must be decreasing.

Student-Specific Practices Toward Effective Schooling

Whereas the "effective teaching" interventions described above are indirectly applied to children (i.e., they are not taught directly to them), some prevention programs do target school children as their primary, active participants. Many of these programs teach self-competence or social skills, cognitive problem-solving skills, and/or self-management skills. These programs' primary goals involve helping children: (a) to avoid situations which could result in inappropriate behaviors and interactions, and (b) to consider the consequences of their actions in all social situations so that misbehavior is never considered a viable option.

Self-Competence or Social Skills Programs

Although sometimes debated in the literature, social self-competence is typically considered the comprehensive "umbrella" under which social skills exist. Social skills training programs most often involve integrated curricula which identify a developmental chronology of interdependent skills that are linked together over time, resulting in a child's appropriate interpersonal and prosocial functioning. Although many social skills training programs are available (Cartledge & Milburn, 1986), they all use the same basic underlying behavioral and psychological processes to teach their skills and nurture behavioral change: modeling, shaping, coaching, guided rehearsal, and generalization (Cardledge & Milburn, 1986; Ladd & Asher, 1985). Overall, these programs can preventively counteract many of the social and societal problems confronting our children (e.g., drugs, delinquency, violence) as the programs directly influence children's prosocial behavior and behavioral control.

Modeling forms the foundation of most social skills programs. These approaches generally teach students: (a) *to attend*, for example, to individuals who are modeling appropriate social skills, interactions, or situational behaviors; (b) *to remember* those modeled behaviors or skills such that new learning can occur and be practiced both in the observed environment and in future environments which require the same behavior; (c) *to motorically reproduce* the behaviors and skills at appropriate times, in appropriate situations, and at optimal frequencies, durations, and/or intensities; (d) *to self-motivate* such that there are incentives for performing new, positive social skills; and (e) *to demonstrate* or practice the skills appropriately across time, setting, and multiple individuals (Bandura, 1977). Pragmatically, most social skills programs also must teach, through behavioral shaping and chaining procedures, specific skills when they do not exist in the child's behavioral repertoire, must coach throughout the modeling process to ensure maximum understanding and motivation, and must use behavioral rehearsal so that all skills are mastered and functional. After instructional modeling, controlled practice and reinforcement opportunities are provided in classroom and other settings, such that the students ultimately exhibit adaptive and prosocial behaviors spontaneously and without the need for external supervision.

Although more detailed discussions of the social skills training processes are available elsewhere (see Cartledge & Milburn, 1986; Michelson, Sugai, Wood, & Kazdin, 1983; Strain, Guralnick, & Walker, 1986 for comprehensive treatments), a brief discussion of coaching and guided rehearsal procedures, and an overview of social skills training is in order. Coaching, as contrasted with modeling, is a direct instructional method which uses the coach's verbal instructions to guide a child through a particular social skill or interactive behavioral pattern. At times, this may require that the coach "shadow" the child, prompting (e.g., by whispering) the appropriate behavioral or verbal responses needed to a particular situation. Or, it might involve a more intricate and planned process consisting of presenting the rules for appropriate behavior, behavioral rehearsal with the coach or a peer, and direct feedback on the rehearsal with suggestions for improved, future performance (Elliott, Gresham, & Heffer, 1987).

Guided rehearsal, meanwhile, is an extension of behavioral rehearsal (see Goldfried & Davison, 1976) wherein a child practices a modeled or taught skill in a structured role-play format. This process may involve: (a) covert responding, where the child imagines the behavioral components necessary to enact the particular social skill and his or her ability to perform those components successfully; (b) verbal responding, where the child describes these components and their enactment while considering various behavioral alternatives, resolutions, and consequences to problem situations that might involve the particular social skill; (c) motor responding, where the child formally acts out the role-play, discusses and evaluates his or her performance, and then replays the scene, incorporating the suggestions from the evaluation/discussion phase; and (d) a final evaluation process, prior to practicing the skill in a real classroom situation, which may utilize self-evaluation, self-reinforcement, and other self-mediating mechanisms (Bandura, 1977). Guided rehearsal obviously can be integrated into a comprehensive process of modeling. Although the differences between guided rehearsal and coaching exist, future research is still needed to clarify these differences and to determine whether they are meaningful and functional.

To summarize, the many social skills programs available generally are oriented toward the development and generalization of prosocial behaviors, the encouragement of social problem-solving and conflict resolution and the prevention of misbehavior before it becomes a child's entrenched pattern of behavior. Some of the more cited and researched social skills programs are:

1. *Structured Learning* (SL) (Goldstein, Sprafkin, Gershaw, & Klein, 1979, 1986), a planned, integrated social skills curriculum which utilizes modeling, role-playing, feedback, and transfer of training procedures (the latter, to encourage generalization from the training setting to real life situations) to teach new and adaptive social skill behaviors to children with social interactive difficulties.
2. *Spivak and Shure's Interpersonal Cognitive Problem-Solving* (ICPS) (Shure & Spivak, 1978; Spivak, Platt, & Shure, 1976; Spivak & Shure, 1974), a 46-lesson curriculum which focuses on students' ability to: (a) recognize and be sensitive to interpersonal problems, (b) generate alternative solutions to these problems, (c) use "means-ends" thinking to develop step-by-step approaches to problem resolutions, (d) consider the consequences of one's actions on self and others, and (e) understand how others feel.
3. *Bash and Camp's Think Aloud Program* (Bash, 1978; Bash & Camp, 1986; Camp & Bash, 1978), developed initially to improve self-control in young aggressive boys, and now comprising an organized, curricular program focusing on the cognitive and social problem-solving skills of elementary school children.
4. *Weissberg and Gesten's Social Problem-Solving Curriculum* (Weissberg, Gesten, Leibenstein, Doherty-Schmid, & Hutton, 1980), a 34-lesson preventive program which uses highly structured 20 to 30 minute lessons addressing students' identification of self and other feelings, their problem sensing and identification, their generation of alternative solutions during problem situations, their consideration of solution consequences, and their integration of problem-solving behavior.

Despite their similarities, not all social skills programs are alike. Special services providers must evaluate social skill programs as closely as when they choose standardized tests. Research demonstrating a program's effectiveness, reliability, and utility must be reviewed, and qualitative considerations, such as the clarity of the program's manual and instructions and the audio-visual supports that accompany the program, also should be evaluated. A social skills program should be matched to the population with whom it will be used. Clearly, the preventive use of social competency and social skills programs should be as strategic and as effective as any other type of behavioral or social-emotional intervention.

Cognitive Problem-Solving Skills Programs

Cognitive behavior modification and self-control training techniques are often important components of the social skills and problem-solving intervention packages discussed above. Nonetheless, they can be used individually and to prevent student misbehavior as long as the techniques are mastered and appropriate generalization strategies have been taught and reinforced. Historically, Meichenbaum (1977) is most associated with the cognitive behavior modification techniques relevant to social interventions. Typically, these techniques begin with an adult model who demonstrates a skill or task (e.g., impulse control or the ability to share a toy or activity) to some children and end with the group performing the task as guided by their own internal speech.

In total, Meichenbaum's basic cognitive behavioral procedure consists of:

1. An adult model perform(ing) a task while talking to himself out loud (cognitive modeling);
2. The child perform(ing) the same task under the direction of the model's instructions (overt, external guidance);
3. The child perform(ing) the task while instructing himself as he (goes) through the task (overt self-guidance);
4. The child whisper(ing) the instructions to himself as he (goes) through the task (faded, overt self-guidance); and
5. The child perform(ing) the task while guiding his performance via private speech (covert self-instruction). (Meichenbaum, 1977, p.32)

While the group is learning specific tasks or skills, Meichenbaum suggests that they also: (a) define the specific task or problem being addressed, (b) attend to the problem and its solution by using self-instruction and self-monitoring techniques, (c) apply self-reinforcement for acceptable behavior or successful task completion, and (d) use self-evaluation to facilitate coping skills, self-correction, and future planning. Meichenbaum's procedure can be expanded to facilitate generalization by talking about and role-playing the different situational uses of each task and skill with the group, and by having students practice these cognitive techniques across people, settings, and time.

These cognitive approaches have been used successfully to decrease aggressive and disruptive behavior, to improve socially immature and inadequate behavior, to reduce social withdrawal behavior, and to teach more adaptive and appropriate social responses across a wide range of specific behaviors and populations (Gresham, 1981; Kerr & Nelson, 1983). They also have been recommended (Kendall & Braswell, 1985) to help decrease children's impulsivity and to increase their academic and social success in the classroom. Finally, other cognitive restructuring techniques from the rational-emotive therapy literature (Bernard & Joyce, 1984; Ellis & Bernard, 1983) have taught children to guard against the irrational or inaccurate beliefs, assumptions, attitudes, and expectations that interfere with and often counteract positive behavioral patterns. All of these cognitive approaches constitute a group of powerful preventive interventions, with impressive past successes and enormous future applications (Meichenbaum, 1977).

Self-Management Skills Programs

In essence, the discussion of social skills and cognitive behavioral programming already has alluded to the basic self-management skills usually identified in the literature: self-monitoring, self-evaluation, self-reinforcement, and self-instruction (Mace, Brown, & West, 1987). Although these approaches are more fully defined, discussed, and operationalized elsewhere in this volume (see Mace & Shea), it is important to note that many students learn these behaviors and strategies without specific instruction or attention. For misbehaving children, however, these skills often relate significantly to their social and behavioral problems. Thus, preventive programs that focus on social skills must include instruction and reinforcement in self-management skills. Clearly, it is difficult to successfully implement a social skills program without cognitive and self-management components. Although these components can be taught individually to children in preventive programs, special services providers must understand the components' individual and collective effects, especially how they interact when integrated into a social skills programs.

Skill, Performance, and Self-Management Deficits

Student-specific practices toward effective schooling and the programs described above must discriminate among and differentially address skill, performance, and self-management deficits (Gresham, 1981; Knoff, 1988; Ladd & Mize, 1983). This section will conclude with a brief discussion of these three deficit areas.

Skill deficits occur when children do not have (i.e., have never learned or been exposed to) the necessary skills to interact appropriately with peers or adults in different social situations. These children often lack the conceptual knowledge that defines appropriate social behavior, they are unable to analyze specific situations to determine what social goals are appropriate, they do not have the applied skills and behaviors necessary to succeed interpersonally in social situations, and they are unable to discriminate the social subtleties that suggest one interactional approach over another (Ladd & Mize, 1983). Preventively, interpersonal knowledge and problem-solving skills must be *taught* to these children, and then practiced and reinforced in multiple settings and situations such that the behaviors become automatic, appropriate to specific situations, and generalized across persons, settings, and circumstances.

Performance deficits occur when children have the necessary knowledge and skill to interact appropriately in diverse situations, yet they fail to perform accordingly. This may occur due to situation-specific characteristics which interfere with appropriate behavioral responses (e.g., the presence of a peer group which reinforces an antisocial response), anxiety or other affective responses which successfully compete with those responses, lack of motivation or environmental incentives, poor generalization processes, or other interfering or competing antecedent or consequent conditions. Performance deficits also may occur when a child manifests behavior (e.g., aggressive behavior, conduct disordered behavior) that is incompatible with the performance of prosocial behavior. Unfortunately, many teachers assume that most misbehaving students are manifesting performance deficits, for example, that they are resisting teacher directions or defying adult authority. This may not be the case, however, especially when many students are entering school without basic prosocial and interpersonal skills and experiences, and when many schools are not teaching these skills because of their focus on the "fundamentals" of reading, writing, and arithmetic. Whereas prevention programs generally teach students behaviors that help them to resist the situational variables across settings that cause performance deficits (e.g., resisting peer pressure, recognizing new environments where prosocial skills are applicable), these deficits are typically addressed by remedial programs. This is especially true because performance deficits involve behaviors already in a child's behavioral repertoire and because these problems already exist in identified groups of specific children.

Self-control deficits involve children's inability to control their own aggressive or impulsive behavior such that they are unable to exhibit prosocial behaviors. Self-control deficits leave a child without the ability to control his or her behavior or impulses and can be due to poor learning histories or to situational circumstances that interfere with and/or impede previously learned behaviors and strategies. In the latter case, children often know what social behaviors are appropriate and expected, yet they are unable to monitor and evaluate their behavior and its effects on others or are unable to make necessary behavioral changes and adaptations. Preventive interventions with these children often focus on aggression and impulse control techniques that help the individual: (a) to stop out-of-control behavior, (b) to evaluate individual situations and plan appropriate social responses, and (c) to carry out these responses with (d) subsequent self-evaluation (always) and self-reinforcement (when successful).

CONCLUSION

The discussion has focused on the effective schools and schooling literature and research as a way to emphasize the importance of promoting student success and preventing classroom misbehavior and discipline problems. By facilitating such success, it is suggested that many discipline problems will be avoided and that school staffs will be able to focus even more of their attention to quality, effective education and instruction. Whereas successful prevention programs can save a great deal time, money, and effort — both in the short- and long-run — the reality is that our schools are more attuned to remedial or band-aid approaches that try to address existing problems as they occur from situation to situation. Organizationally, this must be changed, but realistically, it will take a three to five year process that most school systems do not want and/or know how to begin. The beginning of this process involves an organizational needs assessment that involves the community and the school district and a resulting, strategic plan of organizational change and multifaceted commitment — by parents, school personnel, community support systems, and the school children themselves. The foundation of this needs assessment is systematic and comprehensive problem-solving. The end product is a school system and community that is maximizing its social and educational efforts, and is impacting its own future for the better.

Clearly, research in this area needs to continue. Indeed, the prevention research is considerably dwarfed by the remedial or direct-service research that, in many ways, is easier to complete and more accessible because so few prevention programs in this area are occurring. But, prevention research has a broader potential impact. It impacts on social policy, social progress, social awareness, *and* on the children who come from the broken homes, the abusing homes, the economically disadvantaged homes, the homes and backgrounds that increase the potential for student disruption and worse. If we can impact the children, their academic and social success, their attainment of high school degrees and good jobs, and their ability to positively influence the next generation, then we may have less need for the remedial and intensive interventions that we unfortunately find ourselves using in today's schools.

REFERENCES

Allen, G. J., Chinsky, J. M., Larcen, S. W., Lochman, J. E., & Sellinger, H. V. (1976). *Community psychology and the schools: A behaviorally oriented multilevel preventive approach.* Hillsdale, NJ: Lawrence Erlbaum Associates.

Anderson, R. H., & Snyder, K. J. (1982). *A meta-analysis of effective schooling research.* Tampa, FL: University of South Florida.

Baker, S., Swisher, J., Nadenichek, P., & Popowicz, C. (1984). Measured effects of primary prevention strategies. *Journal of College Student Personnel, 25,* 297-308.

Bandura, A. (1977). *Social learning theory.* Englewood Cliffs, NJ: Prentice-Hall.

Bash, M. A. (1978). *Think aloud classroom resource manual* (Grades 1-2). Denver, CO: Denver Public Schools.

Bash, M. S., & Camp, B. W. (1986). Teacher training in the think aloud classroom program. In G. Cartledge & J. F. Milburn (Eds.), *Teaching social skills to children: Innovative approaches* (2nd ed.), (pp. 187-218). New York: Pergamon.

Becker, W. C., & Armstrong, W. R. (1968). Production and elimination of disruptive classroom behavior by systematically varying teacher's behavior. *Journal of Applied Behavior Analysis, 1,* 35-45.

Berliner, D. C. (1985). Effective classroom teaching: The necessary but not sufficient condition for developing exemplary schools. In G. Austin & H. Garger (Eds.), *Research on exemplary schools.* New York: Academic.

Berliner, D. C. (1988). Effective classroom management and instruction: A knowledge base for consultation. In J. L. Graden, J. E. Zins, & M. J. Curtis (Eds.), *Alternative educational delivery systems: Enhancing instructional options for all students* (pp. 309-325). Washington, DC: National Association of School Psychologists.

Bernard, M. E., & Joyce, M. R. (1984). *Rationale-emotive therapy with children and adolescents: Theory, treatment strategies, preventative methods.* New York: Wiley.

Borg, W. R. (1975). Teacher classroom management skills and pupil behavior. *Journal of Experimental Education, 44,* 52-58.

Brophy, J. (1981). Teacher praise: A functional analysis. *Review of Educational Research, 51,* 5-32.

Brophy, J., & Everston, C. M. (1976). *Learning from teaching.* Boston: Allyn and Bacon.

Brophy, J., & Good, T. L. (1986). Teacher behavior and student achievement. In M. Wittrock (Ed.), *Handbook of research on teaching* (pp. 328-375). New York: Macmillan.

Camp, B. W., & Bash, M. A. (1978). *Think aloud group manual* (Rev. Ed.). Denver, CO: University of Colorado Medical Center.

Cartledge, G., & Milburn, J. F. (1986). *Teaching social skills to children: Innovative approaches* (2nd ed.). New York: Pergamon.

Charles, C. M. (1985). *Building classroom discipline: From models to practice* (2nd Ed.). New York: Longman.

Children's Defense Fund. (1988). *A call for action to make our nation safe for children: A briefing book on the status of American children in 1988.* Washington, DC: Author.

Cowen, E. L., Pederson, A., Babigian, H., Izzo, L. D., & Trost, M. A. (1973). Long-term follow-up of early detected vulnerable children. *Journal of Consulting and Clinical Psychology, 41,* 438-446..

Dawson, M. (1987). Beyond ability group: A review of the effectiveness of ability grouping and its alternatives. *School Psychology Review, 16,* 348-369.

Denham, C., & Lieberman, A. (Eds.). (1980). *Time to learn.* Washington, DC: National Institute of Education.

Elam, S. M. (1983). The Gallup education surveys: Impressions of a poll watcher. *Phi Delta Kappan, 65,* 26-32.

Elliott, S. N., Gresham, F. M., & Heffer, R. W. (1987). Social-skills interventions: Research findings and training techniques. In C. A. Maher & J. E. Zins (Eds.), *Psychoeducational interventions in the schools: Methods and procedures for enhancing student competence* (pp. 141-159). New York: Pergamon.

Ellis, A., & Bernard, M. E. (1983). *Rationale-emotive approaches to the problems of childhood.* New York: Plenum.

Gallup, G. H. (1983). Fifteenth annual Gallup Poll of the public attitudes toward the public schools. *Phi Delta Kappan, 65,* 33-47.

Gelfand, D., Ficula, T., & Zarbatany, L. (1986). Prevention of childhood behavior disorders. In B. Edelstein & L. Michelson (Eds.), *Handbook of prevention* (pp. 133-152). New York: Plenum.

Gesten, E. L., & Jason, L. A. (1987). Social and community interventions. *Annual Review of Psychology, 37,* 427-460.

Goldfried, M. R., & Davison, G. C. (1976). *Clinical behavior therapy.* New York: Holt, Rinehart, & Winston.

Goldstein, A. P., Sprafkin, R. P., Gershaw, N. J., & Klein, P. (1979). *Skillstreaming the adolescent: A structured learning approach to teaching prosocial behavior.* Champaign, IL: Research Press.

Goldstein, A. P., Sprafkin, R. P., Gershaw, N. J., & Klein, P. (1986). The adolescent: Social skills training through structured learning. In G. Cartledge & J. F. Milburn (Eds.), *Teaching social skills to children: Innovative approaches* (2nd ed.), (pp. 303-336). New York: Pergamon.

Graden, J. L., Zins, J. E., & Curtis, M. J. (Eds.). (1988). *Alternative educational delivery systems: Enhancing instructional options for all students.* Washington, DC: National Association of School Psychologists.

Greenwood, C. R., Hops, H., Delquardi, J., & Guild, J. (1974). Group contingencies for group consequences in classroom management: A further analysis. *Journal of Applied Behavior Analysis, 7,* 413-425.

Gresham, F. M. (1981). Social skills training with handicapped children: A review. *Review of Educational Research, 51,* 139-176.

Herman, S. H., & Traymontana, J. (1971). Instructions and group versus individual reinforcement in modifying disruptive group behavior. *Journal of Applied Behavior Analysis, 4,* 113-119.

Jason, L. A., Durlak, J., & Holton-Walker, E. (1984). Prevention of childhood problems in schools. In M. Roberts & L. Peterson (Eds.), *Prevention of problems in childhood* (pp. 311-341). New York: Wiley.

Jones, F. (1979). The gentle art of classroom discipline. *National Elementary Principal, 58,* 26-32.

Jones, R. S., & Tanner, L. N. (1981). Classroom discipline: The unclaimed legacy. *Phi Delta Kappan, 62,* 494-497.

Kendall, P. C., & Braswell, L. (1985). *Cognitive-behavioral therapy for impulsive children.* New York: Guilford.

Kerr, M. M., & Nelson, C. M. (1983). *Strategies for managing behavior problems in the classroom.* Columbus, OH: Merrill.

Knoff, H. M. (1984). A conceptual review of discipline in the schools: A consultation service delivery model. *Journal of School Psychology, 22,* 335-345.

Knoff, H. M. (1987). School-based interventions for discipline problems. In C. A. Maher & J. E. Zins (Eds.), *Psychoeducational interventions in the schools: Methods and procedures for enhancing student competence* (pp. 118-140). New York: Pergamon.

Knoff, H. M. (1988). Effective social interventions. In J. L. Graden, J. E. Zins, & M. J. Curtis (Eds.), *Alternative educational delivery systems: Enhancing instructional options for all students* (pp. 431-453). Washington, DC: National Association of School Psychologists.

Kounin, J. S. (1977). *Discipline and group management in classrooms.* Huntington, NY: Krieger Publishing.

Ladd, G. W., & Asher, S. R. (1985). Social skill training and children's peer relations. In L. L'Abate & M. A. Milan (Eds.), *Handbook of social skills training and research* (pp. 219-244). New York: Wiley.

Ladd, G. W., & Mize, J. (1983). A cognitive-social learning model of social-skill training. *Psychological Review, 90,* 127-157.

Mace, F. C., Brown, D. K., & West, B. J. (1987). Behavioral self-management in education. In C. A. Maher & J. E. Zins (Eds.), *Psychoeducational interventions in the schools: Methods and procedures for enhancing student competence* (pp. 160-176). New York: Pergamon.

Meichenbaum, D. (1977). *Cognitive-behavior modification: An integrative approach.* New York: Plenum.

Michelson, L., Suigai, D. P., Wood, R. P., & Kazdin, A. E. (1983). *Social skills assessment and training with children: An empirically based handbook.* New York: Plenum.

O'Leary, K. D., Kaufman, K. F., Kass, R. E., & Drabman, R. S. (1970). The effects of loud and soft reprimands on the behavior of disruptive students. *Exceptional Children, 37,* 145-155.

Paine, S. C., Radicchi, J., Rosellini, L. C., Deutchman, L., & Darch, C. B. (1983). *Structuring your classroom for academic success.* Champaign, IL: Research Press.

Shure, M. B., & Spivack, G. (1978). *Problem-solving techniques in childrearing*. San Francisco: Jossey-Bass.

Slaving, R. (1987). Grouping for instruction in the elementary school. *Educational Psychologist, 22*, 109-127.

Spivak, G., Platt, J. J., & Shure, M. B. (1976). *The problem-solving approach to adjustment: A guide to research and intervention*. San Francisco: Jossey-Bass.

Spivak, G., & Shure, M. B. (1974). *Social adjustment of young children: A cognitive approach to solving real-life problems*. San Francisco: Jossey-Bass.

Strain, P. S., Gurainick, M. J., & Walker, H. M. (Eds.) (1986). *Children's social behavior*. Orlando, FL: Academic.

Weissberg, R. P., Gesten, E. L., Leibenstein, N. L., Doherty-Schmid, K., & Hutton, H. (1980). *The Rochester social problem-solving (SPS) program: A training manual for teachers of 2nd-4th grade children*. Rochester, NY: University of Rochester.

Ysseldyke, J., & Christenson, S. (1987). *The instructional environment scale*. Austin, TX: Pro-Ed.

The School-Based Prevention of Childhood Crises

Jonathan Sandoval

University of California, Davis

SUMMARY. This paper sets forth the research on the school-based prevention of crises reactions to childhood stress. Four types of crises are considered: life transitions, traumatic events, developmental crises, and psychopathological crises. Each may be prevented by specific programs such as orientation programs for school entrance, informational programs to prevent child abuse, conflict resolution programs, and suicide prevention programs. General programs termed competence enhancement programs may address and ameliorate a variety of stressors. Prevention programs aimed at the entire school system are also discussed, including such activities as creating and supporting crisis response teams. Additionally, a number of issues for future study and research are identified.

Few children pass through the public schools without living through a time of crisis which disrupts their academic progress and causes concern on the part of their parents and teachers. Events such as divorce, the death of a loved one, moving to a new community, a serious illness, suicidal ideation, or peer conflicts are common among children and adolescents and frequently develop into crises (Sandoval, 1988a).

The effects of these events on the lives of children are well known, yet it has been only recently that school personnel have recognized and accepted their responsibility to work preventatively and intervene constructively in the lives of children. Previously,

---

Requests for reprints should be directed to: Jonathan Sandoval, Department of Education, College of Letters and Science, University of California at Davis, Davis, CA 95616.

© 1990 by The Haworth Press, Inc. All rights reserved.

mental health concerns were delegated to non-school personnel. However, currently special services providers recognize that the extremely disruptive nature of a crisis reaction on a child's learning cannot be ignored. Moreover, there is a reciprocal effect in that successful school adjustment often leads to a better resolution of crisis events on the part of the child. In addition, the school is the only institution left in our society where true preventative measures may be taken. Also, in many states, the community mental health system has gone bankrupt and there are few alternatives to school-based intervention. Fortunately, school staffs are now more willing than ever to address the needs that children may have for coping with potentially stressful life events. Special services providers must take leadership initiatives in this regard.

DEFINITION AND THEORY

The pioneering community psychiatrists who began the study of emotional crises, Donald C. Klein, Erich Lindemann, and Gerald Caplan, recognized that it was relatively difficult to predict which children or adults would experience a crisis reaction to a traumatic event. As a result, Klein and Lindemann (1961) made the distinction between an *emotionally hazardous situation* and a *crisis*. A hazardous situation, which can be determined relatively objectively, is any sudden change in an individual's social relationships that occurs as a result of a natural event or maturation. They use the term hazard to suggest that although individuals are at risk, many are able to negotiate the hazard to a safe resolution.

A crisis occurs when a person reacts to the hazard in a maladaptive way. The individual suffers an acute and prolonged disturbance that is associated with being unable to escape from the situation and being unable to use appropriate coping mechanisms or problem solving skills. Thus a crisis reaction is functionally related to children or adults not having the coping skills necessary to overcome the hazard.

Individuals in crisis are in a state of psychological disequilibrium (Caplan, 1964). They are temporarily out of balance because they cannot use customary problem solving resources and cannot escape from what is for them an emotionally significant problem, and there is a need to restore them to a previous level of functioning. Many have observed that it is possible to take advantage of the temporary disruption with the concomitant motivation for change to give the individual in crisis more skills resulting in a better overall adjustment following the crisis. The idea is that being in a crisis situation presents people with an opportunity to grow and change. There is, however, some debate as to whether or not this should be a goal of crisis counseling and intervention, (e.g., see Slaiku, 1984).

It is generally recognized that it is beyond the school's scope to prevent most hazards from occurring. In the process of considering how school staffs might prevent crises from developing, it is natural to turn to the current research and theory on stress and wellness (Selye, 1974). Hazardous events obviously may create stresses in individuals and crises result when stress exceeds a certain level, which may vary from person to person. Prevention efforts in the school, then, are most appropriately directed at providing coping skills as a general strategy for helping individuals prevent crisis reactions to stress.

Moos and Billings (1984) have suggested that coping skills may be classified into three domains, each with three specific skills. The first domain, *appraisal-focused coping* consists of skills which help the person to find meaning in and to understand the hazardous event. The skills are (a) *logical analysis and mental preparation*, (b) *cognitive redefinition or reframing*, and (c) *cognitive avoidance or denial*. Thus, when a hazardous event occurs, the child's first reaction may be to examine the event rationally, step by step, and prepare for what will probably happen next. Alternately, the child may reframe the hazard in a number of ways until a satisfactory understanding is achieved, or may keep all or part of the crisis at a distance until he or she is more able to attack it.

The second domain, *problem-focused coping*, consists of skills which help the person confront reality proactively and solve the problem created by the hazardous event. The skills are (a) *seeking information and support*, (b) *taking problem-solving action*, and (c) *identifying alternative rewards*. Given a hazardous event, the child may try to learn more about what is occurring and turn to others for help, may engage in problem solving, or seek out activities and relationships as a substitute source of satisfaction to those sources lost to the hazardous event.

The third domain, *emotion-focused coping*, consists of skills which enable the child to manage the feelings generated by the hazardous event and to maintain affective equilibrium. The skills are (a) *affective regulation*, (b) *emotional discharge*, and (c) *resigned acceptance*. A child may manage a hazardous situation by maintaining control of emotions, may vent them in a way that brings relief, or may learn to accept the situation with an appropriate sense of loss. As I will point out later, many preventative activities and programs are designed to activate, improve and contextualize (i.e., relate to a specific event) one or more of these nine skills.

This paper will be concerned with the prevention of crisis reactions, or efforts that are directed at the entire school population and thus are applicable for use in the regular classroom. The entire spectrum of crisis prevention, intervention and counseling has been covered in a separate volume (Sandoval, 1988a).

Two distinctions will be useful before reviewing prevention programs. Prevention efforts may be either macrosocial focused or microsocial or person focused (Conyne, Zins, & Vedder-Dubocq, 1988). Macrosocial approaches consist of efforts aimed at large scale social change that will alter the environment within which children function in the school. Changing the school organization is one macrosocial approach. Others include increasing school personnel's knowledge, and developing more effective system wide policies and procedures.

Microsocial or person-centered approaches aim at building competencies of children so that they may function more effectively in coping with situations that are hazardous. I will discuss microsocial approaches first and more specifically.

A second distinction is between direct and indirect prevention efforts. Direct efforts are those conducted with individual children in schools. They may be part of a teaching program, an advising program, or a counseling program. Indirect methods focus on those who work with children, usually teachers, administrators and parents, but could include school crossing guards, custodians, school secretaries, and bus drivers. Indirect methods consist of training, consciousness raising, consultation, and using the media. Macrosocial approaches are usually indirect, but not always.

Different types of crises may be distinguished from one another. Baldwin (1978) developed a very useful taxonomy which can be simplified to four crisis types when dealing with school-based situations. This paper will examine: (a) crises of life transitions, (b) crises associated with coping with traumatic stress, (c) developmental crises, and (d) psychopathological crises and emergencies. Within each of these four types are a variety of specific crises familiar to special services providers, and for which a number of regular classroom approaches exist. Many curricular approaches have been organized as direct programs for children but also have indirect prevention components consisting of teacher and parent awareness programs, screening, and consultation. Competency enhancement programs do not fit this taxonomy and will be discussed in a separate section.

FOUR TYPES OF CRISIS PREVENTION

Assisting with Life Transitions

Crises associated with life transitions are usually viewed by adults as normal and even to be looked forward to. Adults sometimes forget that the child often has little or no control over what is occurring and that the transition usually creates stress. The major transitions that children experience during the school years are entering school, moving from grade to grade, moving from one school or community to another, and even moving from one group to another within a classroom, or beginning a special education program. All these transitions may bring about disruption and disorientation but some result in a more serious crisis reaction.

A transition from one social status to another (e.g., from only child to sibling, from immature to sexually mature adolescent) may also cause a crisis. Other life transitional crises involving a change in status are the birth of a sibling, or in adolescence coping with dating and sexuality. Life transitions differ from other kinds of crises because the events are anticipated, but nevertheless can result in a child failing to cope effectively with the new demands.

The general approach to preventing crises associated with life transitions is to provide anticipatory guidance and support groups. Anticipatory guidance is a process of orienting a child, both intellectually and emotionally, to the new situation he or she will face. The coping skills fostered are logical analysis and mental preparation, seeking information and support, and affective regulation.

Orientation programs are fairly common for children entering school and making a transition from one school to another (e.g., elementary school to junior high school). School entry programs have been examined by Klein and Ross (1965), Signell (1976), and by Zins and Ponti (1985). Examples of school transition programs are reported by Bogat, Jones, and Jason (1980) and by Felner, Ginter, and Primavera (1982). Typically, these programs involve bringing the children and their parents into the classroom during an orientation meeting, so they may learn about the new environment. Peers have been used as orientators and models in many programs. In one study, a homeroom teacher was used to orient beginning high school students, and students were assigned to common core courses (Felner et al., 1982). Orientation programs may be scheduled far in advance of the transition or only days and weeks ahead of time. Materials have been developed for parents to assist them in preparing their children to deal with the new expectations and experiences. Important elements of the orientation program are to be sure that children understand the behavioral expectations of the new setting, and to anticipate new feelings that might be stimulated.

Moving to another community may represent an entirely different kind of problem because moves are often associated with other kinds of crises such as parental divorce. I have explored this problem in depth elsewhere (Sandoval, 1988b). Orientation programs alone may not be as successful as programs that include additional services such as tutoring designed to help children adjust to different curricular demands in the new environment (Pillen, Jason, & Olson, 1988).

Particularly for older children, programs may be developed that include support groups. The group setting allows children to explore fears and anxiety, as well as to gather specific factual information about the new setting that may be of interest or concern to them.

There is not a great deal of research on orientation programs in the literature. Those studies by Jason and his colleagues (Bogat et al., 1980; Jason & Bogat, 1983; Pillen et al., 1988) have been done on the somewhat unique population of parochial school children moving into public schools after the closure of the parochial school. Nevertheless, special services providers should be involved in the design, planning and execution of the programs that do exist at the school site, particularly, verifying to see that the affective component of the orientation program is handled adequately. Regular school personnel may be less comfortable in handling stoney emotional reactions and may welcome the assistance.

Coping with Traumatic Stress

Another category of hazards are traumatic events. These include externally imposed stressors such as the sudden death of a family member, a catastrophic illness, hospitalization, parental disablement, divorce, physical abuse, pregnancy, sexual assault, or even unexpected academic failure. The main feature of a traumatic event is that it is unexpected and outside of the child's control. As a result, children often feel overwhelmed emotionally and unable to marshall traditional coping mechanisms because of the unfamiliar situation and status in which they find themselves.

Most of these traumatic events are relatively rare or are considered to be outside the school's responsibility. However, the prevention of crises related to a number of potentially traumatic events has been attempted. Child abuse has been the subject of a number of curricular approaches in the schools. These programs are designed to help children avoid the situations where abuse may occur, or to report incidences of child abuse. Another set of curricular programs have been directed at accident prevention (Peterson, 1988), and the prevention of AIDS (Brooks-Gunn, Boyer, & Hein, 1988; Flora & Thoresen, 1988; Melton, 1988). Some schools have instituted units on death and dying (Thomas, 1984) which address prevalent feelings and attitudes toward death. Various programs have been developed on divorce and related problems that can affect children (e.g., Pedro-Carroll & Cowen, 1985). Most of these curricular approaches also include teacher and parent awareness programs, as well as instructional components.

Typical child sexual abuse prevention programs for children (see Tharinger, Krivacska, Laye-McDonough, Jamison, Vincent, & Hedlund, 1988, for a review) focus on definitions of sexual abuse in terms of improper touching. They teach concepts such as having the right to say "no" or taking action when abuse is attempted, having the right to control or own one's body, and trusting feelings or intuition to determine if touching is appropriate. Other assertiveness skills such as yelling and running away are often included in programs for younger children. Many programs contain elements devoted to secrets and the idea that some secrets need to be shared with caring adults. Children are assured that there is a support system available and that they are not responsible for abuse. These program elements are intended to promote disclosure of abuse. Abuse prevention programs are designed to contextualize appraisal-focused coping and problem-focused coping.

A natural method of introducing the topic of traumatic events and supplying children with models for how to cope with them is through bibliotherapy, or introducing appropriate books in English or reading classes. A number of excellent bibliographies exist on specific topics such as death (Wass, 1980), or on a whole host of topics (e.g., Fassler, 1978).

Many of the prevention programs teach the coping skills of logical analysis and mental preparation, but bibliotherapy has the potential to be particularly effective in assisting children gain problem-focused coping skills through modeling. To the extent that literature evokes emotion, reading about crises may assist in affective regulation. It is important to point out, however, that there is little evaluative research on bibliotherapy to verify its effectiveness. At present, this lack of data should service as a caution.

Because many of these traumatic crises are unusual and relatively rare and cannot be anticipated, consultation seems to be a major source of prevention. As consultants, special services providers can help teachers think creatively about specific children in their classrooms encountering traumatic situations so that teachers gain skills that will help them with other children. Consultants are able to help the teachers perceive how the child's problems may result from a reaction to the crisis and help the teacher develop ways of approaching and addressing the child's special needs during this time. During traumatic stress, it is usually important to eliminate other unrelated stressors on the child, thereby reducing the coping demands made on the children. When the children have developed appropriate coping strategies to deal with the problem, normal demands can be reinstituted.

The theory and research on prevention programs in the area of child abuse has brought to light a great deal of controversy about the effectiveness of prevention programs (see Tharinger et al., 1988, for a discussion). These controversies echo debates in the prevention of other traumatic crises. A number of researchers have pointed out that young children are unable to understand and retain the information presented to them on child abuse. Others believe that there are flaws in the studies that have brought this result to light. Another concern about child abuse prevention programs is that they have many unanticipated results. Critics charge they frighten children and or create anxiety rather than reducing it. Still other experts criticize these programs on the basis that they create the notion that children are responsible for preventing their own abuse, which is a rather difficult assumption to accept. A final criticism directed at child abuse prevention programs is that they do not take into account the developmental status of the children, and they isolate abuse from general developmental concerns. The programs stress verbal learning and do not allow children, for example, to use fantasy, play, or kinesthetic learning style (Kraizer, 1986). Tharinger et al. (1988), particularly, believe that child abuse programs also should address children's needs for information about sexuality, as well as abuse. As these issues are resolved in the child abuse literature, important implications may be drawn for other kinds of prevention programs.

Facilitating the Resolution of Developmental Crises

Developmental crises typically occur in adolescence when maturation brings into being a number of conflicts related to dependency, values, sexual identity, and relations with authority, related to the adolescent's quest to establish a personal identity. As the demands of adolescence are struggled with, a number of crises need to be resolved. These crises might involve conflicts with parents, conflicts with peers, and conflicts regarding sexuality, particularly homosexuality and promiscuity. Developmental crises are different from transition crises in that previous developmental resolutions of the challenges of earlier stages influence whether or not recent developmental changes become hazardous. For school aged children, Erikson (1962) describes the crisis of industry versus inferiority. The child's success in learning the culturally sanctioned activities of childhood (i.e., learning in school, sports, music, etc.), has positive mental health ramifications. A child who does not become competent in sanctioned areas encounters a number of hazards, and school failure often results in a crisis.

Developmental crises usually are handled by indirect programs which make parents and teachers aware of what is occurring in children, and developing various kinds of group activities where some of these developmental issues may be explored. Much of what is done, however, must focus on consultation both to the teachers and to the parents, as well as to programs, designed generally to facilitate children's achievement of competence. Programs focused on giving social skills or other kinds of general coping mechanisms can help them deal with various hazardous situations. These programs will be discussed in the section on competence enhancement.

Conflict resolution programs have been developed to manage a number of different kinds of hazardous events. These programs consist of training a cohort of student leaders (both elected and natural leaders, such as gang leaders) to manage a peer-run dispute resolution program. The conflict resolution team is taught listening and mediation skills and provided with authority, time, and space to negotiate: (a) conflicts between students or groups of students in a school, or (b) conflicts between teachers and students. The conflict resolution program usually functions as an alternative to the traditional disciplinary system operating in a school (i.e., being sent to the vice principal or dean). Many of these programs have been in place in schools for a long time but have not been rigorously researched or evaluated. The special services provider must evaluate carefully any such programs undertaken.

Anticipating Psychopathological Crises

A final category of crises spring from hazards that may be internal or external in origin but result in extremely devastating crises and the child may at some point be institutionalized. Individuals experiencing a pathological crisis or emergency are often a danger to themselves or others and it is the pervasive and life-threatening nature of these crises that sets them apart from other crises. External circumstances that may result in such a crisis are the availability of drugs or alcohol in a community or abnormal social disorganization in the environment such as the existence of antisocial gangs. Internal hazards may be those that result in psychopathology, such as, the existence of depression, which may lead to the crisis of suicidal ideation and action.

In typical suicide prevention programs for adolescents, school personnel and parents are taught the behavioral warning signs that a person is contemplating suicide (Davis, Sandoval, & Wilson, 1988). These warning signs are embedded in a general informational program that highlights a number of myths as well as facts about suicide. Suicide is usually placed in the context of a maladaptive response to adolescent stress. Program participants also receive assistance in gaining listening skills and are informed about local resources to help suicidal individuals. An important component is how to get professional help for suicidal students. Unlike drug education or AIDS education, students are not taught assertive behavior to avoid certain risky situations. The focus of suicide prevention is on creating an informed community of peers and adults who can intervene early with suicidal youth.

Both drug abuse and suicide have been the subject of a number of curricular approaches in the schools (e.g., Davis et al., 1988; Rhodes & Jason, 1988). Both of these areas of education are fraught with controversy, and many of the issues are similar to those surrounding the sexual abuse prevention literature. For example, critics such as Shaffer, Garland, and Bacon (1987) claim suicide prevention programs may reach only those who are not in the need of the program, do not teach new concepts, and may have unanticipated, negative outcomes. An alternative to traditional prevention programs are competence enhancement approaches which are intended to prevent both drug abuse and suicide. The belief is that giving children various coping skills will enable them to move into paths that do not lead to drugs or the kind of isolation and depression that may result in suicide. Competence enhancement programs are discussed below.

COMPETENCE ENHANCEMENT PROGRAMS

School-based programs are beginning to appear that have as their goals the improvement of children's social and coping skills, in general, not in relation to any particular hazardous event (e.g., Matson & Ollendick, 1988; Meichenbaum, 1985). This general class of programs has been termed competence enhancement (Cowen, 1985). The name reflects the hope that the skills taught will lead to greater adaptability in future coping with stressful as well as nonstressful events. Examples of competence enhancement programs are Spivack and Shure's Interpersonal Cognitive Problem-Solving (1974), Elias' Improving Social Awareness—Social Problem-Solving (Elias, Gara, Ubriaco, Rothbaum, Clabby, & Schuyler, 1986), Gesten and Weissberg's Social Problem-Solving Training, (Gesten, Weissberg, Amish, & Smith, 1987), and Botvin's Life Skills Training (Botvin, 1983; Botvin & Dusenbury, 1987), although this last program is tied to preventing drug abuse. These skills based programs combine didactic training along with role playing and simulation to establish specific positive habits and dispositions.

One might argue that general social studies curricula or even mathematics curricula directed at intellectual problem solving, such as those developed by Hilda Taba or even John Dewey, although oriented largely at cognitive and broader social problems, supply skills that might help a child through a hazardous situation. The special services provider's role is to support teachers in implementing these curricula and helping students transfer approaches from the classroom to everyday life.

The major research issue in competency enhancement programs is transfer. Not only is there a question as to whether the skills taught generalize to new situations and to crises in particular, but there is a question about whether the knowledge and attitudes taught actually transfer to behaviors of any kind. This problem has been addressed in many program evaluations by the use of simulation, but the question remains of how much behavioral change occurs over time and situation.

SYSTEM FOCUSED PREVENTION

All of the types of crises addressed by individually focused prevention can also be prevented by efforts that are directed at the school as a system and at the community at large. One activity that is particularly important is helping schools develop policies to deal with various kinds of crises. Examples of model policies in the prevention of adolescent suicide have been reported by Davis et al. (1988). For traumatic crises in particular, it is useful to have already created a commitment among school district staff to deal with various kinds of crises. This commitment might manifest itself in such activities as staff and parent awareness programs and recognizing the prevention of crisis as a district and community priority.

Special services providers in non-school roles, (e.g., parent, concerned citizen, elected official), may also work for social change. Change activities directed at the social conditions which produce stresses on individuals, families, and schools cannot help but be preventative. Germain (1988) has written persuasively on the need for child abuse prevention on this level, and Ross-Reynolds (1988) has discussed social change activities that could make an adolescent's self discovery of homosexuality less traumatic. The advocacy model of school psychology (Sandoval, 1986) encompasses such activities.

Besides the societal or community level, program development at the school level can be preventative of many crises. Instituting stress reduction programs, providing administrative consultation and implementing the results of the new school leadership research are places to start. One program that illustrates how environmental changes in the public school can result in better student coping is Comer's (1985) Yale-New Haven Primary Prevention Project. In this project, the children showed academic gains and social progress in a school where governance was improved by means of: (a) community input, (b) parent participation, and (c) increasing the sophistication and knowledge of the school staff.

Creating Crisis Response Teams

Creation of crisis response teams at a district wide or even a school wide level are becoming widespread. These response teams are made up of individuals with special expertise or experience who can help with particular kinds of hazardous situations. Each member of the team has a different role and function. For example, in preparing secondary schools to cope with suicide among the campus community, such roles as contacting the police, dealing with the media, answering questions from students and forming support groups all may be delineated. Members of a crisis team need not come from the school system. Clergy members or mental health practitioners in non-school settings can participate effectively if contacted in advance and if team planning meetings are routinely held in advance of need. Such response teams are particularly helpful for traumatic crises and psychiatric emergencies, such as the murder of a teacher or a student's psychotic episode at school.

Support for Personnel Managing Crises

In addition to creating teams, it is important to recognize that teachers and other educational personnel will experience a certain amount of stress while dealing with children and families in crisis. School personnel, too, will need consultation and other support, including the reduction of stressors acting on them as they deal with very sensitive issues and problems. A very important role for school special services providers will be "backing up" teachers, administrators, parents and peers who are working directly with students in crisis, but the special services provider will need back up also, and this should be planned in advance.

RESEARCH NEEDS

There are a number of difficulties in conducting research on crisis prevention. These have been most frequently highlighted in the efforts at preventing child abuse, drug abuse, and suicide. There are conceptual problems, economic considerations, and design and statistical issues. Among the conceptual difficulties are deciding whether or not prevention should be aimed at the specific hazard in question or should be directed at providing children with more general coping skills. Another general conceptual problem is what should the outcomes be. Should they be knowledge or behavior? Should the behavior change be directed at the child in crisis or at the peers and adults in contact with that child?

Economic considerations include the cost of providing programs to deal with rare events, and finding room in an exceedingly crowded curriculum. If a topic is added to a curriculum, what should be dropped? Given that only a fixed amount of time is available for instruction, which curricular topics should be dropped in favor of a suicide or drug prevention program?

Design and statistical issues center around having adequate control groups, randomization of subjects to groups, and the fact that, in many cases, crises are rather rare events. In California, for example, legislators specified that suicide prevention programs should be evaluated by a reduction in suicides. This stringent requirement proved difficult to meet, given the rare nature of well-documented, completed suicides. The legislators were skeptical even though documentation of consumer satisfaction and increases in referral rates suggested the programs were effective.

CONCLUSION

This paper has only skimmed the surface of the problems and prospects of crisis prevention in the regular classroom. Table 1 summarizes the features of various crisis prevention programs operational in the schools. There are a number of issues *still* unresolved, but school personnel can be effective in promoting school wide and district wide policies and programs aimed at helping children. Children can continue to learn effectively in the classroom even though they may be experiencing a crisis in their lives.

TABLE 1

Guidelines for Four Types of Crisis Prevention Programs

CRISIS TYPE	PROGRAM ELEMENTS	FEATURED COPING SKILLS
Life Transitions	Information for child Anticipation of positive and negative consequences Creation of sense of community	Appraisal-focused
Traumatic Stress	Information for child and caregivers Practice avoidance behavior Provide models System preparedness	Appraisal-focused Emotion-focused
Developmental	Developmental information for caregivers Consultation Develop peer networks	Problem-focused
Pathological	Information for peers, parents, caregivers Practice avoidance behaviors Practice getting help Create peer identifiers	Problem-focused

REFERENCES

Baldwin, B. A. (1978). A paradigm for the classification of emotional crises: Implications for crisis intervention. *American Journal of Orthopsychiatry, 48,* 538-551.

Bogat, C. A., Jones, J. W., & Jason, L. A. (1980). School transitions: Preventative intervention following an elementary school closing. *Journal of Community Psychology, 8,* 343-352.

Botvin, G. J. (1983). *Life skills training.* New York: Smithfield Press.

Botvin, G. J., & Dusenbury, L. (1987). Life skills training: A psychoeducational approach to substance-abuse prevention. In C. A. Maher, & J. E. Zins, *Psychoeducational interventions in the schools* (pp. 46-65). New York: Pergamon.

Brooks-Gunn, J., Boyer, C. B., & Hein, K. (1988). Preventing HIV infection and AIDS in children and adolescents. *American Psychologist, 43,* 958-964.

Caplan, G. (1964). *Principles of preventative psychiatry.* New York: Basic Books.

Comer, J. (1985). The Yale-New Haven primary prevention project: A follow-up study. *Journal of the American Academy of Child Psychiatry, 24,* 154-160.

Conyne, R. K., Zins, J. E., & Vedder-Dubocq, S. (1988). Primary prevention in the schools: Methods for enhancing student competence. In J. Graden, J. E. Zins, & M. J. Curtis (Eds.), *Alternative educational delivery systems: Enhancing instructional options for all students.* Washington, DC: National Association of School Psychologists.

Cowen, E. (1985). Person-centered approaches to primary prevention in mental health: Situation-focused and competence-enhancement. *American Journal of Community Psychology, 13,* 31-49.

Davis, J. M., Sandoval, J., & Wilson, M. P. (1988). Strategies for the primary prevention of adolescent suicide. *School Psychology Review, 17,* 559-569.

Elias, M. J., Gara, M., Ubriaco, M., Rothbaum, P. A., Clabby, J. F., & Schuyler, T. (1986). Impact of a preventive social problem solving intervention on children's coping with middle-school stressors. *American Journal of Community Psychology, 14,* 259-275.

Erikson, E. (1962). *Childhood and society* (2nd ed.). New York: W. W. Norton.

Fassler, J. (1978). *Helping children cope.* New York: The Free Press.

Felner, R. D., Ginter, M., & Primavera, J. (1982). Primary prevention during school transitions: Social support and environmental structure. *American Journal of Community Psychology, 10,* 277-290.

Flora, J. A., & Thoresen, C. E. (1988). Reducing the risk of AIDS in adolescents. *American Psychologist, 43,* 965-970.

Germain, R. B. (1988). Maltreatment of children. In J. Sandoval (Ed.), *Crisis counseling, intervention and prevention in the schools* (pp. 73-92). Hillsdale, NJ: Lawrence Erlbaum Associates.

Gesten, E. L., Weissberg, R. P., Amish, P. L., & Smith, J. K. (1987). Social problem-solving training: A skills-based approach to prevention and treatment.

In C. A. Maher, & J. E. Zins, *Psychoeducational interventions in the schools* (pp. 26-45). New York: Pergamon.

Jason, L. A., & Bogat, G. A. (1983). Evaluating a preventive orientation program. *Journal of Social Science Research, 7,* 39-49.

Klein, D. C., & Lindemann, E. (1961). Preventive intervention in individual and family crisis situations. In G. Caplan (Ed.), *Prevention of mental disorders in children* (pp. 283-306). New York: Basic Books.

Klein, D. C., & Ross, A. (1965). Kindergarten entry: A study of role transition. In H. J. Parad (Ed.), *Crisis intervention: Selected readings.* New York: Family Service Association.

Krazier, S. K. (1986). Rethinking prevention. *Child Abuse and Neglect, 10,* 259-261.

Matson, J. L., & Ollendick, T. H. (1988). *Enhancing children's social skills.* New York: Pergamon Press.

Meichenbaum, D. (1985). *Stress inoculation training.* New York: Pergamon Press.

Melton, G. B. (1988). Adolescents and prevention of AIDS. *Professional Psychology: Research and Practice, 19,* 403-408.

Moos, R., & Billings, A. (1984). Conceptualizing and measuring coping resources and processes. In L. Goldberger & S. Breznitz (Eds.), *Handbook of stress: Theoretical and clinical aspects* (pp. 109-145). New York: Macmillan.

Pedro-Carroll, J. L., & Cowen, E. (1985). The children of divorce intervention program: An investigation of the efficacy of a school-based prevention program. *Journal of Consulting and Clinical Psychology, 14,* 277-290.

Peterson, L. (1988). Preventing the leading killer of children: The role of the school psychologist in injury prevention. *School Psychology Review, 17,* 593-600.

Pillen, B. L., Jason, L. A., & Olson, T. (1988). The effects of gender on the transition of transfer students into a new school. *Psychology in the Schools, 25,* 187-194.

Rhodes, J. E., & Jason, L. A. (1988). *Preventing substance abuse among children and adolescents.* New York: Pergamon.

Ross-Reynolds, G. (1988). Intervention with the homosexual adolescent. In J. Sandoval (Ed.), *Crisis counseling, intervention and prevention in the schools* (pp. 219-238). Hillsdale, NJ: Lawrence Erlbaum Associates.

Sandoval, J. (1986). Models of school psychological service delivery. In S. N. Elliott & J. C. Witt, *The delivery of psychological services in schools* (pp. 139-169). Hillsdale, NJ: Lawrence Erlbaum Associates.

Sandoval, J. (Ed.) (1988a). *Crisis counseling, intervention, and prevention in the schools.* Hillsdale, NJ: Lawrence Erlbaum Associates.

Sandoval, J. (1988b). Children and moving. In J. Sandoval (Ed.), *Crisis counseling, intervention and prevention in the schools* (pp. 151-162). Hillsdale, NJ: Lawrence Erlbaum Associates.

Selye, H. (1974). *Stress without distress.* New York: The New American Library.

Shaffer, D., Garland, A., & Bacon, K. (1987). *Prevention issues in youth sui-*

cide. Report prepared for Project Prevention, American Academy of Child and Adolescent Psychiatry. New York: Adolescent Study Unit, College of Physicians and Surgeons of Columbia University.

Signell, K. A. (1976). Kindergarten entry. A preventive approach to community mental health. In R. H. Moos (Ed.), *Human adaptation* (pp. 37-48). Lexington, MA: D. C. Heath.

Slaiku, K. A. (1984). *Crisis intervention. A handbook for practice and research*. Boston: Allyn and Bacon.

Spivack, G., & Shure, M. B. (1974). *Social adjustment of young children: A cognitive approach to solving real-life problems*. San Francisco: Jossey-Bass.

Tharinger, D. J., Krivacska, J. J., Laye-McDonough, M., Jamison, L., Vincent, G. G., & Hedlund, A. D. (1988). Prevention of child sexual abuse: An analysis of issues, educational programs, and research findings. *School Psychology Review, 17*, 614-634.

Thomas, J. L. (Ed.). (1984). *Death and dying in the classroom: Reading for life*. Phoenix, AZ: Ornyx Press.

Wass, H. (1980). *Death education: An annotated resource guide*. Washington: Hemisphere.

Zins, J E., & Ponti, C. R. (1985). Strategies for enhancing child and adolescent mental health. In J. E. Zins, D. I. Wagner & C. A. Maher (Eds.), *Health promotion in the schools: Innovative approaches to facilitating physical and emotional well-being* (pp. 49-60). New York: The Haworth Press.

Reducing Academic Related Anxiety

Thomas J. Huberty

Indiana University

SUMMARY. This paper discusses anxiety from psychological and educational perspectives, with emphasis upon developing and implementing interventions in school settings. Definitions and characteristics of anxiety are presented, followed by discussion of anxiety as a problem in academic and personal-social functioning. Discussion occurs about identification, assessment, and the development of specific intervention techniques. Included are suggestions of how special services providers can assist in working with academic related anxiety in regular and special education.

Anxiety is experienced by every person at each stage in life and for many reasons. It can occur in a variety of settings, be elicited by a number of stimuli, and can have one of several effects on a person's behavior and task performance. Anxiety is a normal and often useful reaction in many situations. The definition of anxiety has not received consensus, however. Kratochwill and Morris (1985) suggest that "the terms 'fear,' 'phobia,' and 'anxiety' have been used in a variety of ways across and within behavioral models" (p. 95), leading to some inconsistency in the definition of the term "anxiety." The most popular distinction among these terms is that fears and phobias are reactions to specific objects and situations, whereas anxiety is more likely to be reported as a subjective, internalized state (e.g., Jersild, 1954). Johnson and Melamed (1979) refer to anxiety as "apprehension without apparent cause."

Requests for reprints should be directed to: Thomas J. Huberty, Institute for Child Study, Indiana University, Bloomington, IN 47408.

© 1990 by The Haworth Press, Inc. All rights reserved.

TRAIT AND STATE ANXIETY

Cattell (1966) and Cattell and Schier (1963) proposed that *trait anxiety* and *state anxiety* occur in both children and adults. *Trait anxiety* is defined as a relatively stable tendency to respond with anxiety across a variety of situations. Persons considered to have a high level of trait anxiety are more likely to perceive situations as potentially dangerous or threatening than are most people. *State anxiety* is more likely to be manifested in specific situations, such as taking tests, and are not necessarily reported by persons with high trait anxiety. Consequently, for some children, anxiety may be associated with a specific situation, whereas for other children, it may be more pervasive and require different assessment and intervention approaches.

INDICATORS OF ANXIETY

Because anxiety is considered to have an internalized component (Werry, 1986), it cannot be directly observed. Werry (1986) divides anxiety symptoms into four categories: subjective, physiological, behavioral, and cognitive. *Subjective* symptoms are not observable and must be obtained either by the child's statements or responses to self-report scales and questionnaires. *Physiological* symptoms that occur most often in children are recurrent, non-specific stomach pains, tics, and enuresis. *Behavioral* symptoms include motor restlessness, facial expressions of anxiety, and compulsive and escape-avoidance behavior (e.g., school refusal). *Cognitive* symptoms include inattention, distractibility, academic failure, and poor memory.

The presence of anxiety is inferred by observations of overt behavior and by reports from the individual. Overt behavioral manifestations

> ... may include distractibility, impulsive acts, inattention to schoolwork, excessive movement, problems either in getting to sleep or staying asleep, "sweaty" hands and skin, heart palpitations, rapid breathing, nausea, headaches, stomach aches, and unusual fatigue. In extreme reactions, actual flight

from the anxiety-producing situation or physical immobility might occur. (Huberty, 1987, p. 46)

Verbal statements or responses to self-report anxiety questionnaires or scales by anxious individuals may include difficulties with concentration, excessive worry about present or future events, memory difficulties, varying degrees of unhappiness, frustration, discomfort in family or social relationships, or expectations of negative outcomes.

WHEN ANXIETY BECOMES PROBLEMATIC

Any behavior can become problematic under any of the following conditions: (a) when the frequency, intensity, or duration of the behavior is of such magnitude that interference with the normal functioning of the individual occurs, (b) when the behavior manifested is characteristic of an earlier developmental level and is contributing to current problems, (c) when the behavior is an inappropriate and ineffective alternative to more adaptive and appropriate behavior, (d) when the behavior is inappropriate for the setting and circumstances, or (e) when the behavior is pervasive and contributes to the overall maladaptive functioning of the person. Any of these conditions may cause concern and indicate the need for intervention in school, family, or social settings. It is incumbent upon potential interveners to determine the nature of the problems and the appropriate courses of action. "Chronic anxiety, left unidentified and untreated, could lead to disabling effects such as deterioration in cognitive performance, physical ailments, substance abuse, and in extreme situations, suicidal or homicidal reactions" (Argulewicz & Miller, 1985).

TYPES OF ANXIETY DISORDERS

There are three types of anxiety disorders commonly associated with children, according to the American Psychiatric Association's *Diagnostic and Statistical Manual of Mental Disorders — Third Edition, Revised (DSM-III-R)*, (American Psychiatric Association, 1987). The three types are *separation anxiety disorder* characterized by anxiety when a child is separated from "major attachment figures" (usually parents) and avoids being away from home and parents; *overanxious disorder*, characterized by excessive worry about future events, such as examinations, injury, meeting the expectations of others, oversensitivity to others' attitudes, or somatic complaints; and *avoidant disorder*, characterized by excessive avoidance of new persons, strangers, or events, and tendencies to cling to familiar persons. The significant aspects of these disorders are that they are pervasive and affect many areas of the child's life and are in excess of expected developmental patterns in terms of intensity, frequency, and duration.

ANXIETY AND SCHOOL PERFORMANCE

Anxiety has been studied concerning its relationships to academic achievement and the establishment and maintenance of social relationships. There is much research on social anxiety, test anxiety, and relationships to academic performance. Some examples of this research follow.

Social anxiety is a phenomenon often reported by children, particularly in the adolescent years. Social anxiety, however, may not be easily distinguishable from other manifestations of anxiety, such as social withdrawal. Typically, children who experience social anxiety want to be involved with others, but, for a variety of reasons, feel uncomfortable. They have interests in being with others, but are unable to compete effectively, are abnormally unassertive, or exhibit inappropriate behavior in social situations. Rogers (1972) suggests that adolescents who demonstrate social anxiety are socially oriented, show a fear of being ostracized, have low self-confidence, and are unusually shy. Bamber (1977, 1979) also found fear of social rejection to be prevalent in a sample of Northern Ireland adolescents. It may be that students who experience social anxiety may also have some social skills deficits that prevent them from emitting the appropriate behavior under particular circumstances.

Much research has been conducted about *test anxiety*. Sarason (Sarason, Davidson, Lighthall, Waite, & Ruebush, 1960) first addressed the concept of test anxiety in children. He viewed it from a psychoanalytic perspective as beginning in the preschool years and resulting from a fear of rejection by parents who had unreasonably high expectations for the child's achievement. If the child became afraid of failure, repression of aggressive and hostile impulses were substituted with dependency, anxiety, and low self-esteem. Other studies have suggested that test anxiety is more adquately conceptualized from motivation, social learning, and attention problem perspectives (Hill, 1972; Nottleman & Hill, 1977; Wine, 1971).

School phobia is an anxiety-related problem about which much has been written, but only occurs in about 1.7% of school-aged children (Kennedy, 1965). The child showing school phobia resists going to school, despite no obvious reasons to be afraid. School phobia is distinguished from separation anxiety by the nature of the child's relationship to the parent. If the child refuses to go to school, even when accompanied by the parent, it may be labeled simple school phobia. When separation anxiety occurs, the child may accompany the parent to school, but then show anxiety or fear when separated from the parent (Wielkiewicz, 1986).

Relationship to Learning and Performance

Several studies have indicated that anxiety can have negative effects on problem-solving and school performance. Anxiety has a debilitating effect on school performance from grades one through five and high-anxiety children are more likely to receive lower grades and to be retained in a grade (Hill & Sarason, 1966). Specifically how anxiety affects performance has been the subject of several studies. Hill (1972) and Wine (1971) have suggested that anxiety experienced in testing situations may interfere with the child's ability to properly direct attention toward tasks. Anxious children are more likely to demonstrate off-task behavior (Nottleman & Hill, 1977), are more easily distracted (Dusek, Mergler, & Kermis, 1976), and perform better when given training in memory-related problem-solving strategies (Stevenson & Odom, 1965). Sarason (1975) interprets these types of findings to indicate that the child tends to worry about performance, leading to distractibility and negative self-evaluations that affect problem-solving. Reynolds and Paget (1983) suggest that anxiety can affect a person's selection of the best problem-solving strategies and thereby contribute to lowered performance and achievement.

INTERVENTIONS WITH ANXIOUS STUDENTS

Knowing when and how to intervene with a child experiencing anxiety is not always evident. Intervention is indicated when anxiety occurs under any of the following conditions: (a) when it occurs in situations where anxiety typically is not expected; (b) when its frequency, intensity, or duration is excessive for the situation; (c) when it is not expected based upon the person's age and/or developmental status; or (d) when it causes behavioral or performance problems for a person. It also is important to consider whether anxiety is the primary problem or whether it is secondary to another problem (e.g., depression). If it is secondary to another problem, then the situation must be assessed and different treatment must be considered. For example, if the child's primary problem is depression and anxiety is merely an accompaniment, it will be necessary to evaluate the family, school, and possibly medical factors.

Interventions with students who might have anxiety-related problems require four components: (a) identification of students who might either demonstrate anxiety or be at risk to develop it, (b) assessment of students who have been identified as demonstrating anxiety, (c) development of an appropriate intervention plan, and (d) implementation of an intervention plan.

Identification of Anxious Students

In addition to the characteristics of anxiety indicated above, there are some "early warning signs" that may be of value when attempting to identify students who may be experiencing anxiety. These signs are:

1. Significant problems with interpersonal relationships
2. Excessive withdrawal and/or shyness
3. Low academic achievement
4. Achievement not consistent with ability
5. Presence of handicapping conditions
6. Experiencing extreme out of school stress

7. Few or no friends
8. Developmental immaturity
9. Excessive absences or tardiness at school
10. Physical complaints or symptoms
11. Signs of stress, such as crying
12. Problems with concentration, memory, and following directions
13. Inconsistent or erratic school performance
14. Distractibility, inattentiveness, and impulsiveness
15. Speech difficulties (e.g., rapid speech, articulation errors)
16. Social skills deficits
17. Recent traumatic events (e.g., divorce, death of parent)
18. Excessive fears of objects and situations

Special services providers can be very instrumental in the identification of anxious students. By being aware of the indicators of anxiety, they will be in a position to assist regular and special class teachers to identify anxious students. Anxiety is not easily identified by untrained persons, and may be equated with inattentiveness, distractibility, withdrawal, or any of a number of other behaviors. At the early screening and identification phase, special services providers can do any or all of the following: (a) observe children in classrooms and note anxious behaviors of the students, (b) provide informal consultation to teachers about children suspected of being anxious, (c) provide or participate in inservice training about the nature of anxiety and its potential effects upon academic and social functioning, and (d) provide teachers with information so that they are better able to identify the anxious student.

Assessment of Anxiety

Any intervention requires a thorough and systematic assessment of the behaviors of concern and should consist of multi-method, multi-source, and multi-setting approaches. A variety of methods have been used to assess anxiety in children, such as projective techniques, objective personality inventories, self-report measures, behavior rating scales, interviews, and direct behavioral assessment. All of these methods have advantages and disadvantages, and it is not possible to review all of them here. The most useful methods for assessing academic related anxiety in children are behavior rating scales, self-report anxiety scales, and direct behavioral assessment.

Behavior Rating Scales

The two most well-researched behavior rating scales that contain anxiety scales are the Revised Behavior Problem Checklist (Quay & Peterson, 1983) and the Child Behavior Checklist (CBCL) (Achenbach & Edelbrock, 1983). Both scales have adequate reliability and validity. The CBCL has the added advantage of being useful from age 2 through 16 and usually is completed by a parent. It also has forms for teacher reports from age 6 through 16, which allows for comparisons across raters and settings, as well as a youth self-report form. Although behavior rating scales may provide important information about anxiety, they typically are "trait" measures and may not accurately reflect the type and degree of anxiety that a child experiences in a particular situation. Consequently, they may not be very useful as outcome measures.

Self-Report Measures

One of the most reliable and valid self-report measures is the Revised Children's Manifest Anxiety Scale (Reynolds & Richmond, 1978), a revision of the Children's Manifest Anxiety Scale (Castenada, McCandless, & Palermo, 1956). The scale is essentially a trait measure and has three factors: social/concentration problems, physiological anxiety, and worry/oversensitivity, plus a lie scale. The Children's Anxiety Scale (Gillis, 1980) contains 20 items that assess global trait anxiety, and has adequate reliability. Another scale is the State-Trait Anxiety Scale for Children (Spielberger, 1973), but it should be used as a research instrument at this time. These and other self-report measures may be helpful in obtaining information about the subjective stress that a child is experiencing, a procedure recommended by Kratochwill and Morris (1985). Many self-report scales are prone to the effects of the response style of the child, however, and may not always be accurate measures of the child's subjective state. Reynolds and Paget (1983) speculate, for example, that younger children may tend to "yea say" and report higher levels of anxiety than they experience. Thus, although self-report measures may be helpful in assessment of anxiety, literal interpretation of the scores and individual items should be done with caution.

Direct Behavioral Assessment

Although many authors (e.g., Mash & Terdal, 1981) consider assessment methods such as behavior rating scales to be a part of behavioral assessment, this section refers to the direct measurement of behavior, using methods such as self-monitoring and observation. These methods are relatively easy to implement, are reliable and valid, and facilitate the measurement of outcomes (Kratochwill & Morris, 1985). If one is interested in using behavioral assessment methods to differentiate anxiety from fear, the effort becomes problematic because of the overlap of similar behavioral manifestations. Moreover, anxiety is conceptualized as having a subjective component, and these internal states are not amenable to direct behavioral assessment. Nevertheless, many of the methods used to assess fears can be adapted to assess anxiety.

To conduct direct behavioral assessment, the target behaviors must be identified and delineated in specific terms so that they can be readily observed and recorded. For example, if an "anxious" behavior is "cannot concentrate on classwork," then direct behavioral assessment might include the child or observer recording the number of times the child does not attend to assigned tasks. Another approach might be to record how long the child remains off-task during one of the periods when concentration is problematic. In most situations, frequency or duration recording can be used to collect baseline data of the behaviors. Another useful method is to compile a list of behaviors presumed to reflect anxiety, put the child in a situation where the behaviors might be observed, and record the frequency or duration of their occurrence. The list of behaviors can be based upon those identified above (early warning signs) or upon those that are of particular concern.

A useful adjunct to observation of the identified child is the use of peer normative comparisons, whereby one or more other children in the same setting are observed for the same behaviors. Frequency or duration recording is used for the same behavior for all children observed and the results are compared. If the identified child's baseline rates are significantly higher than those of the peer(s), anxiety-related problems may be present. Conversely, if the baseline rates are high but comparable across children, there might be contingencies in the settings that are maintaining the behaviors. If all baselines are low (including the identified child), suggesting that the reported problem behavior is not as severe as indicated, then the source of the referral should be more thoroughly evaluated (e.g., the teacher). It may be necessary to return to the problem identification stage in order to better understand and assess the situation.

A method that may be helpful in evaluating the individual subjective component of anxiety involves self-reporting and recording of feelings of anxiety. If subjective feelings can be made sufficiently specific to the point that the child can identify them, such as how often s/he experiences anxiety about taking a test, these feelings could be recorded by the student on a card or sheet of paper. A measure of intensity also could be developed, such as a five-point rating scale with "1" indicating that a minimal amount of anxiety was experienced to a "5," indicating that the anxiety was so severe that trembling occurred. A variety of scales with descriptors could be developed. Baseline data can be collected on frequency and intensity in this manner that can be useful in monitoring and evaluating the outcomes of intervention. The success of this approach is dependent upon the child's ability and willingness to identify and record the anxious experiences.

Special services providers can be particularly helpful in both regular and special classes when evaluating students suspected of experiencing anxiety. Many of the behavior rating scales and self-report scales require training for interpretation, as does direct behavioral assessment. Identification of problematic behaviors, observation, recording, peer normative comparisons, and monitoring of behaviors can be done effectively by special services providers. The ultimate goal of direct behavioral assessment is to define the behaviors and to obtain accurate baseline data.

Specific Interventions

The most effective intervention methods for fears and anxiety are those broadly defined as behavioral approaches. Morris and Kratochwill (1985) identify five major types of behavioral techniques for fear reduction that can be used with anxiety-related problems: systematic desensitization, flooding, contingency management, modeling, and self-control. It is not possible to review all of the techniques here, and many of them require extensive specialized training and also are not practical to use in school settings (e.g., flooding). Also, few of these techniques have been researched extensively with children; thus, empirical evidence for their effectiveness is essentially unknown for large groups of children. Nevertheless, these methods may be effective for individual children. The following discussion will focus upon those techniques that are most appropriate for problems likely to occur in school, and can be implemented by special services providers.

Systematic desensitization is a counterconditioning technique that involves first identifying the anxiety problem situation and then developing a hierarchy of situations that differ in the degree to which they elicit the anxiety. The hierarchy is developed by identifying the situation which produces the highest level of anxiety. This situation is placed at the top of the hierarchy and the next least anxiety-producing situation is identified. Ultimately the hierarchy consists of several steps ranging from little or no anxiety at the bottom to the most anxiety-producing step at the top. Once the hierarchy is established, then the student is taught to relax. With the student in a relaxed state, a counselor orally presents the lowest step on the hierarchy. When anxiety generated by the step is no longer present, then the next step is presented. The sequence continues until the student expresses no anxiety about the situation represented by the highest step on the hierarchy. The entire intervention may require several sessions, including any necessary revisions of the hierarchy.

An example of a hierarchy for a student experiencing test anxiety might include the following (9 = highest anxiety, 1 = lowest anxiety):

9. Inability to write responses
8. Picking up the pencil to write responses
7. Reading the instructions
6. Opening the test booklet
5. Sitting at the desk
4. Walking to the desk
3. Entering the room
2. Walking to the room where the test is taken
1. Leaving the house

A variation of this technique can be used in school settings, and is termed *in vivo* desensitization in which a similar hierarchy might be established, but is not paired with relaxation. A counselor gradually exposes the student to each of the steps. If anxiety is reported, then the next lower step on the hierarchy is repeated. The technique continues until the student is able to perform the necessary steps in the hierarchy without anxiety. In some cases, successful completion of a step on the hierarchy may be paired with some type of reinforcement, such as praise or a tangible reward. This technique is more practical in a school setting and can be implemented by a variety of personnel, although consultation with a professional trained in desensitization is recommended. Systematic desensitization that includes relaxation training requires more specialized training.

In vivo desensitization may also be used with school phobia in which a hierarchy is established to gradually return the phobic child to school. The hierarchy is developed in collaboration with the child, parent, and teacher. An example of a partial hierarchy is the following (11 = highest anxiety, 1 = lowest anxiety):

11. Child is in the classroom with activities occurring around him/her
10. Child is alone in the classroom
9. Child is alone in the classroom with the teacher
8. Child enters the classroom alone
7. Child enters the classroom with a parent
6. Child walks to the classroom alone
5. Child walks to the classroom with parent

4. Child enters the school building alone
3. Child enters the school building with the parent
2. Child gets into the car with the parent
1. Child gets dressed and prepares to go to school

A final hierarchy may require more steps, depending upon (a) the severity of the phobia, (b) the actual behaviors the child must perform, and (c) the degree of cooperation of adults. In many cases, positive reinforcement may be a useful adjunct in working with the school phobic child. This type of approach may be helpful as long as the child's behavior is not related to problems within the family structure. If such problems do exist, interventions that may or may not directly include the parents may be indicated (Wielkiewicz, 1986).

Contingency management techniques include positive reinforcement, shaping, stimulus fading, and extinction. Positive reinforcement may be useful in treating social withdrawal behaviors associated with anxiety problems. In these cases, the desired behavior is positively reinforced as it occurs, for example, initiation of a conversation with a stranger. Positive reinforcement has been found to be effective in working with social withdrawal (Kirby & Toler, 1970) and selective mutism problems (Kratochwill, 1981). *Shaping* involves reinforcement of a behavior that becomes increasingly closer to the desired behavior. In the example of the school phobia hierarchy, the child could be reinforced at each step in the hierarchy, as s/he more closely approximates (gets closer to) the ultimate behavioral goal.

Modeling involves having the child observe another person properly demonstrate the desired behavior without showing anxiety. The behavior to be modeled should be clearly identified (e.g., initiating a conversation) and, if possible, divided into identifiable components. Then, as the student observes the model, a counselor or facilitator accompanies the child and helps to emphasize the appropriate behaviors. This technique may be particularly helpful in social situations, such as speaking to a group. An additional technique that can follow the observation is for the student to rehearse the desired behavior while being observed and then guided with gentle physical prompts, and verbal statements and reinforcement. This technique is sometimes referred to as "participant modeling" and has been found to be more effective than only watching a model without practice (Graziano, Mooney, Huber, & Ignasiak, 1979).

Self-control techniques are designed to help students manage their own anxiety by engaging in behaviors such as self-talk, self-monitoring, and self-reinforcement. In using these techniques, it is assumed that if the child is willing and able to assume the responsibility for his/her own intervention program, it is more likely to be effective over a long period of time. These techniques require some training and practice on the part of the school personnel involved before implementing them and may not be practical in many situations.

In the interventions described, special services providers can be valuable contributors to the planning, development, and implementation of intervention plans to reduce academic related anxiety. Their role may involve determining initial baseline data, establishing or collaborating in the development of the intervention plan, and they may be the primary persons involved in the implementation. The role that the special services provider takes will depend upon the nature of the problem, the person's previous experience with anxiety-related problems, and the degree of support and resources available.

CONCLUSION

Anxiety is a very complex problem and can be both a cause and effect of academic and personal-social problems. At the school level, anxiety becomes a concern when it affects or has the potential to negatively affect students. Knowledge of the characteristics of anxiety, its potential effects on students, and possible assessment and intervention techniques are essential. Special services providers, through their unique roles and knowledge base, can help students and regular education personnel to work effectively with academic related anxiety.

REFERENCES

Achenbach, T. M., & Edelbrock, C. S. (1983). *Manual for the Child Behavior Checklist and Revised Child Behavior Profile.* Burlington, VT: Department of Psychiatry, University of Vermont.

American Psychiatric Association. (1987). *Diagnostic and Statistical Manual of Mental Disorders* (3rd ed.) (rev. ed.). Washington, DC: Author.

Argulewicz, E. N., & Miller, D. C. (1985). Self-reported and teachers' rankings of anxiety among first-grade children. *School Psychology Review, 14,* 75-78.

Bamber, J. H. (1977). The factorial structure of adolescent responses to a fear survey schedule. *Journal of Genetic Psychology, 17,* 229-238.

Bamber, J. H. (1979). *The fears of adolescents.* New York: Academic Press.

Castenada, A., McCandless, B., & Palermo, D. (1956). The children's form of the Manifest Anxiety Scale. *Child Development, 27,* 317-326.

Cattell, R. B. (1966). Patterns of change: Measurement in relation to state, dimension, trait change, and process concepts. *Handbook of multivariate experimental psychology.* Chicago: Rand-McNally.

Cattell, R. B., & Schier, I. H. (1963). *Handbook for the IPAT Anxiety Scale* (2nd ed.). Champaign, IL: Institute for Personality and Ability Testing.

Dusek, J. B., Mergler, N. L., & Kermis, M. D. (1976). Attention, encoding, and information processing in low and high test anxious children. *Child Development, 47,* 201-207.

Gillis, J. S. (1980). *Child Anxiety Scale.* Champaign, IL: Institute for Personality and Ability Testing.

Graziano, A. M., Mooney, K. C., Huber, C., & Ignasiak, D. (1979). Self-control instruction. *Behavior Therapy and Experimental Psychiatry, 10,* 221-227.

Hill, K. T. (1972). Anxiety in the evaluative context. In W. W. Hartup (Ed.), *The young child: Reviews of research* (Vol. 2). Washington, DC: National Association for the Education of Young Children.

Hill, K. T., & Sarason, S. B. (1966). The relation of test anxiety and defensiveness to test and school performance over the elementary school years. *Monographs of the Society for Research in Child Development, 31,* (2, Serial No. 104).

Huberty, T. J. (1987). Children and anxiety. In A. Thomas & J. Grimes (Eds.), *Children's needs: Psychological perspectives* (pp. 45-51). Washington, DC: National Association of School Psychologists.

Jersild, A. T. (1954). Emotional development. In L. Carmichael (Ed.), *Manual of child psychology* (2nd ed.) (pp. 833-917). New York: Wiley.

Johnson, S. B., & Melamed, B. G. (1979). The assessment and treatment of children's fears. In B. B. Lahey & A. E. Kazdin (Eds.), *Advances in clinical child psychology* (Vol. 2). New York: Plenum.

Kennedy, W. A. (1965). School phobia: Rapid treatment of fifty cases. *Journal of Abnormal Psychology, 70,* 285-289.

Kirby, F. D., & Toler, H. C. (1970). Modification of a preschool isolate behavior: A case study. *Journal of Applied Behavior Analysis, 3,* 309-314.

Kratochwill, T. R. (1981). *Selective mutism*. New York: Lawrence Erlbaum.

Kratochwill, T. R., & Morris, R. J. (1985). Conceptual and methodological issues in the behavioral assessment and treatment of children's fears and phobias. *School Psychology Review, 14*, 94-107.

Mash, E. J., & Terdal, L. G. (1981). Behavioral assessment of childhood disturbance. In E. J. Mash & L. G. Terdal (Eds.), *Behavioral assessment of childhood disorders*. New York: Guilford.

Morris, R. J., & Kratochwill, T. R. (1985). Behavioral treatment of children's fears and phobias: A review. *School Psychology Review, 14*, 84-93.

Nottleman, E. D., & Hill, K. T. (1977). Test anxiety and off-task behavior in evaluative situations. *Child Development, 48*, 225-231.

Quay, H. C., & Peterson, D. R. (1983). *Interim manual for the Revised Behavior Problem Checklist*. Coral Gables, FL: University of Miami.

Reynolds, C. R., & Paget, K. D. (1983). National normative and reliability data for the Revised Children's Manifest Anxiety Scale. *School Psychology Review, 12*, 324-336.

Reynolds, C. R., & Richmond, B. O. (1978). What I Think and Feel: A revised measure of children's manifest anxiety. *Journal of Abnormal Child Psychology, 6*, 271-280.

Rogers, D. (1972). *Adolescence: A psychological perspective*. Monterey, CA: Brooks/Cole.

Sarason, S. B. (1975). Test anxiety, attention, and the general problem of anxiety. In C. D. Spielberger & I. G. Sarason (Eds.), *Stress and anxiety* (Vol. 1). Washington, DC: Hemisphere.

Sarason, S. B., Davidson, K. S., Lighthall, F. F., Waite, R. R., & Ruebush, G. K. (1960). *Anxiety in elementary school children*. New York: Wiley.

Spielberger, C. D. (1973). *State-Trait Anxiety Inventory for Children*. Manual. Palo Alto, CA: Consulting Psychologists Press.

Stevenson, H. W., & Odom, R. D. (1965). The relation of anxiety to children's performance on learning and problem-solving tasks. *Child Development, 36*, 1003-1012.

Werry, J. S. (1986). Diagnosis and assessment. In R. Gittleman (Ed.), *Anxiety disorders of childhood* (pp. 73-100). New York: Guilford.

Wielkiewicz, R. M. (1986). *Behavior management in the schools*. New York: Pergamon Press.

Wine, J. (1971). Test anxiety and direction of attention. *Psychological Bulletin, 76*, 92-104.